Managing Nonprofit Financial and Fiscal Operations

Managing Nonprofit Financial and Fiscal Operations

DALE SWOBODA

GEORGALU SWOBODA

MANAGEMENTCONCEPTS

MANAGEMENTCONCEPTS

8230 Leesburg Pike, Suite 800

Vienna, VA 22182

(703) 790-9595

Fax: (703) 790-1371

www.managementconcepts.com

Printed in the United States of America

Library of Congress Cataloging-in-Publication Data

Swoboda, Dale

  Managing nonprofit finanacial and fiscal operations / Dale Swoboda, Georgalu Swobada.

  p.cm.

  ISBN 978-1-56726-229-2

1. Nonprofit organizations--Finance. 2. Nonprofit organizations--Management. I. Swoboda, Georgalu. II. Title.

  HG4027.65.S96 2009

  658.15--dc22

                          2008027187

10   9   8   7   6   5   4   3   2   1

ABOUT THE AUTHORS

Dale Swoboda, DPA, has a doctorate in public administration from Arizona State University. He is senior professor at Walden University, where he teaches courses in intellectual traditions of public policy and administration, management, and nonprofit finance and budgeting. Dr. Swoboda has experience as a consultant and business owner, a state government agency manager and executive, a contracts administration manager, and a regional planner. Dr. Swoboda has published scholarly articles, symposia contributions, and book chapters about Medicaid HMO cost savings challenges, contracting techniques, taxation issues, management ethics, higher education affordability, and media coverage of budget/finance issues. His current research interests are in management, useful knowledge, and government and nonprofit finance and budgeting.

Georgalu Swoboda, MAM, MS, is the Executive Director of Big Brothers Big Sisters of Central Missouri. She has provided management consulting and other services to public and nonprofit agencies by planning and leading events, conferences, leadership programs, and fundraising efforts. She has over 30 years of nonprofit administration experience. Ms. Swoboda was an equal opportunity specialist directing the operations of the Phoenix Women's Commission and the Human Relations Commission in Phoenix, Arizona. Additionally, she was a program and management consultant for the Young Women's Christian Association (YWCA). She was also Executive Director of the San Antonio YWCA and other smaller YWCAs in Texas. Ms. Swoboda is currently a part-time instructor of a graduate-level course at Walden University, "Nonprofit Marketing and Fundraising."

Many creative people around the world work in health services, education and research organizations, social and legal services, religious institutions, and arts and culture organizations described as *nonprofit* by the Internal Revenue Service. While the nonprofit classification means the organizations aren't making money for stockholders, a lot of profits are in fact generated: these organizations inspire and implement so much positive social change. This book is dedicated to the board members, employees, and volunteers of these extraordinary organizations.

CONTENTS

Preface xiii
Acknowledgments xxi

Chapter 1: Introduction 1
    What Is a Nonprofit Organization? 2
    Why Do Nonprofit Organizations Exist? 2
    Financial Condition of the Nonprofit Sector and
    Level of Participation in the Economy 3

Chapter 2: The Underpinnings of Financial and Fiscal Operations 9
    What Is Financial and Fiscal Administration? 10
    The Importance of Financial and Fiscal Administration 13
    The Financial and Fiscal Administration Network 14
    How and Where Does the Network Fit within an Organization? 17
    Value, Risks, and Rewards in Financial and Fiscal Administration 19
    To Whom are NPOs Accountable
    for Financial and Fiscal Administration? 21
    Board Member Financial and Fiscal Responsibilities 21
    Staff Member Financial and Fiscal Responsibilities 23
    Volunteer Responsibilities 23
    Vital Internal Factors Affecting NPOs 24
    Vital Legal Factors Affecting NPOs 28
    How Do Financial and Fiscal Responsibilities
    Differ among the Sectors of the Economy? 31

Chapter 3: Strategic Financial Planning 39
    A Strategic Planning Metaphor 40
    The Financial and Fiscal Administration Network:
    The Strategic Plan 40
    Strategic Planning Defined 42
    Why Do Strategic Planning? 43
    The Strategic Planning Process 44
    External Factors Affecting Strategic Plans 52

Internal Factors Affecting Strategic Plans 53
Money, Goals, and Objectives 54
Operational versus Capital Budgeting 57
Financial and Fiscal Administration in a Strategic Plan 58
Revenue Planning 59
Cost, Expenditure, and Investment Planning 60

Chapter 4: Budgeting and Its Complexities 67
The Financial and Fiscal Administration Network: The Budget 68
What a Budget Is 68
What a Budget Does 70
The Budget Process 72
Comparing Federal, State, Local, Business,
and Nonprofit Budgeting 75
Budgetary Decision-Making Models 75
Types of Budgets and Budget Evolution 78
Budgets and People 85
Important Budget Considerations 86

Chapter 5: Accounting 97
The Finance and Fiscal Administrative Network: Accounting 98
The Reasons for Accounting 99
The Accounting Function 99
The Bases of Accounting 109
Funds 112
Double-Entry Accounting (DEA) 115
Reporting Requirements Unique to NPOs .121
The Importance of Documentation 122

Chapter 6: Evaluating Finances and Assessing Financial Conditions . .131
The Financial and Fiscal Administration Network:
Financial Evaluation 132
The Purposes and Reasons for Monitoring NPO Finances 133
Types of Audits 137
The Independent Audit Process 139

Preparing for an Independent Audit 145
How to Increase the Success of an Audit .147
The Auditing Profession 148
Assessing Financial Condition 150
Financial Ratios 157

Chapter 7: Revenues, Revenue Management, and Forecasting 165
The Financial and Fiscal Administrative Network:
Revenue Management 166
The Importance of Philanthropy 166
Nonprofit Funding Sources 167
Legal Limitations on Fundraising 174
Trends and New Ideas in Revenue Sources 176
Revenue Administration 179
Determining Prices 181
Forecasting Revenue 184
Tax Credit Policy 194

**Chapter 8: Expenditure Management: Spending, Purchasing,
and the Time Value of Money** 203
Value, Time, and Money 204
Criteria-Based Spending Decision Making 211
Procurement: Theory and Practice 218

Chapter 9: Cash and Investment Management 229
Cash Is King 230
Cash Payment Strategies 230
Technology Strategies:
Wire Transfers and Online Banking 232
Managing Cash Needs 233
Investment Management 244

Chapter 10: Risk and Reward: Financial Risk and Risk Management . .255
Risks and Rewards 256
Nonprofit Financial Risks 256

Liability 261
Financial Risk Management 262
Related and Unrelated Business Risk 266
Partnerships with Corporations 268

**Chapter 11: Capital Budgeting, Evaluating Capital Investment
Decisions, and Debt Management** 279
Capital Budgeting and Cost of Capital 280
Capital Budgeting and the Strategic Plan 281
Capital Decision Making 282
Financing Capital Projects 291
Capital Debt Policy 294

**Chapter 12: Personnel Compensation: Salaries,
Benefits, and Retirement** 301
Planned Compensation: Salary, Benefits, and
Retirement Packages 302
Components of a Compensation System 303
Compensation Administration 311

Index 325

PREFACE

Nonprofit organizations (NPOs) are among civil society's noblest actors. While they are businesses that provide services to communities without concern for profits and losses, they do fret terribly about revenues and expenditures. NPOs often partner with governments and businesses to produce and distribute services that the public and private sectors cannot or will not provide alone. This book is about how NPOs raise, manage, and spend money to provide those services.

Looking Backward: Recent History

The stirring first line of *A Tale of Two Cities*, written a century and a half ago by Charles Dickens, begins, "It was the best of times, it was the worst of times," and those words never seemed more applicable than they do today. Since the millennium began, five momentous and unconnected events interrupted the normal economic cycle in the United States. These events had an enormous financial impact on virtually every NPO in the United States. The first event occurred September 11, 2001, when the worst foreign attack on American soil shook the homeland. Hurricane Katrina, the second event, hit the Gulf Coast region of the country in August 2005. It was the costliest natural disaster (in terms of property losses and displacement of residents) in the history of the nation. These two violent events affected many citizens, businesses, governments, and NPOs in profound ways. They exacerbated a recession.

Two more momentous events, the invasions of Afghanistan and Iraq by U.S. forces, put upward pressure on federal deficits that led to a pulling back on nonmilitary spending. Citizens also cut back—both on purchases and on donations to nonprofits—as concern for the future arose. Businesses experienced reductions in consumer demand, and broad-based donations by businesses decreased. Government budgetary problems lasted several years. Budget cuts included reductions for programs operated by NPOs across the country at every level—national, regional, state, and local.

By 2003, the economy had begun to recover. Government budgets improved, as did government funding of NPOs. Consumer demand increased. NPOs reported near-record donations in 2005 of $260.3 billion, an amount surpassed only in the year 2000.[1] As citizens became more confident in the future, consumer demand increased, economic activity grew, and both citizens and corporations resumed their financial support NPOs.

Then a fifth and very positive momentous event occurred in 2006, when the richest man in the world did something that had not been done since Andrew Carnegie set up his charitable foundation in the early twentieth century. Bill Gates, the founder of Microsoft Corporation, gave approximately $30 billion of his own fortune to the Bill and Melinda Gates Foundation, which was created in 2000 to fight difficult diseases like malaria and tuberculosis in developing countries and to provide education and library technology in the United States. This was a staggering and unprecedented donation. Shortly thereafter, the second richest man in the world, Warren Buffett of Berkshire Hathaway, pledged to donate $30 billion of his fortune to the Bill and Melinda Gates Foundation, thereby doubling the foundation's staggeringly bountiful resources. This kind of generosity is reassuring.

The roller coaster ride for NPOs at the outset of the millennium, however, serves notice. Bad things happen to good organizations—instantaneously or over time—and the folks who are running NPOs had better be prepared to handle them. Good, professional, and ongoing financial and fiscal administration is the best way to prepare an NPO for meeting most challenges and threats.

Nonprofit Financial and Fiscal Administration

The independent (nonprofit) sector has a major role in maintaining and improving civil society. Financial and fiscal activities play a vital role in nonprofit operations. To affect civil society in a positive way, nonprofits must raise revenue, purchase equipment and services, guarantee salaries and benefits, account for money, obtain insurance, and provide goods and services to target populations. The nonprofit sector generates a diverse set of products and delivers them to various target populations who are seeking services in the areas of health care, education and research, social and legal services, religion, and arts and culture.[2]

NPOs are responsible for a full ten percent of the economic activity in the United States.[3] Consequently, there is a need in today's ever-expanding nonprofit sector for managers who understand the complexities of financial and fiscal administration and who can apply the strategies of budgeting and financial management within their organizations. This book provides theoretical, professional, and practical information to those managers.

NPOs are unique participants in the culture and the economy, and effective NPO managers must be aware of the special financial and fiscal needs and requirements imposed on the industry by government and other external factors. This book will help prepare readers to understand and manage the financial responsibilities of NPOs by focusing on both common and unique financial concepts and by emphasizing the integrated financial responsibilities of executive, financial, program, and development staff and boards of directors.

Looking Forward: The Focus

Financial and fiscal administration is an important responsibility of nonprofit administration. *Fiscal administration* is defined as the management of budgets. *Financial management* oversees the areas of accounting, procurement, cash and investments, and other functions related to the day-to-day operations of an organization. The momentous events identified in the previous section remind us how important it is for the nonprofit industry and all its subsectors to understand how such events impact the economy and how changes in the economy impact NPO missions and operations. Agency boards and staff members must guarantee to their stakeholders that prudent, professional, and planned financial and fiscal management will be an operating certainty.

This book is designed in the context of the increasing professionalization occurring in the nonprofit sector. An estimated 640,000 managers at the senior and executive level—those most responsible for financial and fiscal administration—will be needed to meet the leadership requirements of the nonprofit sector through the year 2016 due to growth and employee retirement.[4] This book addresses a gap in the nonprofit management curriculum: financial and fiscal management of NPOs.

The Book Roadmap

Each of the chapters of this book is organized around basic topics of financial or fiscal function. The end of each chapter has two discussion questions and a real-world exercise emerging from the topics discussed in the chapter. In addition, most chapters identify an innovation in finance or budgeting developed and practiced by NPOs.

Chapter 1 defines nonprofit organizations, what they do, and why they exist. The chapter also lays out a snapshot of the financial size and condition of the nonprofit sector.

The primary objective of Chapter 2 is to discuss theoretical concepts that provide a foundation for learning finance and budgeting. Chapter 2 explains the role of finance and budgeting in the achievement of organizational success. It explains what a financial and fiscal system is and how important it is to the success of an organization. Chapter 2 also examines how the functions of the system interact, discusses the major financial and budgeting responsibilities of nonprofit governing boards, staff, and volunteers, and briefly talks about the financial reporting requirements of tax-exempt and nonprofit organizations. It closes by extensively comparing and contrasting the financial and fiscal operations of for-profit and government organizations to agencies in the nonprofit sector.

Chapter 3 delves into one of the most intriguing and important areas for a modern organization—strategic planning. This topic is at the beginning of the book because it provides readers a view of how mission, program, and finance come together in a single planning process. The purpose of this management tool is to obtain the commitment of everyone in the organization and move them toward the same vision, mission, goals, and objectives. The chapter also shows why the strategic plan must be flexible.

Chapter 4 covers the complexities of the standard budgeting process. The chapter starts by comparing nonprofit budgeting to federal, state, and local budgeting. It also discusses how the budget derives from the strategic plan and describes a step-by-step budgeting process. Finally, Chapter 4 describes various budget strategies.

Chapter 5 reveals the accounting and reporting functions of NPOs. It discusses accounting both as the practice broadly impacts all organizations and especially as it impacts the nonprofit sector. Accounting keeps the organization running on a daily basis and reports how money is used. Chapter 5 explains all of the components of the accounting function, including day-to-day operations and reporting at various points during a fiscal year. A key aspect of this discussion is what accounting contributes to the maintenance of the organization.

In Chapter 6, the focus is on evaluation. Evaluation involves primarily auditing and the evaluation of financial conditions. The discussion covers the theoretical and practical values involved in establishing trust through regular financial audits. The chapter explains the reasons—trust, accuracy, risk reduction—NPOs should require audits. It also discusses program audits that are analytical examinations of the economy, efficiency, and effectiveness of a program or an organization. The chapter discusses the use of financial ratios that paint the financial picture of pledges and contributions, grants and endowments, expenditures and commitments, and responsiveness to the results of an audit.

Revenue, the vital nourishment of an NPO, is discussed in Chapter 7. The chapter begins with the philosophy of philanthropy and giving. It discusses various sources of revenue, including fundraising, tax management, grants, and others, and it describes and analyzes the legal and contractual limits to fundraising. Tax credits are an important topic also covered in Chapter 7. Finally, the chapter talks about revenue management strategies that organizations should employ.

Chapter 8 balances Chapter 7 with a discussion of expenditures and purchasing, and gives criteria that can be used in making spending decisions. The time value of money—that is, inflation—is covered, as is cost and value analysis. The chapter ends with a discussion of purchasing management involving both competitive and noncompetitive bidding.

Chapter 9 discusses cash and investment management. Topics under cash management include cash flow budgets and strategies, managing the flow of cash through a budget year, petty cash, and cash reserve management. On the investment side, a comparison and discussion of short- and long-term investments provides the reader with an understanding of the usefulness of these financial instruments to an NPO. This discussion includes the limits of investing strategies set by both the law and by agency policies.

Chapter 10 covers the topics of risk, insurance, liability, and risk management. It also covers the risk associated with starting and managing related and unrelated ventures that both cost and, ideally, earn money. Business ventures are popular and often useful methods of acquiring revenue. Starting a business-type venture requires knowledge of the laws and regulations covering earned income and the tax treatment of revenue from these ventures. These topics are covered from both a legal and a business perspective.

Chapter 11 covers capital budgeting, debt, and capital investment decision-making. Many NPOs have the opportunity to decide whether to rent capital facilities and items or to purchase them. Thus, decision-making techniques become important. The chapter talks about capital budgeting and its relationship to the strategic plan and then discusses the critical topic of debt and debt management.

Finally, Chapter 12 discusses internal controls and personnel management issues. This includes compensation, benefits and personnel costs, pensions, and 403(b) plans. The topics are discussed in the context of costs and cost savings strategies.

These chapters present an abundance of complex information. Nevertheless, the non-mathematically inclined need not worry: our goal is to provide understandable information that adds value to the learning process. We hope readers find the information both enlightening and practical.

Dale Swoboda

Georgalu Swoboda

Columbia, Missouri

NOTES

1   Holly Hall, "Coming on Strong," *Chronicle of Philanthropy,* June 29, 2006.

2   E. T. Boris, "Civil Society: The Foundation of Democratic Participation," Dissemination Paper #7 (Washington, DC: Inter-American Development Bank, 1998).

3   Christopher Gunn, *Third Sector Development: Making Up for the Market* (New York: Cornell University Press, 2003).

4   Brennen Jensen, "640,000 New Senior Managers Will Be Needed to Run Nonprofit Groups in Next Decade," *Chronicle of Philanthropy,* April 6, 2006.

ACKNOWLEDGMENTS

The authors want to recognize their indebtedness to a number of people. First, Myra Strauss of Management Concepts deserves credit for listening and responding to our ideas. It was an inspiring moment in the life of this book. Many important people working at Walden University have been supportive with their patience and understanding. We would especially like to thank Denise DeZolt, Gary Kelsey, and Marion Angelica. Joan Swoboda's generosity and creativity are valued; you did a great job! Michael Devereux deserves our attention for his careful and very helpful editing and for showing up in our lives after years of absence, ironically at about the same time this project was born.

CHAPTER 1
Introduction

Because of their unique missions in the civil society of the United States, NPOs have a special fiduciary responsibility to their clients, to their volunteers, and to their communities. This book contains a lot of useful knowledge to help NPOs fulfill that responsibility. This chapter provides the basis of understanding the nonprofit sector in terms of its component parts and the degree of its participation in the national economy.

TOPICS
- What Is a Nonprofit Organization?
- Why Do Nonprofit Organizations Exist?
- Financial Condition of the Nonprofit Sector and Level of Participation in the Economy
- Summary

WHAT IS A NONPROFIT ORGANIZATION?

NPOs vary in size from local, all-volunteer organizations to huge national and international systems employing thousands and with revenues in the billions of dollars. One of the characteristics that distinguishes NPOs from for-profit entities is economic in nature, and is captured in the word *nonprofit*. Private organizations that have no owners who receive a distribution of profits at the end of a fiscal year are known as *NPOs*. But being nonprofit is not the only distinguishing characteristic of NPOs. For example, NPOs are generally tax-exempt. An NPO provides services and goods to a targeted group, cause, or mission that the for-profit sector cannot or does not provide. An NPO is generally overseen by an official board consisting of people who are appointed because of their interest in an organization's mission, their crucial expertise, or because they are good at raising funds. NPOs cannot exist without such interest, expertise, or funding. Additionally, there are supporters of NPOs who do not serve on the board. These supporters include donors and volunteers, whose interest in the success of NPOs motivates them to voluntarily contribute their time, expertise, and abilities to mission fulfillment.

An organization's mission is the soul of an NPO. The mission drives an NPO to do what it does. Expertise is the brain and the intelligence of an NPO. Fundraising and management provide the lifeblood. This book addresses how these three aspects—mission, expertise, and fundraising and management—coalesce under a complex of financial and fiscal administration.

WHY DO NONPROFIT ORGANIZATIONS EXIST?

NPOs existed in the United States before it became a nation; these organizations provide a history and tradition usually associated with religious organizations.[1] Independent organizations, like the YMCA, Boy Scouts of America, and local United Way or similar organizations have been responding to the unmet needs of our civil society for a century or more. Independent organizations exist because some needs—health care, education, social and legal services, culture and arts—were not being met by either the government or the for-profit sector. Such philanthropy grew as NPOs took on more and more of the burden that the marketplace did not, could not, or would not take on. NPOs contribute to civil society by becoming providers of or supplementing health care, education, social, legal, and cultural infrastructures. It is hard to imagine that the United States would be the economic and social force it is today without the growing contribution of the nonprofit sector.

FINANCIAL CONDITION OF THE NONPROFIT SECTOR AND LEVEL OF PARTICIPATION IN THE ECONOMY

This book focuses on the financial and fiscal responsibilities of the nonprofit sector. This quest for knowledge and understanding begins with a snapshot of the national picture of finances in the nonprofit sector. This information depicts the wide variety of products and services that define the nonprofit sector and underscores the magnitude of nonprofit participation in the U.S. economy and in civil society. The descriptions of the size and the growth of the nonprofit sector underscore the need for this book.

The *Independent Sector's* 2005 estimate of the number of NPOs in the United States was 1.9 million. That number represents a tripling between 1987 and 2005. The nonprofit sector accounts for 9.5 percent of total non-farm employment in the United States and 6.1 percent of national income. NPOs vary by size, by type, and by the diversity of their goals, missions, locations, and revenue sources. Employment in the nonprofit sector grew at a faster rate (2.8 percent) between 1997 and 2001 than both the government sector (1.6 percent) and the business sector (1.8 percent). The *Nonprofit Almanac* reports that in 2001, total independent sector employment was 11.7 million workers.[2]

Most nonprofits in the United States are small in financial and fiscal terms compared to ExxonMobil ($339 billion) and the Pentagon (over $200 billion). In 2004 the nation's YMCAs collectively had the largest budget of all nonprofits, at $4.8 billion.[3] According to the *Christian Science Monitor*, the top 50 nonprofit operating budgets in the nation range from the YMCA's high to the American Diabetes Association's $206.4 million (last in the list). The combined assets of the nonprofit sector in 2004 was estimated at $2.95 trillion.[4]

There are five major service subsectors included in the nonprofit sector—health services, education and research, social and legal services, religious organizations, and arts and culture. The statistics in this discussion come from *The Nonprofit Almanac: Dimensions of the Independent Sector*, a publication of the National Center for Charitable Statistics and Giving USA.

Health Services

The health services subsector is the largest nonprofit in terms of revenue, employment, and payroll. This has been true for a long time and will likely be true for a long time to come largely due to the aging Baby Boomer generation. The types of organizations in this subsector include hospitals, nursing facilities and personal care services, specialized treatment facilities, public clinics, home health care, outpatient services, drug and alcohol treatment centers, and others of a similar nature.

- In 2001, this subsector's total estimated revenue accounted for 49 percent of total revenue in the nonprofit sector.

- In 2004, donations to health care decreased by an inflation-adjusted 0.7 percent.

- Approximately 42 percent of all paid workers in the nonprofit sector worked in health services in 2001, down from 44.5 percent in 1997.

- Health services workers consistently earn around 54 percent of total wages and salaries in the nonprofit sector.

- The primary revenue source in the health services subsector is private payments, which accounts for 47 percent of its funding.

Education and Research

The education and research subsector comprises institutions of teaching and learning and related organizations. It includes colleges and universities; pre-school, elementary, secondary, and correspondence schools; libraries; and other educational and research institutions.

- This subsector consistently has the second largest amount of total revenue. Private payments from dues, tuition, fees, and services made up 56 percent of total funds.

• In 2004, donations to educational organizations increased by an inflation-adjusted 9.4 percent.

• In 2001, the education and research subsector had approximately 22 percent of all paid workers in the nonprofit sector. More than half worked in higher-education settings.

Social and Legal Services

Organizations that make up the social and legal services subsector include organizations that deliver the following types of services: individual and family assistance, civic and community services, social and fraternal assistance, legal aid, child and residential care, job training, youth counseling, and housing assistance.

• Employment in social and legal services grew at a faster rate than in other subsectors. Its share of total employment in the independent sector grew from 13.0 percent in 1997 to 18.5 percent in 2005.

• This subsector consistently has the third-highest share of total revenue in the nonprofit sector, but that share is growing.

• In 2004, donations to social and legal services agencies increased by an inflation-adjusted 9.4 percent.

• Government payments generally make up 50 percent to 55 percent of total revenue received by the social and legal services subsector. It is the subsector that is most reliant on government support and is therefore the most sensitive to public policy changes.

Religious Organizations

Religious organizations (including religious congregations of all faiths) are unique in that private contributions account for most of their funds.

• In 2004, donations to religious organizations increased by an inflation-adjusted 2.5 percent.

• In 1998, religious organizations' share of independent-sector employment was 11.6 percent, compared with 11.8 percent in 2005.

- The primary revenue source in this sector is private contributions, which account for 95 percent of its funding.

- Most of the donations made to nonprofits go to religious organizations.

Arts and Culture

Included in the arts and culture subsector are museums, orchestras, botanical and zoological gardens, performing arts groups, ballet groups, nonprofit radio and television, literary organizations, and other humanities-oriented organizations.

- In 2004, donations to arts and culture agencies decreased by an inflation-adjusted 6.6 percent.

- The primary revenue source is private donations, which account for 44 percent of its funding.

SUMMARY

The nonprofit sector is a healthy and growing part of the U.S. economy. But does an efficient and effective nonprofit sector really make a difference in the country's economic health as a whole? It may be difficult to conclude, except anecdotally, that this nation's economy would be any different without nonprofit boards, staff, and volunteers, but the experiences of these participants indicates that life in the United States would be deficient without them. Studies that delve into the contributions of NPOs generally conclude that the nonprofit sector is a vital part of the economic and social infrastructure because of its financial contributions.

NOTES

1   David C. Hammack, "Nonprofit Organizations in American History," *American Behavioral Scientist* 45 (2002): 1638–1674. Boris, E. T. "Civil Society: The Foundation of Democratic Participation," Dissemination Paper #7 (Washington, DC: Inter-American Development Bank, 1998).

2   *Independent Sector,* "Nonprofit Almanac," 2002. Online at http://www.independentsector.org/ programs/research/NA01main.html (accessed May 14, 2008).

3   The Christian Science Monitor, "The 50 largest US charities ranked by total income," *The Christian Science Monitor* (November 21, 2005): 16–17.

4   *Independent Sector,* "Independent Sector Survey Measures the Everyday Generosity of Americans." Online at http://www.independentsector.org/programs/research/GV01main.html (accessed May 19, 2008). Also, Giving USA, *Giving USA 2006: The Annual Report on Philanthropy for the Year 2005* (Glenview, IL: Giving USA Foundation, 2006).

CHAPTER 2
The Underpinnings of Financial and Fiscal Operations

This chapter provides a theoretical and practical overview of the financial and fiscal system that any organization should build, protect, and use in carrying out its programs. It introduces and discusses the five components of a financial and fiscal network: the strategic plan, management, the budget, accounting, and evaluation. The major participants in the network—board members, staff, volunteers—and their financial and fiscal responsibilities are discussed. Also introduced are the major factors affecting success in NPO finance and budgeting. Like all the chapters that follow, this one includes discussion questions, exercises, and a discussion of an innovation in the practice of financial and fiscal administration in the nonprofit sector.

TOPICS

- What Is Financial and Fiscal Administration?
- The Importance of Financial and Fiscal Administration
- The Financial and Fiscal Administration Network
- How and Where Does the Network Fit within an Organization?
- Value, Risks, and Rewards in Financial and Fiscal Administration
- To Whom are NPOs Accountable for Financial and Fiscal Administration?
- Board Member Financial and Fiscal Responsibilities
- Staff Member Financial and Fiscal Responsibilities
- Volunteer Responsibilities
- Vital Internal Factors Affecting NPOs
- Vital Legal Factors Affecting NPOs
- How Do Financial and Fiscal Responsibilities Differ among the Sectors of the Economy?
- Summary
- Useful Websites
- Discussion Questions
- Exercise
- Innovation: Malcolm Baldrige National Quality Award for Nonprofits

WHAT IS FINANCIAL AND FISCAL ADMINISTRATION?

What is financial and fiscal administration? What are its components? How do those components fit with other functions within an NPO? How do they affect decision making about legitimate concerns of the organization and the realities of the larger political-economic-social system? What technologies are appropriate to financial administration? What role does the financial management specialist play in the organization? What is a board? What do staff members of an NPO do with respect to financial and fiscal operations? These are critical questions that this chapter of the book will begin to answer.

Financial and fiscal administration is much more than fundraising. Obtaining dollars is just the beginning of financial operations. Financial and fiscal administration is also much more than the relationship of revenues and expenditures. It also includes the following activities:

- Accounting
- Assessing Financial Conditions
- Auditing
- Banking
- Budgeting
- Cash Management
- Cost Analysis
- Debt Administration
- Expenditure Administration
- Forecasting
- Investment Administration
- Pension Administration
- Purchasing
- Revenue Management
- Risk Management

There are two types of theories that help answer the questions posed at the beginning of this section. One is foundational and ideal—*rational theories*. The other is sensible and realistic—*real-world theories*. These theories, like all good theories, try to explain the world by making generalizations. In this case, the generalizations are about financial and fiscal administration. They provide an aggregated view of the world of NPOs. These theories are important. They have been tested and proven over the years.

First, a *rational theory of finance* would have us understand NPO financial and fiscal administration as representing a business theory that states that an organization is very rational in its quest for efficiency and, ultimately, profits. It assumes that the knowledge and practice of all sectors of the U.S. economy operate identically to a business model, with the assumption that there is a basic nature of financial and fiscal administration that cannot vary. A rational theory is a basic financial theory that reverently worships at the altar of wealth; the belief in the maximization of shareholder wealth is the one all-consuming goal to achieve. A state of *Pareto optimality* is the ideal. Pareto optimality refers to the achievement of a state where any change in the economy to make somebody better off will make others in the economy worse off. In other words, complete efficiency has been achieved. *Shareholder* translates into stakeholder in an NPO, including clients of the organization, donors of time and money, board members, employees, and other interested unrelated parties.

The financial manager has the job of maximizing results by efficiently leading the organization to a point at which every stakeholder can trust in an NPO's financial and fiscal operations. In the rational environment, financial decision making follows the rational model, that is, managers seek to find the most efficient means of satisfying preferences. The types of organizations described in a rational theory are those that operate in a *closed* environment. That is, they are unaffected by the decisions of other organizations in the environment. Rationality, as it applies to financial and fiscal decision making, has value in that it portrays an ideal organization. A rational theory, then, does not go far enough in explaining the world of fiscal management, because financial and fiscal administrators must obviously operate in the real world.

Theoretical Tenets of a Rational Financial Practice

Goal: Profit-making

Goal: Maximization of Shareholder Wealth

Strategy: Rational Decision Making

Strategy: Closed to the Environment

Strategy: Efficiency Orientation

This rational theory does not always reflect reality in an operational sense, but it is the basis of understanding important concepts and processes. In the real world, organizations might not be able to fulfill ideal expectations. For example, there may be competing needs and demands of NPOs that require the use of money to fund programs that are not as productive as other uses of the money might be. A *real-world theory* shares the belief in the maximization of shareholder wealth, and it is founded on rationalism. But real-world theory differentiates itself from its rational counterpart in that it acknowledges that other factors act to limit rational decision making. It operates in an open environment.

Theoretical Tenets of Real-World Financial Practice

Goal: Profit-making

Goal: Maximization of Shareholder Wealth

Strategy: Incremental Decision Making

Strategy: Open to the Environment

Strategy: Balance Competing Needs

Because individuals act in their own best interests and compete for outcomes, decisions can only be made incrementally. That is, giant leaps of change in society seldom occur. Instead, small steps are taken toward changes. An excellent example of this is the conflict during the Clinton Administration during the 1990s over the health care system. Some quarters wanted to create a single-payer health care system to ensure affordable health care for everyone, while others blocked that attempt on the basis that markets are the best means of delivering a quality health care system. The result was that only small changes were made in the system. Political influences on financial priorities provide an example of outside factors that affect financial decision making. Likewise, NPOs may face competing uses of funds, which requires a prioritizing process that could benefit some interests while ignoring others. Financial managers are relied upon to develop strategies for making finances work without regard for the effects of outside influences.

Note that in both theories, financial managers have the task of sorting out the details. Thus, all of the economic sectors—private, public, and nonprofit—are dependent upon the vital skills of financial and fiscal managers.

THE IMPORTANCE OF FINANCIAL AND FISCAL ADMINISTRATION

Money is vital to all organizations and individuals. Money means a great deal to people. Money is the marker for all things. No organization can operate without money. No organization in the nonprofit sector has ever had enough money to do all of the things it wanted to do and is commissioned to do. What does all this say about the role of NPO finance? According to the National Academy of Sciences, knowledge about the social world of civic society is insufficient if it does not include metaphoric and symbolic understanding of important concepts.[1] An NPO can be viewed as a human body that comprises the shell, the parts, the organs, and the important fluids. The staff and board constitute an organization's brain. They control the decisions that are made on behalf of the organization. Other parts of a working organization, such as programs, fundraising, marketing, human resources, legal services, and so on, represent the various organs within a body. The brain and organs need a vital fluid in order to thrive. While money may not be the heart of organizational endeavors, it is an organization's lifeblood. Nothing can be done without it. Taking nothing away from the importance of the concept of *mission,* which is the heart of any NPO, how money is raised and spent by NPOs is arguably more important than any other activity of NPO administration. Blood must get pumped through the heart.

The other parts of an organization cannot thrive without the lifeblood. The arteries, veins, capillaries, lymph nodes, and other components of a circulatory system represent the functions of a financial system. One of the first things a health care worker does when a patient is examined is to measure a person's pulse. The pulse is a good indicator of how the whole system is working. To see if there is a problem with the body of the person, you have to keep checking the pulse to see if the heart is still pumping blood through the system. Ignoring the pulse and other indicators would be poor health management. Just as ignoring the function of the circulatory system can allow disease to kill a body, ignoring the financial and fiscal administration system can allow disease of that system to kill an organization.

Financial and fiscal administration determines the quality of service that can be provided to a target community. At the end of each fiscal year, the people responsible for financial and fiscal operations determine which areas need to be funded for the next fiscal year, and then the budgeting plan is created accordingly. Financial and fiscal managers try to make sure that an organization anticipates mission success and failure and that it minimizes operational disruptions. Timely information on the status of programs is essential for managers to make choices about services they provide. Financial and fiscal administration systems provide the means for managing and ultimately delivering those services. Nonprofit financial administration, then, is concerned with how money is raised and spent by board members, volunteers, and professional administrators.

THE FINANCIAL AND FISCAL ADMINISTRATION NETWORK

Good financial management today means you have to do the following:

- Invest wisely.
- Prepare annual financial statements that routinely receive clean audit opinions.
- Pay your bills on time.
- Collect what is owed you.
- Implement and maintain meaningful management standards.
- Reduce the number of audit findings.
- Ensure that your major internal controls are known and used.

The Whatcom Council of Nonprofits (2006) offers the following eight best practices for nonprofits in the area of financial management:

- Generating sufficient revenue

- Tying the budget to outcomes

- Maintaining the board-approved budget

- Proper filing of legal financial documents

- Maintaining accurate records according to accepted accounting rules

- Establishing adequate annual internal controls

- Periodic reporting to managers

- Maintaining a diversified funding base.[2]

To reach the state of good financial management, an organization should follow an ideal as close as possible and strive to accomplish fiscal and financial administration goals. A financial and fiscal administration network contains the following four major functions that are framed by the strategic plan (see Figure 2.1):

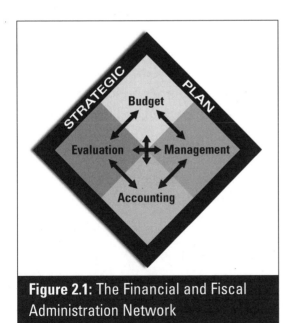

- Budget

- Management

- Accounting

- Evaluation

Figure 2.1: The Financial and Fiscal Administration Network

The network is more than technology. It includes all processes, plans, and participants involved in the financial operations of an organization. The interlocking aspects of the four functions are important and can be seen in Figure 2.1. Equally important is how the functions should be integrated. As shown in the figure, theoretically speaking, the strategic plan surrounds the functions and responsibilities of the financial and fiscal administration network. The network consists of several components: a base (strategic plan); four functions/responsibilities (budget, management, accounting, evaluation); and six two-way flow arrows. While it is shown in its complete form here, the network is used in this book to depict how the various components operate individually. The network can be thought of as a puzzle. Most children who have played with puzzles have experienced great frustration when a puzzle could not be finished. It was not right; it was incomplete. Similarly, when a component of the network depicted in Figure 2.1 is deficient or not working well in an organization, it impedes achievement of that organization's goals. The organization works best when all the components of the network are in place and working well.

A strategic plan, of course, is the base upon which the other components of the financial and fiscal network operate. It should drive and explain why the other functions operate as they do. It explains the vision, mission, plans, goals, objectives, and expectations of where an organization wants to be in both the long term and the short term. The annual budget is a reflection of where an organization is being led. The strategic plan is discussed in Chapter 3. Most of the book's chapters allude to the connection to the strategic plan.

A fiscal year for any organization begins and ends with the budget. The budget is the process where decisions are made, where plans are developed, and where policies are set in motion for a year or for another prescribed period of time. For that year or the prescribed time period, the budget function controls financial decisions and operations. Note in the figure the two-way arrows between the various functions. The budget function links directly to the three other functions, both driving them and responding to them. The budget contains the standards under which the other functions operate. Budgeting is discussed in Chapter 4 of this book.

Managers use budget standards and accounting reports to fulfill the desired outcomes of an organization's mission. Managers need to operate the financial and fiscal system and make sure that the people they supervise operate within the prescriptions of the budget. Managers are also responsible for providing accurate information for the accounting function and the audit/evaluation function. Unlike the other functions, management is not confined to one chapter of this book. It is a function that cannot be isolated in the way the other functions can. Management is pervasive and is the application—to all functions—of the guidance set out in the strategic plan. The strategic plan contains directions about how priorities will be implemented, namely, through the budget. The management function, primarily the day-to-day operations of the organization, is discussed beginning in Chapter 7.

The accounting function provides both control over finances and information about the budget to managers and to auditors. Accounting for and reporting on how dollars are used are especially important in most NPOs, where grants require accounting for special funds that limit the use of money. Accounting information is necessary for auditing and evaluation in order to ensure that accounting was done properly and that the numbers themselves are accurate. Accounting is discussed in Chapter 5.

The evaluation function provides assessment in the form of financial and management audits and program evaluation, both of which feed back into the budget and the strategic plan and often lead to adjustments to both the budget and the strategic plan. The evaluation function is where course corrections are identified and developed for consideration in both the present and for future periods of time. Managers are subject to audit and evaluation results. They also receive feedback from the results of audits and evaluations. What they learn should guide them as to how to improve management of their budgets. Chapter 6 discusses auditing and program evaluation.

HOW AND WHERE DOES THE NETWORK FIT WITHIN AN ORGANIZATION?

How does financial and fiscal administration fit into the larger administrative and policy picture? Financial management often implies both short- and long-term financial analysis and budgeting. An NPO must look at its mission and goals, short- and long-term strategic management and planning, and often the organization must make an intelligent estimate of how much funding will be needed (creating budgets to fulfill these needs), always searching for new and better ways of achieving its financial goals. This is obviously an ongoing process.

For-profit organizations operate with the mission to maximize the wealth of their shareholders by selling goods and services for a profit. In this context, financial analysis and planning for short-term gain is crucial to the organization's success. NPOs, as part of the social and cultural infrastructure, are mission-driven. Responsibility, both cultural and social, and creation of a social infrastructure are of primary concern, and financial planning is therefore centered on financing the organization's needs so it may continue to serve the community.

Keeping careful track of financial resources is such a vital element of successful management that no one questions its necessity, yet the diversion of resources away from direct mission accomplishment in order to support the financial function is extremely hard for members of an organization to accept. Unfortunately, however, the books of an NPO do not keep themselves, and the price of good financial management tools remains steep. Bad things can happen when an organization does not find the time and the means by which to sharpen its financial control.

Financial management provides the affordability horizon and direction for programs, sustains the organization, influences policy decisions and the ability to fulfill the mission, and establishes a threshold of accountability. All other organizational functions depend on fiscal planning, financial policy decisions, and the availability of funds. In many NPOs, the commitment to mission is so pervasive throughout the culture that most staff, except for the accountants and top executives, view financial and fiscal management as a necessary evil that frequently inhibits the realization of greater ideals. And that is only if the staff ever thinks about financial and fiscal management at all. The reality, however, is that to be effective at its mission, an NPO needs to integrate the principles of financial and fiscal management into all aspects of operations.

As we will see, an effective financial and fiscal administration network will contribute to financial success. One of the great difficulties in organizations is the access to financial information. Modern automated systems notwithstanding, there are numerous horror stories about what can happen when one section of an organization does not communicate with the others. In the worst case, the automated system itself may be the horror if it does not provide adequate communication. In an organization where staff members receive only quarterly reports, which may not be compiled until a month after the quarter has closed, four full months may have passed before a problem (for example, a program with actual revenue far below budgeted projection) can be detected and acted upon. Too great a delay in responding to financial management problems can cost NPOs unnecessary expenses.

Monitoring the budget is roughly the same in the both the profit and nonprofit sectors. The difference in the nonprofit sector is often the inflexibility of the use of funds, especially those funds coming from granting organizations. Unused money cannot be transferred easily to other uses. The perspectives of the public, nonprofit, and for-profit sectors differ somewhat in perception and in nomenclature, but the theories, concepts, goals, and even the outcomes are quite similar.

The choice of functional emphasis can have a serious impact on an organization's ability to carry out its mission. For example, for many years, the leaders in an organization focused solely on how money was raised and not how it was spent. Rewards, both symbolic and financial, were based on reaching financial objectives such as fundraising and budget goals. When the board decided to give rewards based on the quality of the programs provided and mission outcomes instead of financial performance, the staff argued for higher budgets that included more money for programs and more money to hire qualified program staff. It is the role of financial and fiscal administrators, through the guidance of the strategic plan, to find an appropriate balance between financial objectives and appropriate spending on mission.

VALUE, RISKS, AND REWARDS IN FINANCIAL AND FISCAL ADMINISTRATION

There is a fishbowl factor that all sectors of the economy must be concerned about in managing finances: many stakeholders are watching. In many organizations in the nonprofit sector, there is a need to integrate the various sources of funding sought in order to be able to meet the all-important mission. It is the job of the financial management system to make sure that the money is taken in and sent out to where it needs to go. As in any other aspect of an organization, professional leadership makes the difference in creating and maintaining an effective finance system. The financial manager is responsible for the overall fiscal functioning of the organization. Organizations either do not exist or, at the least, do not exist efficiently and effectively without an integrated financial and fiscal managerial network that includes accounting, management, and evaluation of financial operations and outcomes. The U.S. Office of Management and Budget has stated that "financial management systems must be in place to process and record financial events effectively and efficiently, and to provide complete, timely, reliable and consistent information for decision makers . . . ."[3]

More than likely, an organization without an integrated financial and fiscal administration network would experience significant waste, not meet basic needs, and be in a poor management position that would affect everything from balancing the books to the morale of the organization's personnel. Many NPOs are experiencing these conditions. An integrated financial and fiscal managerial network ensures an organization is free to concentrate on its objectives without finance being a showstopper. When one function is not being addressed adequately, or is even left out, an organization can end up in chaos. Some organizations are lucky and succeed in spite of ignoring or undervaluing one of the four functions of an integrated financial and fiscal administration network. Clearly, you can have all four financial functions in place and value them all, but if one is ignored it affects all parts of an NPO.

Often budgeters have to have wisdom like Solomon or must at least pretend to have such wisdom. At the city council, NPO board, or legislative level, coping with budget pressures, regardless of the type of organization, involves either increasing revenues in some way or cutting expenditures. There are often good things that come out of bad things. Outside of the world of finance, people who pull together learn to appreciate what they have. Financial disasters can lead to renewals as well. Organizations begin to work on the margin out of necessity. As each dollar becomes more important, greater care is taken with regard to that dollar.

TO WHOM ARE NPOS ACCOUNTABLE FOR FINANCIAL AND FISCAL ADMINISTRATION?

NPOs are unique social entities because they are private organizations that serve the community without a need to maximize the wealth of owners or shareholders. Each NPO has a board of directors that monitors the operations of the organization. Donors, members, and other stakeholders hold the board accountable. While the board has final approval of the financial activities from a policy perspective, the executive director and staff members carry out day-to-day financial and fiscal responsibilities. Management is a key factor to the success or failure of any business, especially in an NPO. The board of directors must have a good sense of the programs and services that are offered and needed by the community. In the end, the board has to answer to the public and the government for financial accountability.[4]

To whom are financial and fiscal professionals accountable? They are accountable not only to those who run an NPO but also to clients, beneficiaries, donors, and other supporters as well as funding partners like governments, foundations, and corporate partners. They are also accountable to the Internal Revenue Service. All NPOs (except churches, other religious institutions, and those with budgets under $25,000) are required to file IRS Form 990 with the Internal Revenue Service. This form discloses "financial and organizational leadership information."[5] Executives and other staff are usually responsible for fiscal activities and held accountable by board oversight.

BOARD MEMBER FINANCIAL AND FISCAL RESPONSIBILITIES

People who serve on NPO boards provide a great service to civil society. They deserve to be honored for the time they spend on behalf of NPOs and the energy they expend, because they do it generally for free. Board members are expected to make an annual contribution to the NPO they oversee or to personally identify or solicit funds for the NPO from outside sources in order to demonstrate their commitment to the organization.[6] This *give, get, or open doors* responsibility is becoming prominent in the nonprofit sector. The board has several fiduciary responsibilities that include:

- Approving comprehensive written financial policies for revenues, purchasing, accounting, investing assets, reserve funds, salaries and benefits, and all financial activities.

- Passing a budget that meets the organization's needs and overseeing the budget they approve.

- Ensuring that an accurate financial audit occurs.

Board members take on a certain amount of financial risk in accepting their roles as directors or officers of the organization, although liability is limited by state laws. Their fiduciary responsibility requires them to exercise diligence toward the financial health of their organizations. The assumption made, however, is that they face very little financial risk, because no one would sue someone working at an NPO because of the respect paid to them for their willingness to serve.[7] Directors and officers (D&O) liability insurance can also be purchased to limit the financial liability of board members.[8]

In the case of NPOs, business skill alone does not guarantee effective performance in a nonprofit board. Of what use is business experience on a nonprofit or governmental board? Bottom-line thinking is useful in a business setting, where the demands of the marketplace are predetermined and the board's responsibility is to maximize income and minimize inefficiency. J. Carver tells us that in the case of a nonprofit board, however, "the board must substitute for the rigors of the marketplace."[9] It is the board that has the legal and moral responsibility to set the limits and make sure its policies are carried out as they were designed. It is its job to understand the marketplace in which the NPO operates and to know the needs of the clients.[10]

Board members are often chosen for strategic reasons, not necessarily because of their interest in the organization in question. Many are chosen because they may be able to bring in funding, some are chosen because they are powerful in the community, others are selected because they are high-ranking public officials, and still others seek an appointment to a board. Board selection is a very political process.[11]

STAFF MEMBER FINANCIAL AND FISCAL RESPONSIBILITIES

Delegation and oversight are demanded of NPO boards. Individual board members can help staff when the time comes, but they cannot be the implementers of their own policies. Bruce Collins notes, "How the organization's board delegates its authority varies with business needs and management style."[12] In most cases, board members have functions and responsibilities outside the NPO. Managers and program people are responsible for implementation of policy. The administration of financial and fiscal functions is especially complex, and board members, who generally come from a cross section of professions, need their NPO director to spend time training them on how the mission, strategic plan, programs, and budgets relate to one another. Regardless of how that is done, an organization's director and the staff he or she supervises are delegated the primary responsibility of carrying out the financial directives and policies of the board. Much of the authority that gets delegated is spelled out in state statutes, incorporation papers, bylaws, and other documents. Where such authority is not clearly understood, or where specific responsibilities need to be clearly spelled out, written policies need to be drawn up. This process begins with the simple yet important financial decision about who may sign a check and for what amount.[13]

VOLUNTEER RESPONSIBILITIES

A unique characteristic of the nonprofit sector is the contribution of volunteers drawn from among working professionals, students, retirees, housewives, and others who have time available to produce successful mission outcomes for the various types of NPOs. Volunteers come from all sectors and subsectors. While volunteers are not generally given responsibilities with the revenues and expenditures of the NPOs, they provide services to them and do have a major function. They save the organization money and provide expensive services that NPOs cannot afford to purchase. In 2006, the hourly value of volunteer time was estimated to be at a national average of $19.51, according to *Independent Sector*.[14] Volunteers contribute to the productivity of the nonprofit sector by providing accounting, administrative, fundraising, event management, communications services, and client supervision expertise. It is probably not an exaggeration to say that the nonprofit sector would not have achieved the success it has without the valuable services of volunteers.

VITAL INTERNAL FACTORS AFFECTING NPOS

Leaders of organizations were discussed in previous sections. Leadership is probably the key to success for any organization in any sector of the economy. The modern organization will not likely be successful by only relying on leadership. In addition to leadership, there are three other factors, in terms of financial and fiscal administration, that the modern organization must rely on, especially as they apply to the generation of revenues and spending of resources. The factors are *ethics, communication*, and *technology*. Leaders and managers must concentrate on these factors because of several highly scrutinized financial scandals that affected not only corporations like Enron, WorldCom, and others, but also such well-known NPOs as the United Way, the Rainbow Coalition, and the American Red Cross. All of these organizations became subject to scrutiny in the 1990s and the early part of this century for failing to maintain their integrity.

Ethics

Many NPOs operate under an ethics and accountability code to which board and staff members are expected to subscribe. To operate under a shared understanding of ethics is in the best interests of any organization, and doing so will help any organization meet its mission and goals. It is extremely important for NPO boards and staff to establish ethical and communication policies and philosophies to establish a system of trust. If done correctly, stakeholders will gain and maintain trust in the organization. NPO staff members must know the chain of command.

Not following the chain of command gets many organizations in trouble. People without an ethical base will ultimately fail. Regardless of the individual responsibilities for financial matters, all parties have a duty to each other to know what is in the budget and to make sure that they are operating within its parameters. All parties have a responsibility to discuss large deviations (plus or minus) that may affect an NPO's bottom line. Poor planning or unwillingness to accept the plan is an ethical problem from almost any perspective. The ultimate responsibility for an area should be left to the one whose job description includes the area of concern.

An excellent and relevant code of ethical principles is that of the Association of Fundraising Professionals (AFP).

AFP members aspire to:

- Practice their profession with integrity, honesty, truthfulness, and adherence to the absolute obligation to safeguard the public trust.

- Act according to the highest standards and visions of their organization, profession, and conscience.

- Put philanthropic mission above personal gain.

- Inspire others through their own sense of dedication and high purpose.

- Improve their professional knowledge and skills, so that their performance will better serve others.

- Demonstrate concern for the interests and well-being of individuals affected by their actions.

- Value the privacy, freedom of choice, and interests of all those affected by their actions.

- Foster cultural diversity and pluralistic values, and treat all people with dignity and respect.

- Affirm, through personal giving, a commitment to philanthropy and its role in society.

- Adhere to the spirit as well as the letter of all applicable laws and regulations.

- Advocate within their organizations adherence to all applicable laws and regulations.

- Avoid even the appearance of any criminal offense or professional misconduct.

- Bring credit to the fundraising profession by their public demeanor.

- Encourage colleagues to embrace and practice these ethical principles and standards of professional practice.

- Be aware of the codes of ethics promulgated by other professional organizations that serve philanthropy. [15]

Communication

Poor communication is a deficiency that can affect any of us and can bring down any organization. Like any business or any government organization, communication is the key to success. If there is a sin that can lead an NPO into organizational hell, it is poor communication. It is the first and the deadliest of sins that an organization can commit, and it is likely the only organizational sin that stands all on its own, because all the other sins within an organization are based on either poor or no communication.

Both external and internal communications are vital to financial success in an organization. While fundraising is clearly more important than many other functions, it should not be the only contact an NPO has with stakeholders. Letting the community know the status of the financial condition can be helpful in fundraising efforts. Nonprofits operate in a fishbowl, so they should strive to be open organizations in order to create appropriate relationships with funding organizations, supporters, clients, and all other stakeholders. Without effective communication to all users, serious problems can ensue. Management too often informs the staff of important commitments and changes after they occur, which results in frustration and resentment. Staff members need to not only be aware of changes prior to implementation but be made part of the change management whenever possible.

In their book, *Financial Management for Nonprofits*, J.G. Seigel and J.K. Shim write, "Financial information should be recorded, reviewed, summarized, and reported."[16] While information hoarding may be a sort of power ploy, none of us are invincible, and unforeseen events may occur. In the event of an emergency, someone needs to be able to continue the mission of the agency. In such an emergency, or in the event of the unavailability of the person with the information, someone still needs to make decisions and take actions to meet the needs and goals of the agency.

Technology

Modern technology has become essential to most organizations and is worthy of special attention in this discussion. It is true that some NPOs still operate with technologically disadvantaged systems that cannot transfer data easily and have poor reporting capabilities.[17] Some NPOs are so small and poorly funded that computer technology may be unobtainable. But in order to conduct business effectively and to improve communications, NPOs need to keep up with technological innovations and enhancements. For some nonprofits, technology is not always the priority it ought to be because funds are limited. Overall, NPOs tend to be unsophisticated and unprepared for technological change and advancement, and the so-called digital divide separates organizations as well as people. One useful recommendation is to view information technology not as a cost but as an investment. Organizations should structure information technology systems wisely with a vision that recognizes the following:

- Existing systems
- Implications of updates or changes in information management with consideration of effects on staff, clients, members, and other stakeholders
- Key board members and staff

Simply put, this means that an NPO should do nothing that would unnecessarily hurt existing technology and functional operations. NPOs should share ideas and invest in the necessary training so that the use and application of technology are most effective.

If an NPO has an opportunity to make room in the budget for updated technology, it should do so. If the NPO buys the right equipment and is well prepared to take care of the equipment, there may only be a need for a one-time budget allowance for computers. It may be possible for an NPO to cut back on one program or another for a year while it updates its technological equipment and software. In the end, it is better to be technologically advanced in order to reduce the number of people and the amount of time needed to find information.

Computer hardware and software have achieved the status of utility, the same category as water, sewer, and electric services. And due to the constant change in technology, computer hardware and software should be replaced every three or four years. A word to the wise: Automating a bad system may only allow errors to be made at a faster pace.

VITAL LEGAL FACTORS AFFECTING NPOS

This section takes a close look at the main purposes of NPOs from a legal perspective as they apply to finance and budgeting. It helps lay the foundation for understanding the rest of the concepts in the chapters that follow by showing the limitations imposed on NPOs by government and other influences. It examines legal and financial requirements that affect NPOs, such as the all-important 501(c)(3) designation as granted and administered by the Internal Revenue Service (IRS), the IRS Form 990, the Sarbanes-Oxley Act, and other important requirements that dictate many NPO financial and fiscal administration activities.

The 501(c)(3) Internal Revenue Service Designation

Most NPOs aspire to achieve the IRS tax status of 501(c)(3). In fact, of the 1.9 million recognized NPOs in the United States, 1.5 million have achieved that status.[18] There are privileges that come with that designation that benefit the financial operation of NPOs. When the designation is approved, it allows the organization to create tax-exempt revenue through the sale of services and products related to the organization, through grants from funding sources, and through donations from individuals and organizations. The designation gives donors to NPOs the right to deduct a portion of their donation from their income tax bill. The designated organizations are exempt from sales and income taxes for their primary related operations. These organizations achieve eligibility for certain grants from government and private foundations. There are tests of eligibility for the designation as 501(c)(3). The first is mission-related and involves several identifiable types of missions. The IRS and state agencies review and examine any organizations that seek to become a designated organization. The organization must prove to have one of the following missions:

- Educational
- Religious
- Charitable

- Scientific

- Literary

- Public safety

- Fostering certain national or international amateur sports competitions

- Prevention of cruelty to children and animals

The second IRS test is a political test. An organization seeking to become and operate as a 501(c)(3) cannot participate in or contribute to any political campaign for a particular candidate either by developing and distributing campaign literature or having a close relationship with the candidate.

Another area of the 501(c)(3) designation that affects financial and fiscal responsibilities deals with unrelated business activities. These activities are considered to be substantially unrelated to the NPO in terms of the products or services it provides and have profit as a motive. Unrelated business activities can be exempt if the activity is operated by the NPO or benefits the organization's clients without compensating those operating the business. NPO revenue from an unrelated business activity may be subject to income taxes.

Nonprofit Financial Reporting to the Internal Revenue Service

NPOs report mostly to the Internal Revenue Service. The IRS Form 990 (Exhibit 1.1, partial view) is the principal reporting instrument used. Forms 990 are subject to being audited onsite at NPOs by IRS agents.

The Form 990 requires tax-exempt NPOs to complete a revenue and income statement, a balance sheet, a statement of how functional expenses were allocated, a segregated expenses section, and a detailed report on all revenue, including donations, membership fees, investment income, and grant revenue. The reader should find the box in the upper right-hand corner of Exhibit 1.1 under *2005*. The statement in bold type, *Open to Public Inspection*, is worth noting because it is a directive that an NPO's financial status is open to the public. Anyone can gain access to any tax-exempt NPO's Form 990 through websites like www.guidestar.com. A creative NPO will scan the Forms

Form **990**	**Return of Organization Exempt From Income Tax**	OMB No. 1545-0047
Department of the Treasury Internal Revenue Service	Under section 501(c), 527, or 4947(a)(1) of the Internal Revenue Code (except black lung benefit trust or private foundation) ▶ The organization may have to use a copy of this return to satisfy state reporting requirements.	2005 **Open to Public Inspection**

A   For the 2005 calendar year, or tax year beginning _____ , 2005, and ending _____ , 20 ____

B Check if applicable:	Please use IRS label or print or type. See Specific Instructions.	C Name of organization	D Employer identification number
☐ Address change			
☐ Name change		Number and street (or P.O. box if mail is not delivered to street address) Room/suite	E Telephone number ( )
☐ Initial return			
☐ Final return		City or town, state or country, and ZIP + 4	F Accounting method: ☐ Cash ☐ Accrual
☐ Amended return			☐ Other (specify) ▶
☐ Application pending	• Section 501(c)(3) organizations and 4947(a)(1) nonexempt charitable trusts must attach a completed Schedule A (Form 990 or 990-EZ).		H and I are not applicable to section 527 organizations.

H(a) Is this a group return for affiliates?   ☐ Yes ☐ No

G   Website: ▶ _____

H(b) If "Yes," enter number of affiliates ▶ _____

J   Organization type (check only one) ▶ ☐ 501(c) ( ) ◀ (insert no.) ☐ 4947(a)(1) or ☐ 527

H(c) Are all affiliates included?   ☐ Yes ☐ No
(If "No," attach a list. See instructions.)

K   Check here ▶ ☐ if the organization's gross receipts are normally not more than $25,000. The

H(d) Is this a separate return filed by an

Exhibit 1.1: Internal Revenue Service Form 990: Reporting to the Internal Revenue Service (IRS) (Partial View)

990 of other agencies with similar missions to compare itself on financial factors that will be discussed in Chapter 6.

State Agency Oversight

States, naturally, differ on required reporting by NPOs. There are four financial and fiscal bylaw requirements of NPOs that are found in the laws of most of the states in the United States:

- Capital (common) stock may not be issued to raise funds

- Assets cannot be distributed for personal benefit

- Profit making as a principal purpose is not allowed

- Assets cannot be used for political purposes except where mission is affected (must be specified and justified)[19]

Financial reporting to state oversight agencies usually follows the lead and the structure of the IRS and Form 990.

Grants from Government and Private Funding Organizations

Organizations that receive grants from private funding sources and federal, state, and local organizations must follow financial accounting requirements.

NPOs, in some cases, may be required by granting agencies to obtain regular financial audits by an independent third party. Of course, the requirements vary among the granting agencies. Some of the organizations that may be used as resources for understanding requirements for managing grant funds include the Financial Accounting Standards Board (FASB), the American Institute of Certified Public Accountants (AICPA), and the U.S. Federal Office of Management and Budget (OMB). Individual state and local governments and private organizations have individual guidelines and should be considered the primary source of information.

The Sarbanes-Oxley Act

The corporate scandals of the early 2000s involving ENRON, WorldCom, and others underscored the importance of the auditing function and its contribution to restoring trust, ascertaining the reliability of operations, and even promoting economic development. The unfortunate scandals led to the enactment into law of the Sarbanes-Oxley Act (SOX) of 2003, which materially affected the auditing profession.[20] While this law is directed at corporations in the business sector, it also has implications for NPOs, especially those that conduct annual audits. Hiring an auditor who also provides consulting and outsourced accounting services to the organization is no longer considered a good business practice because of the scrutiny applied under the terms of SOX. Such a relationship can cause the appearance of a conflict of interest that some might suspect will influence the findings of an audit.

HOW DO FINANCIAL AND FISCAL RESPONSIBILITIES DIFFER AMONG THE SECTORS OF THE ECONOMY?

Every functional area in the business and government world is needed in NPOs as well. As seen in Table 2.1, the three traditional sectors of the U.S. economy—government, nonprofit, and for-profit—are similar in terms of financial and fiscal responsibilities. That does not mean, however, that NPO administrators can call up their friends in government and business and ask specific questions about financial and fiscal issues. While financial and fiscal

	PUBLIC	NONPROFIT	PRIVATE
Financial Goals	Promote economic growth, stabilize prices, and increase employment.	Support specialized agency missions.	Maximize profits and shareholder wealth.
Job Categories	Fiscal Analyst, Treasurer, Accountant, Auditor, Chief Financial Officer (CFO).	Financial Analyst, Assistant or Divisional Treasurer, CFO.	Financial Analyst, Credit Manager, Tax Manager, Assistant or Divisional Treasurer, CFO.
General Responsibilities	Fiscal management. Appropriations and spending. Manage unique capital assets (e.g., Mt. Rushmore). Investing.	Fundraising. Fiscal and accounting activities. Investing.	Sell goods/services for a price. Investing, fiscal and accounting. Price-setting.
General Education Requirements	Minimum: Bachelor's degree in accounting, or public or business administration.	Minimum: Bachelor's degree in accounting, public nonprofit, or business administration.	Minimum: Bachelor's degree in accounting or business administration.
Salaries (expressed as average or mean)	Local CFO $67,688; local treasurer $46,200, fiscal analysts $52,480; tax examiners, collectors & revenue agents $42,250.	CFO $60,675; planned giving officer $62,019; development director $55,807; major gifts officer $56,850.	CFO at a large firm: up to $295,000; financial analyst - $23 to 47,000; credit manager $30-63,000; tax manager $57-105,000; asst. or division manager $47-78,000.
Knowledge Requirements	Financial, cost accounting, tax collection, data processing, cash and securities management, financial planning, pension fund management.	Financial, cost accounting, data processing, cash and securities management, financial planning, pension fund management.	Financial, cost accounting, taxes, data processing, cash and securities management, financial planning, credit analysis, investor relations, pension fund management.
Ethics and Accountability	Public interest fiduciary responsibilities as protectors of the public treasury.	The public and donor trust and confidence protected and upheld by the actions of the sector.	Responsible to owners and raising ethical awareness, providing guides and education on ethics.

Table 2.1: Comparison of Key Responsibilities of Financial and Fiscal Professionals

functions may be the same or similar, the sectors experience different influences and therefore must apply the functions differently. The information in Table 2.1 is aggregated and represents averages of the whole population. It is a starting point for understanding both the uniqueness and the similarity of NPO financial and fiscal operations. The factors on the left axis of the table are the descriptive factors of finance and budgeting that fit all sectors: financial goals, types of jobs, responsibilities, education requirements, salaries, knowledge requirements, and ethics. These factors define the professionals in charge of raising and using funds. As readers scan across the columns, they can discern differences and similarities among the sectors.

The items found in Table 2.1 provide a framework that can assist in the development of an understanding of the theories, concepts, and applications covered in this book. Clearly, finance professionals in the nonprofit sector are more like their counterparts in the other sectors than they are different. The main differences among the economic sectors lie in the first factor, financial goals. This factor is also important because it demonstrates that NPOs are unique among the sectors, and it defines the focused role of providing services to specific target populations within society. The chapters that follow will cover these financial goals in sufficient detail to provide useful knowledge for students of NPO financial and fiscal administration.

SUMMARY

Chapter 2 has laid the groundwork for understanding the content and concepts of the rest of the book. Financial and fiscal administration was illustrated as a network of four critical functions integrated to ensure that an NPO carries out its mission. The chapter explained the roles and responsibilities of important contributors to an NPO's financial operations, including board members, staff, and volunteers. It also outlined important internal and external factors that affect the outcomes of an NPO as it strives for mission success. Finally, Chapter 2 compared the roles of financial professionals in the nonprofit sector to those working in government and in the business sector.

USEFUL WEBSITES

Students may find the following websites useful in gaining a broader understanding of the contents of this book. These websites were current as of September 2008. Readers are urged to conduct their own search for useful websites.

- Nonprofit Alliance (http://www.allianceonline.org/faqs.html)
- Tax Information for Nonprofits (http://www.mapnp.org/library/tax/np_tax.htm)
- Independent Sector (http://www.independentsector.org)
- Index Calculators (http://www.bls.gov/)
- Inflation Calculator (http://www.westegg.com/inflation/)
- Cash Management Strategies for Nonprofits (http://www.kdv.com/cash.html)
- Forecasting Principles (http://www.marketing.wharton.upenn.edu/forecast/welcome.html)
- The New Nonprofit Almanac & Desk Reference (http://www.independentsector.org/PDFs/NAExecSum.pdf)
- Nonprofit Fundraising and Grantwriting (http://www.mapnp.org/library/fndrsng/np_raise/np_raise.htm)

DISCUSSION QUESTIONS

1. Be the board member. To serve on an NPO's board, you take on several substantial financial and fiscal responsibilities. Nothing is more important than the development of a sound budget to control and direct those activities. Assume you have been appointed to a board and receive from the executive director a handshake and an orientation manual. Budget time is a couple of months away. What steps would you take to prepare yourself for the budget process?

2. Communication within an organization is an asset. Knowledge
    hoarding is power, as seen in the following scenario: An NPO that
    provided exceptional services to its clientele is run by an executive
    director who was always in the news discussing the organization's
    wonderful accomplishments for the community. The executive director
    was extremely controlling and kept the budget information and several
    other key pieces of financial information from the staff. Unfortunately,
    the executive director became ill, and no one else in the organization
    knew how to maintain the momentum of the organization. Several of
    the staff members were new, but not even senior long-time employees
    were in a position to provide much information. The executive director
    was dynamic and did accomplish many wonderful things for the
    community, but he failed to delegate and share information. He clearly
    did not follow the theory that competent and trustworthy knowledgeable
    financial professionals should be asked to review managerial financial
    reports. The board did very little to provide any budgetary oversight.
    What would you do to ensure information sharing in an organization
    if the executive director did not return to take his job back? What
    actions should this organization take if the executive director did
    return?

EXERCISE

Table 2.1 describes the differences and similarities of the three major
economic sectors in the United States. Scan the table and separate the similarities and differences into two columns. Consider the fact that some of
the similarities and differences have greater value than others. Discuss
whether the nonprofit sector varies more from the government sector or
from the private sector. Overall, are the three sectors more alike than different or vice versa?

INNOVATION:
MALCOLM BALDRIGE NATIONAL QUALITY
AWARD FOR NONPROFITS

A national organization that has for years recognized businesses and universities for demonstrating outstanding operations has added NPOs to the types of organizations it honors. The prestigious Malcolm Baldrige National Quality Award has decided to test a program for awarding NPOs for making quality improvements in their operations. This is an indication of the emergence and recognition of the nonprofit sector. Therefore, the future is bright for the NPO financial and budgeting professional. According to the Baldrige website: [21]

> *The Baldrige Award was created by Public Law 100-107, signed into law on August 20, 1987. The Award Program, responsive to the purposes of Public Law 100-107, led to the creation of a new public-private partnership. Principal support for the program comes from the Foundation for the Malcolm Baldrige National Quality Award, established in 1988. The Award is named for Malcolm Baldrige, who served as Secretary of Commerce from 1981 until his tragic death in a rodeo accident in 1987. His managerial excellence contributed to long-term improvement in efficiency and effectiveness of government. Baldrige awards go to businesses that demonstrate high quality performance in lower costs, productivity improvements and strategic planning that can serve as models for others.*

> *The purpose of the nonprofit pilot is to provide nonprofit organizations an opportunity to participate in the Baldrige evaluation process and to receive feedback reports concerning their strengths and opportunities for improvement relative to the Baldrige criteria for performance excellence. The 2006 pilot was a one-year activity that allows the Baldrige Program to test the applicability of the Baldrige Award's key processes, procedures, and criteria to the nonprofit sector of the United States economy.*

NOTES

1   Committee on Examination of Plant Research Programs in the United States, *Plant Biology Research and Training for the 21st Century* (Washington, DC: National Academies Press, 1992).

2   Whatcom Council of Nonprofits, "Financial Management," *Best Practices for Nonprofits,* 2002. Online at http://www.wcnwebsite.org/practices/financial.htm (accessed May 19, 2008).

3   Office of Management and Budget, "Financial Management System," *Circular No. A-127,* revised version, (Washington D.C.: Office of Management and Budget,1993).

4   Ibid.

5   Fisher Howe, "Nonprofit Accountability: The Board's Fiduciary Responsibility," *Nonprofit Governance and Management,* Victor Futter, ed. (Chicago: American Bar Association, 2002).

6   Ibid.

7   H. Goldschmidt, "The Fiduciary Duties of Non-Profit Directors and Officers: Problems, Paradoxes and Proposed Reforms," May 19, 2006. Online at http://www.law.nyu.edu (accessed May 19, 2008).

8   K. Mathiasen, Board Passages: *Three Key Stages in a Nonprofit Board's Life Cycle* (Washington, DC: National Center for Nonprofit Boards, 1998).

9   J. Carver, "What Use is Business Experience on a Nonprofit or Governmental Board?" *Board Leadership* 58 (2001): 2–8.

10 Ibid.

11 L. Stegink, "What Are My Legal Responsibilities?" *Association Management* 57.1 (2005): 84–86.

12 Bruce Collins, "What Every Incoming Director of a Nonprofit Organizations Should Know: A Checklist," *Nonprofit Governance and Management,* Victor Futter, ed. (Chicago: American Bar Association, 2002).

13 Ibid.

14 *Independent Sector,* "Draft Regulations Released for Redesigned Form 990," 2008. Online at http://www.independentsector.org (accessed April 28, 2008). Also, *Independent Sector,* "IS Announces New Estimate for Value of Volunteer Time." Online at http://www.independentsector.org (accessed May 19, 2008).

15 Association of Fundraising Professionals, "Code of Ethical Principles." Online at http://www.afpnet.org (accessed May 19, 2008).

16 J. G. Seigel and J. K. Shim, *Financial Management for Nonprofits: The Complete Guide to Maximizing Resources and Managing Assets* (New York: McGraw-Hill, 1997).

17 Kevin Corder, "Acquiring New Technology: Comparing Nonprofit and Public Sector Agencies," *Administration & Society* 33 (2001): 194.

18 *Independent Sector,* "Nonprofit Almanac," 2002. Online at http://www.independentsector.org/programs/research/NA01main.html (accessed May 14, 2008).

19 Herrington J. Bryce, *Financial and Strategic Management for Nonprofit Organizations* (San Francisco: Jossey-Bass, 2000).

20 The American Competitiveness and Corporate Accountability Act of 2002: The Sarbanes-Oxley Act. For more information see the U.S. Securities and Exchange Commission website at http://sec.gov/index.htm (accessed May 19, 2008).

21 National Institutes of Standards and Technology, Baldrige National Quality Program. Online at http://www.quality.nist.gov (accessed May 19, 2008).

CHAPTER 3
Strategic Financial Planning

If you do not know where you are going, then how can you expect to get there? It is said that in the NPO industry successful nonprofits in the twenty-first century will be those who are financially empowered.[1] A vital and pertinent question, then, is how does an NPO achieve financial empowerment? This chapter delves into one of the most intriguing and important areas for a modern organization—strategic financial planning. This topic comes early in this book because it provides readers with a view of how mission, program, and finance come together in a single planning process for the betterment of NPOs and their stakeholders. Strategic financial planning is a management tool that is designed to allow organizations to acquire the commitment of everyone in or concerned about an organization, and then move them toward the same vision, mission, goals, and objectives. A vital aspect of the strategic planning process is to anticipate costs in order to identify revenue sources that will fulfill the strategic design. This chapter shows that even in that context, the strategic plan must be flexible and revisable, because circumstances change constantly. Strategic planning provides organized answers to the questions, "Where are you going?" and "How are you going to get there?"

TOPICS

- A Strategic Planning Metaphor
- The Financial and Fiscal Administration Network: The Strategic Plan
- Strategic Planning Defined
- Why Do Strategic Planning?
- The Strategic Planning Process
- External Factors Affecting Strategic Plans
- Internal Factors Affecting Strategic Plans
- Money, Goals, and Objectives
- Operational versus Capital Budgeting
- Financial and Fiscal Administration in Strategic Plans
- Revenue Planning
- Cost, Expenditure, and Investment Planning
- Summary
- Discussion Questions
- Exercise
- Innovation at the Sector Boundaries: Strategic Restructuring

A STRATEGIC PLANNING METAPHOR

Strategic planning has been called a *ritual,* sometimes simple, sometimes complicated, that leads to long-term plans with short-term flexibility. Metaphorically, it resembles the explorations during the fifteenth and sixteenth centuries by crews in ships on the high seas whose brave captains discovered new worlds. In the harbor of Lisbon there is wonderful monument, *Padrao dos Descobrimentos,* that celebrates all of Portugal's famous sea captains, including Henry the Navigator and Vasco da Gama. Though faced with uncertainty, each of these captains had a vision of where he wanted to go. Equipped with the latest charts and the latest technology, each took stock of his situation and determined his abilities and possibilities. Navigators would read the stars, and the captains would sail in a prescribed direction. The mission and goals of these long journeys were to increase the wealth and power of their sponsors as well as the captain's glory. Though they had their plans, the way was full of unknowns; the way was fuzzy. As they sailed, the captains had to adjust for the sailing conditions, unexpected islands, sail-ripping winds, rancid food, sickness, and mutiny. They had to face and overcome these problems while maintaining a planned course. Those who succeeded at their mission changed the world for all time.

Here is an even more ancient way of thinking about strategic planning that captures the importance of flexibility in strategic planning: In prehistory, before the advent of the sail for vessels, boats were subject to the wind. If the wind blew out of the north, the prehistoric mariner went south. He might try to row against the wind for a time, but eventually the vessel headed south. Early sails allowed our ancestors to sail across the wind at right angles to it, and later inventions actually made it possible, by planning a series of tacks, to sail due north, directly into the wind.[2]

THE FINANCIAL AND FISCAL ADMINISTRATION NETWORK: THE STRATEGIC PLAN

Every organization engages in strategic planning, whether its members call it that or not. Someone in every organization has an idea about where the organization needs to go with its mission, an idea that is at least tucked away somewhere in his or her mind, if not actually written on paper. It is important that efforts made toward creating a strategic plan be recognized and valued. In the best case, the strategic goals of an organization are codified in a document that is known and understood by everyone within an organization. Done correctly, a strategic plan is an excellent guide for funding, spending, and investing. A strategic plan is a walking, talking *opportunity cost*. In economics, opportunity cost measures the value of selected projects based on the value of the next best use of dollars. In other words, a decision to spend a given amount of dollars to acquire a good or service is measured against the cost of what you had to give up to acquire that good or service. A strategic plan is the ultimate opportunity cost. If the projects and programs selected to be included in a strategic plan are thoroughly implemented, the funds used for those programs are lost opportunities for years to come.

Strategic planning provides a base for finance and budgeting. Figure 3.1 is derived from Figure 2.1 in Chapter 2, which depicted the Financial and Fiscal Administration Network.

Recall that Figure 2.1 included a base, four diamond shapes representing financial and fiscal functions/responsibilities (budgeting, management, accounting, and evaluation), and six two-way flow arrows among the diamond shapes. The base of that figure, in fact, represents the strategic plan of an organization. It is the foundation on which all the other activities should depend. Financial and fiscal administration plays a key role in a strategic plan because it answers the question, *"How are we going to pay for these great ideas?"* Figure 3.1 removes the four functions and the flow arrows that were depicted in Figure 2.1, leaving only the

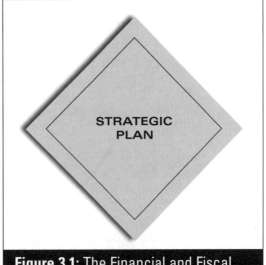

Figure 3.1: The Financial and Fiscal Network Base: The Strategic Planning Function

strategic plan represented as the large base shaped like a diamond figure. The graphic depicts how the strategic plan holds the entire financial system together and how all the functions fit into the plan. The following chapters will add the other functions back to the network graphic so that it will again appear as it was depicted in Chapter 2.

This chapter defines and describes what a strategic plan is, what it does, why it is important to do, the process NPOs must follow, and the internal and external factors involved in carrying the strategic plan. The chapter distinguished between capital and operational budgeting, revenue, expenditures, and investments. It shows that a strategic plan will help an NPO reach its goals and build its relationships with its stakeholders as it carries out the strategic plan in an efficient and effective manner.

STRATEGIC PLANNING DEFINED

A strategic plan is a written document that translates an organization's vision and objectives into a long-term three to five year vision. As both a concept and a tool, strategic planning makes it possible for an organization to define its future in an organized way. The concept of strategic planning for NPOs was born out of their need to succeed in the modern, constantly changing world in which they operate. The success horizon for any organization is, at best, undefined and fuzzy until the organization takes steps to understand where it wants to go. That fuzzy horizon must be brought into focus through a process that looks both at defining the organization's mission and goals for serving clients and figuring out how to pay for reaching its goals. Strategic planning is a deliberate choice an NPO makes to take the opportunity to examine the assumptions that lead in a purposeful direction. A strategic plan is put in place to develop long-term objectives that are consistent with an organization's mission and goals, and that takes into account financial performance. In the strategic planning process, no idea should be ignored, but everyone involved must understand that no organization can do everything. The process will result in making tough choices about what to include and what to exclude.

WHY DO STRATEGIC PLANNING?

You do strategic planning in order to sail due north directly into the wind. You do strategic planning so you can reach your goal regardless of environmental challenges. For most NPOs, multiple projects compete for limited resources. There is never enough money to finance them all, so having a strategic plan in place is a non-negotiable asset for many nonprofits. How will a nonprofit hospital meet the special needs of its community without having a plan and knowing how it will be paid for? Is blind luck a legitimate substitute for strategy? Is creating an annual budget enough? Will an NPO in a growing community with a mission of mentoring at-risk children sustain itself without a plan for attracting enough men and women to become mentors or knowing what level of staff it will need? A community theater with a mission to provide entertainment for the elderly may have the greatest productions in the world, but if it lacks a plan for funding that includes ways and means to make the productions affordable and accessible, will it ever succeed?

While strategic planning is required, it is not perfect as a management tool. It will not guarantee an organization's success, and if the plan is not perceptive and does not point the organization in the best direction, it might never achieve success. To achieve success, the boards and staffs of NPOs have to think both strategically and critically, because proposed strategies can be wrong. To think strategically requires both knowledge and wisdom. In thinking strategically, the organization must stay informed and responsive. It must have the capability of managing both long-term strategies and the daily strategies that must be translated into action. Although reality may interfere, a strategically thinking organization ideally should let the strategic plan permeate throughout the organization so that staff at all levels can make or suggest corrections that are within their level of responsibility and in line with the longer-term strategies and options contained within the strategic plan.

Strategic plans require strong organizational commitment. A strategic board assumes a leadership position by identifying broadly important outcomes, setting priorities, and monitoring the way the staff and volunteers implement major initiatives.[3] Some organizations may not need to think as strategically as others. Clearly, small organizations not motivated by growth, those with guaranteed long-term revenue sources, those with extremely focused missions, those that are strictly regulated by government, boards, or other influential organizations, or organizations that fulfill local missions unaffected by externalities might be able to rely on a one-year horizon as opposed to the three- to five-year horizon associated with strategic planning. An annual plan may be sufficient for these organizations and may take the form of a budget or a separate planning tool.[4] A large, complex organization that is highly susceptible to environmental changes must search continuously for revenue. Other organizations likely to benefit from developing a sophisticated strategic plan include those with a global mission, those committed to growth, those with multiple missions and many options, and those that are highly visible and have aggressive boards.[5]

THE STRATEGIC PLANNING PROCESS

A strategic plan is developed and implemented in order to make progress toward long-term objectives and visionary strategies that take into account financial performance, public image, and social responsibility. The goal is to give an agency control while seeking a shared prosperity with its most important relationships. Although the strategic planning process can be lengthy and receive much criticism for the resources it consumes, strategic planning is a means for adjusting and restructuring the functions and operations of an organization. Thus, as B. Reed and J. Swain write in their book, *Public Finance Administration*, "... as an organization's financial situation changes and as environmental factors change ... the [strategic plan] should reflect the change."[6] The preparation of a strategic plan provides an opportunity to consider programs and activities that can be terminated, reduced in scope, or transferred elsewhere within the financial decisions considered.

Overall, strategic plans are necessary in order to formulate future goals, plans, and budgets. J. Sammer writes, for example, that the process "helps create the most efficient vehicle for getting there."[7] It is a *strategic* process, and it is intentional because it is birthed by specific thoughts, proposals, discussions, debates, compromises, and agreements. These organizational agreements should reflect the best way of navigating the fuzzy and often treacherous horizon. Reaching agreements allows room for creating thoughtful approaches.

The steps presented in this section of the chapter provide one framework for the development of a strategic plan. Other processes might be more appropriate for different types of organizations in different situations.

Strengths, Weaknesses, Opportunities, and Threats (SWOT)

A SWOT (pronounced "swat") analysis is a management tool that helps organizations to identify internal strengths, internal weaknesses, opportunities, and threats that affect their ability to fulfill their missions. It can be used as the basis for strategic planning. The SWOT analysis shown in Table 3.1 provides an approach to ascertaining a fictitious community medical center's strengths, weaknesses, opportunities, and threats. See the next section, which analyzes critical factors involved in strategic financial planning.

A Case Analysis: Applying SWOT

In this approach, the first step is to put weights on various factors that contribute to an organization. The approach assumes that a total weight of 1 will be apportioned among all factors in the analysis. This results in weights of between 0 and 1, which reflect the importance of each of the factors to the organization's mission. Scores closest to 0 are low in importance, while scores closer to 1 are highly important to the NPO. Total weights cannot exceed the value of 1. The weights are depicted in column two in Table 3.1. Each factor, then, is scored to reflect the performance of the NPO using the following scale: 5 = outstanding, 4 = above average, 3 = average, 2 = below average and 1 = poor. In Table 3.1, column three lists the scores provided by evaluators external to the organization, while column five depicts the scores of evaluators who are internal to the organization. To arrive at the level of organizational strength for each factor, the weight for each factor is multiplied by its strength rating. The results are added together to yield a total strength of contribution score. The higher the total score, that is, the closer to a score of 5, the stronger the organization is for a given factor.[8]

FACTORS	WEIGHT	RATING	WEIGHTED SCORE	RATING	WEIGHTED SCORE
Ability to respond to changes in community needs	.04	2	.08	4	.16
Managerial experience	.17	3	.51	4	.68
Line staff experience	.11	3	.33	4	.44
Quality of support services	.07	3	.21	3	.21
Provider availability	.22	3	.66	3	.66
Community reputation	.10	3	.30	4	.40
Environment for new funding sources	.02	2	.04	3	.06
Capacity to serve new clients	.02	2	.04	2	.04
Collection of co-pays	.05	2	.10	2	.10
Community health ratings	.03	3	.09	3	.09
Financial condition	.10	4	.40	3	.30
Client satisfaction	.07	3	.21	1	.07
	1.00		2.97		3.21

Table 3.1 Factor Analysis – Community Medical Center

The NPO should not develop the strength factors and weights but should find an existing instrument or bring in outside expertise. The effective organization will score itself and will also invite outsiders to evaluate the strength factors separately. This will help the NPO avoid bias by taking it out of the scoring.

The results differ markedly between the internal and external evaluators. The latter have discerned that the NPO's performance is relatively low. Clearly, the external evaluators and internal evaluators need to have some discussion in order to determine the basis for the differences and then need to reevaluate performance in order to arrive at recognition of strengths, weaknesses, opportunities, and threats. When agreement is achieved, discussion about how to deal with the SWOT items can begin.

Steps for Creating a Strategic Plan

1. **Know the organization:** Conduct a SWOT analysis. Discover not only the condition of the NPO but also what must be done and what has to be overcome.

2. **Define the mission:** The organization needs to write, refine, and agree on what it wants to accomplish for the community or clients it exists to serve. Get buy-in from all stakeholders.

3. **Define the core values:** Organizations are distinguished by their values. Values are reflected in plans, goals, strategies, and actions. Care must be taken to reflect values correctly.

4. **Evaluate possibilities:** Determine what the organization is capable of accomplishing in the context of strategic goals. Then set the deadlines for achieving goals.

5. **Assess the external environment:** Come to an understanding about what in the environment affects the agency. This will include "competitors."

6. **Set objectives:** This step involves breaking down the strategic goals into specific and measurable objectives that must be reached in the process of achieving the goals.

7. **Prioritize the strategic goals.**

8. **Design programs:** Programs reflect all the aspects of the strategic plan in action. Buildings, staff, and programs are the most visible endeavor of strategic planning.

9. **Determine budget:** While this is part of the program design process, it needs to be distinguished, because seeking viable funding sources and understanding how they are to be used dominates the responsibilities of organization leaders.

10. **Select strategies:** Strategies are ideas about the steps that need to be taken to implement programs. They must be flexible, however, so that they allow for shifting obstacles and targets.

11. **Evaluation cycle:** Performance, whether excellent or poor, is the first and foremost input for the next performance cycle. A formal evaluation

process at the end of a cycle contributes to success.

Strategic planning should err on the side of inclusiveness. While a planning committee of leaders from an organization's staff, board, and consultants should lead the process, individuals and organizations with a stake in the success of an NPO should be invited to participate in ways that are appropriate to their level of involvement and interest in the organization. Ideas and information from board and staff members, funding agencies, leaders of the community as defined by an organization, donors, volunteers and other interested parties are essential to the process. The following is an example of the strategic planning process in a fictitious NPO.

Case Analysis: Succeeding in the Strategic Planning Process

Strategic planning should err on the side of inclusiveness. While a planning committee of leaders from an organization's staff, board, and consultants should lead the process, individuals and organizations with a stake in the success of an NPO should be invited to participate in ways that are appropriate to their level of involvement and interest in the organization. Ideas and information from board and staff members, funding organizations, leaders of the community as defined by an organization, donors, volunteers, and other interested parties are essential to the process. The following is an example of the strategic planning process.

How does a small nonprofit organization with a mission to mentor at-risk children make it to the top 25 percent in the country in rate of participation by volunteers in and percentage of growth in financial support? The NPO belongs to an association with a national organization. It has 250 volunteers and a budget of less than $200,000. The NPO board, the new executive director, and other stakeholders believed that the NPO should be doing a lot better than it was. The mission of the organization is to mentor at-risk children and divert them from bad choices. The programs it operates include one-on-one mentoring between adults and children, mentoring in schools, and team mentoring. Prior to implementing strategic planning, the

NPO recruited mentors from the community and from local colleges and universities for children whose parents requested mentors. As will be seen, the NPO was able to dramatically expand its programs as well as the number of adult mentors and the number of children served. Strategic planning had an important role.

Three years before the good statistics, the agency was not recognized as a star performer on its stage. The NPO turned over its executive director position, and the new executive director came into the job recognizing that possibilities existed to expand and serve more children. She was motivated to find new directions in which the agency could move, and she was experienced in using strategic planning. Within a year she initiated a strategic planning effort and convinced the board and her staff to support the exercise. As a starting point, the board and staff scrutinized the agency using an analysis of strengths, weaknesses, opportunities, and threats (SWOT). The SWOT analysis showed that the organization was fundamentally sound but needed more money, better facilities, a new location, and a higher level of community involvement. Armed with the results of this analysis, the agency went into a planning mode, with everyone pointed in the same direction. The board hired a professional facilitator who led board members and staff through the planning process. With a long-term horizon of six years into the future, fifteen board members and three staff retreated off-site for a long day of planning, not knowing where the professional facilitator would lead the agency with such a long-term horizon.

The first topic the group analyzed and discussed was the agency's mission statement (who they were and who they served). After some disagreement on wording, they came pretty quickly to agreement. The group next turned to identifying their performance status and how they arrived at it. They reviewed the number of mentoring matches in the three previous years and examined research results that showed the outcomes of their efforts at matching mentors and mentees. Not satisfied with these outcomes, they looked at where the agency should be in terms of outcomes. The discussion about growth that followed stimulated some thoughtful questions. The chief factors that tempered any grand ideas about growth were the NPO's core values. The core values revolved around the belief in the community that mentors were a form of intervention for children of single parents—children who tend to be at risk for problems, including incarceration, in their lifetime. Mentors are role models who can be a positive influence on children who might be susceptible to becoming delinquents and might not achieve a status that contributes to a civil society. It is believed that children were worth the effort of intervention. The participants agreed that these mission-oriented values had to transcend any programmed growth ideas. This part of the process was a sensitive area for some people who had ideas that others did not find reasonable or viable. The process participants ultimately agreed on growth ideas that were consistent with the NPO's core values.

A staff person provided statistics showing solid data on the large number of at-risk children in the NPO's community. Another study assessed potential sources of mentors and what might motivate them to become mentors. The two studies gave the staff and board members a clear picture of the percentage of children they were serving as well as a picture of how many more children would need a mentor by the end of the six-year planning horizon. With this information the participants set about crafting a vision statement that would guide the agency during the time horizon. This part of the strategic planning process allowed the staff and board to dream much bigger and grander than they had ever done before, and they began to think about what it would take to make their vision a reality. In the end, the participants set reasonable dream goals for matching mentors and children and selected programs to participate in that met the standards contained in the agency's core values.

To serve these dream goals the agency then had to establish strategic goals and objectives in the following functional categories:

- Volunteer recruitment

- Financial management

- Financial development

- Marketing

- Board and staff development
- Facilities
- Technology

The group brainstormed each of these categories, and in doing so, realized that their big dream needed people, knowledge, and resources beyond what was available in the agency. The dream needed people who could and would assist the agency in making its big dream a reality. Group members identified one community leader in each of the functional categories and invited each of those individuals to meet with the group at the second planning meeting in order to complete the goals and objectives and to start the development of action plans. The planning process ended with the development of action plans that had specific timelines, quantity and quality goals, budgets, staff and volunteer committee assignments, benchmarks, and evaluation plans. As a result of the planning process, new grants that fit the mission and strategic plan were obtained, and the budget more than tripled, A full-time fundraiser and a full-time marketing director were brought on board, and the number of staff also tripled. The agency budgeted for and moved into a quality facility that was large enough to meet its needs and upgrade its image. Information technology was updated and upgraded, and both hardware and software were vastly improved.

This strategic planning process turned out to be an excellent way for the board, volunteers, and staff to work together, and for each of them to buy into the long-term plan for the agency. It resulted in better working relationships among staff members and between the board and the staff members. Three years after the initial planning process, the agency reviewed and updated the strategic plan, which led to goals with even higher numbers of matches to achieve than were set in the original plan. In the fifth year, the dream goal of matches between volunteers and children had been increased from some 250 to over 1,000, and the budget, likewise, was increased to more than three times as much as in the beginning of the strategic planning process.

EXTERNAL FACTORS AFFECTING STRATEGIC PLANS

The case analysis just presented brings strategic planning to life and reflects many of the issues involved in the planning process. The next sections of the chapter consider these issues, beginning with the external factors that strategic planners should take into account.

Every organization, like every organism, exists within an environment that affects it both negatively and positively. And no sector of the economy has to face a more treacherous and dynamic environment than the nonprofit sector. Most organizational environments are constantly stirring and changing. For NPOs, social events, politics, and economics impact everything they do—from purchasing paper clips to negotiating funding grants. Mittenthals argues that "even as advances in technology present opportunities, they also generate new expectations. Needs and community demographics are subject to change. So are methods for delivering programs and services. It is thus essential that NPOs reexamine their programs, services, and operations in light of current realities and future projections."[9] A successful planning process will help an NPO make projections about environmental realities, and it will also allow the organization to anticipate and respond in a positive way and avoid negative effects.

A very common environmental obstacle is politics. The political climate affects NPO budgets in important ways. To many NPOs, this climate means being susceptible to both "big P" politics, that is, politics in the public sector, and "little p" politics, that is, internal and community political affairs. In the public political arena, some NPOs are affected by decisions about direct funding made by legislators at the various levels of government. These NPOs often must make their case in front of public committees and in private meetings, lobbying decision makers the same way associations in all other sectors do. Other NPOs, which receive pass-down funds from government and other nonprofit agencies, are affected indirectly by the amount of funding that these pass-down agencies receive for distribution to the NPO community.

One must not neglect the political influences of power and decision making from NPO executives and board members in the overall process.[10] In some ways, a strategic plan takes some of the politics out of the budgeting process. Eventually, even board members, staff, and other stakeholders with strong points of view will approve strategic plans that at least point an organization in an appropriate direction, although they may be reluctant to change a direction that has been approved and codified. If this occurs, then the budget will reflect the strategic plan.

Truly and profoundly, and despite the best laid plans, other external factors can ruin a good strategic financial plan. The most notable examples are the two shocking events of September 11, 2001 and Hurricane Katrina (in New Orleans and along the southern coast of the United States), which led to belt-tightening in all sectors. Other examples include:

- Competition with other NPOs for limited community dollars

- Changes in the demographics of clients within a service area

- Shifts in donors' priorities

Still, strategic planning sets an organization on a definite course that should result in a flexible action-oriented plan that can be adapted to changing social and environmental conditions.

INTERNAL FACTORS AFFECTING STRATEGIC PLANS

Commitment to the plan is vital. If anyone in an organization is not committed to a strategic plan, it creates an internal obstacle. If board members or staff leaders are not committed to the strategic plan, it probably will not accomplish the vision it creates. Commitment must occur across the entire breadth of an organization. Leaders of an NPO—board members and executive staff—must ensure that the plans are properly interpreted and implemented. Poor leadership that moves NPOs in unworkable directions can kill a strategic plan. Drucker, in fact, warns leaders of organizations not to divert resources toward interesting and unprofitable ideas and projects, that is, not to "concentrate them on very small number of productive efforts."[11]

Staff turnover is another factor that can wreak havoc on a strategic plan. When key people are removed from a staff, either voluntarily or involuntarily, continuity of commitment to a strategic plan is threatened. Changeover of an executive director can be either a positive or a negative factor, depending on the incoming executive's vision and the board's acceptance of the newcomer's vision. Organizational culture may also result in a positive or negative impact on strategic planning. If an NPO staff is unwilling to accept change, that lack of buy-in might be a factor in the failure of a strategic plan. Other internal factors include:

- Ineffective budgetary controls
- A decline in personnel productivity

MONEY, GOALS, AND OBJECTIVES

What strategic planning boils down to is moving an organization in a positive direction toward a rewarding end. Knowing it is headed in that direction is a great advantage to the organization.

What benchmarks provide the necessary feedback? If you don't clearly identify these indicators, the organization will lack direction and may never solve the problem at hand.

An NPO must be able to measure and implement the goals and objectives in its strategic plan. The link between the strategic plan and the annual budget is the operating plan. Larry Scanlan observes that "operating plans allow for budgeted work in terms of goals and objectives for each program area and each management function, and call for reporting the actual progress on a monthly or, perhaps, quarterly basis."[12]

The budget of an NPO that is based on a strategic plan will be tied to goals and objectives. If, for example, an identifiable goal for a museum is to make exhibits and art more attractive to the *unsophisticated* and *non-artsy* consumers among us, it should be easy to develop measures for a phased program, such as the number of staff it will take to oversee such a goal, the costs of materials, the number of consumers desired, the amount of donations such a vision will attract, and the additional revenue attributable to the new goal.

If the budget truly reflects the spirit of the strategic plan, actual performance by goals and objectives can be monitored against the budget. Performance results as measured might result in variances that indicate a need for a program goal or objective to be corrected. If a nonprofit home health agency had expected to provide a certain number of strategic services during a period of time, but falls short or spends more than budgeted, the budget variance can be examined early if it is properly monitored. Monitoring allows for continuous adjustments, and it might also indicate a need for a change in strategic goals in order to replace ineffective goals and outcomes.

Whether poorly crafted or not, a strategic plan is nothing more than words, charts, and graphs on paper if it is not funded and implemented. A strategic plan can either gather dust, the most common use of long-term documents, or it can get the backing of the administration of an NPO. The strategic planning process can be complex, challenging, and even messy, so a truly important aspect of implementing a strategic plan is the concept of *discipline*. A failure of discipline by NPOs is a great challenge to its ultimate success. A strategic process that is not respected is like the old adage of planning: "A failure to plan is a plan to fail." Critical planning questions that guide the development of goals and objectives include:

- What issues restrict your ability to move forward?

- What barriers block the organization's ability to effect change?

- What low-hanging fruit can you easily harvest?

A disciplined focus is an excellent way to demonstrate commitment without the cost of a major initiative. It creates an immediate sense of change and offers instant gratification to your team. Be bold. Remember that if you're too careful, nothing good or bad will ever happen to you.[13]

Moldof provides vital information for understanding the relationship between strategic plans and budgets:[14]

The devil is in the details. Strategic plans should emphasize detailed breakouts of how money has and will be used. Nonprofits are often found to be slack when it comes to creating detailed budgets. For fundraising purposes, this budgetary information can be helpful. Donors like to know how their money *was or will be used; they feel more comfortable about making a contribution when they approve of how their donation will be applied. A strategic plan designates how dollars will be used to achieve specific goals. A fundraiser can take that information and use it as a selling tool: 'Yes, Mr. Smith, I can earmark your donation so that it goes toward the construction of our new arts center. In fact, as you can see, we need $50,000 more and your contribution gets us halfway there.'*

It is clear that annual budgets should emerge from the goals and objectives of a strategic plan. If the board, staff, and other stakeholders did the strategic planning process correctly, the most difficult task will be justifying the proposed expenditures so they can be tied to the mission goals and objectives and not to emotions or undue non-strategic influences that have no place in a strategic budget. Emotions and powerful influences are especially prevalent during lean budget years when actual revenue to expense margin expenditures come too close to exceeding available funds. Even a bare-bones budget can be as strategic as possible at the margin.

Organizations must not be myopic in understanding the budgeting process. There is a clear link between the budgeting process and strategic planning. If an NPO adopts a strategic plan and then ignores its encoded guidance when an annual budget is developed, that NPO has just wasted the entire effort that went into the development of its strategic plan. It is either acknowledging that the plan was poorly constructed or it has abandoned the notion of using it, for one reason or another. Likewise, the implementation of a budget during a fiscal year becomes a fruitless exercise if the directions in the strategic plan are completely ignored.

These two documents, the strategic plan and the annual budget, should be inextricably linked. Both are policy statements and plans. If an NPO puts these documents in order of importance, the strategic plan comes first, followed by the budget. In familial terms, the strategic plan is the parent and the budget is the child. The strategic plan sets the priorities, and the budget converts them into day-to-day operations, that is, it defines them and puts them into action for a given fiscal period. The budget is a plan for acquiring and spending money. In a strategic planning mode of thinking, that means getting and spending money as guided by the strategic planning process. If done correctly, the budget establishes the annual financial benchmarks that measure the outcome of the strategic plan.

OPERATIONAL VERSUS CAPITAL BUDGETING

For many organizations, the strategic plan guides not only the operational budget, but the capital budget as well. While capital and operational budgets are discussed in detail in later chapters, they are talked about here only in the context of a strategic plan. Strategically planning operational and capital budgets provides a big picture of an organization. A capital budget works in the confines of a strategic plan by setting a time-line for making capital acquisitions such as buildings and land and the purchasing or replacing of capital equipment or other fixed assets. It has a longer horizon than operational budgeting because of the long-term nature and high cost of capital projects.

The operational budget has a short-term horizon, usually one year or less. Many parts of an operational budget do not seem to readily lend themselves to strategic thinking in the short term. For example, functional items are unavoidable, including rents, utilities, outsourced services, insurance, and employee benefits like vacations. These obligations simply must be paid or the organization goes out of business. Other costs like payroll size, employee raises, capital spending, and the like are or can be strategic in nature.

In the broadest sense, the strategic plan does not reflect day-to-day operations except as they indicate growth or other types of change. The budget is the tool in which both strategic and functional thinking come to life. A church that has a mission to serve the spiritual and social needs of its current members likely will not have a strategic plan behind its mission, and maintenance will likely be its greatest cost line item. Conversely, a church with a growth mission to reach ten percent of its community should have a strategic plan that not only contains plans for building new facilities but also anticipates all costs associated with growth, including increasing labor costs, costs of maintenance, and other costs associated with its anticipated growth. Sometimes capital and operational budgets can intermingle and undergo conversion as the example of technology in the following example demonstrates.

Information Technology: Capital or Operating Budget Item?

A capital budgeting problem facing many NPOs is the acquisition of information technology. In some quarters, technology is considered to be a capital expenditure with a prescribed life expectancy. The systems of such organizations, however, can become nearly obsolete well before the forecasted life of the assets. It is axiomatic that computers are nearly obsolete the day they are taken out of the boxes they come in. Technology has a much shorter lifespan than most people understand. That misconception puts some NPOs in an operational bind. Information technology consists of necessary functions and equipment that might properly belong in the strategic plan's operating budget section and treated like a utility. An incorrect assumption about the longevity of technology could leave an organization at a disadvantage as programs as well as fundraising, cash management, investment strategies and other financial activities are being carried out. Interestingly, one of the strategies proposed for information technology in some modern organizations is to move it out of the "capital" category altogether and transfer it to the "operational."

FINANCIAL AND FISCAL ADMINISTRATION IN A STRATEGIC PLAN

The goal of strategic finance is to make sure that resources are available when they are needed at the same time that the organization provides for growth and upkeep of facilities. Meeting this goal will ensure that the mission and goals as detailed in the strategic plan can be carried out. For example, the plan should make certain that debt is available to be used (legal or institutional restrictions on debt limit have not been exceeded), that debt is affordable (debt repayment schedules are computed as a part of the operating budget), that the plan includes information on current debt liabilities, and that necessary improvements to infrastructure and assets are being carried out to ensure the best return (replacing inefficient facilities and equipment). The development and use of revenues is another of the topics that will be studied in later chapters, as will spending and investing. These are obviously areas that play an important role in strategic planning. Deciding where an NPO wants to go yields the types of programs and projects in which it wants to become involved. That fact will help direct an NPO to potential funding sources and away from others that will not fit the programs and projects that are part of the strategic vision.

REVENUE PLANNING

Another important aspect of strategic planning is to link future revenues to capital projects and mission-based programs. This important step includes the financing of expensive and long-term programs and projects. An NPO should line up its strategic revenue planning with three factors: mission relevance, financial flexibility, and financial efficiency. Revenue sources must be matched with projects that reflect the values, goals, and mission of an organization. A smart organization will choose funding sources that fit its strategic funding plan rather than the acquisition of easy dollars from funding sources that might obstruct the achievement of strategic goals by diverting resources away from them. The strategic plan should steer the sources of revenue. This could mean that an NPO would move away from its traditional funding sources in favor of new ones that are more aligned with the goals that are adopted in the strategic plan. While forecasting is another topic to be discussed in detail in a later chapter, no organization can do revenue planning without a forecast of the amount of revenue needed for strategic projects and the sources of those funds. As part of the forecasting process, NPOs have to determine possible funding sources and implement an action plan for pursuing those funding sources. This means identifying and estimating levels of the various funding streams, and seeking appropriate sources of funds. NPOs also need to examine other scenarios, including debt possibilities. In addition, the marketplace for revenue sources should be monitored on an ongoing basis. The following revenue sources should be considered.

- **Grants:** NPOs should think strategically about grants and match up the type of projects that have the highest priorities.

- **Donations:** Strategic plans may reveal new targets for donations, that is, potential donors who have not participated in giving to the NPO before.

- **Memberships:** Like donors, new groups might be targeted if they are appropriate and fit the mission.

- **Debt:** NPOs should determine the appropriate amount, mix, and cost of debt that supports the organization's strategic-financial goals.

- **Innovation:** New and/or alternative funding sources should be considered. These include branding, collaborations, fundraising events, and related and unrelated business ventures.

COST, EXPENDITURE, AND INVESTMENT PLANNING

The strategic plan is the basis for a detailed implementation plan. According to Mittenthals, "An implementation plan is an organizational user's guide to the strategic plan. It spells out the cost, duration, priority order, and accountability for each strategy."[15] In other words, an implementation plan uses the benchmarks for spending by NPOs established in the strategic plan. Both cost and time savings can result from a well-conceived and well-constructed strategic plan for operational and capital projects. The intended outcomes of the strategic plan are effective programs and capital assets that exactly meet the needs of an organization in the long term. The plan needs to answer questions that define the organization's needs and correspond to its strategic goals. A key factor in the planning of cost, expenditures, and investing is inflation. While inflation is discussed in detail in Chapter 8, it is important to think about it in the context of strategic planning, because the horizon is long-term. The further out a strategic horizon, the more important the need for considering the impact of inflation on costs. Obviously, reasonable estimates of expenditures can be tied to projects and programs in the short term. It is more difficult to project costs for inputs like materials, labor, services, and maintenance over time. NPOs, therefore, must take a strategic approach to the consideration of costs.

NPOs are generally regulated either by charter or by law with regard to the types and amounts of investment instruments in which they can commit. The prudent organization will include an examination of investments during the strategic planning process. A recent American Hospital Association (AHA) report reads, "To maintain maximum flexibility, lowest possible interest costs, and acceptable levels of risk, organizations must proactively and regularly adjust their portfolios as changes occur in the market and in the portfolios themselves."[16] Depending on performance in the relevant markets, investments might provide significant revenue to invest in the strategic projects and programs. Detailed discussions about investing money are found in Chapters 9 and 11.

SUMMARY

The importance of strategic planning in the administration of finance and budgeting cannot be overstated. While not every NPO will have the success of the one in the case study in this chapter, it was not a sensational accident that led that NPO to realize its good fortune. Instead, it was the strategic thinking and action the NPO practiced that led to its success. Most of the concepts covered in this chapter will be explained and discussed in detail in later chapters. Their connection to strategic planning is solid and undeniable. Concepts such as revenue, expenditures, costs, operational and capital budgeting, inflation, debt, and investing are vital components of a strategic plan for any NPO in search of a successful new horizon.

DISCUSSION QUESTIONS

1. The argument is made in this chapter that strategic planning represents a vital component of an organization's success, in particular as a collaboration tool that facilitates budgeting and forecasting across the organization both horizontally and vertically. How can an idealistic NPO engage in the development of realistic, actionable plans rather than over-generalized and lofty dreams? How can an NPO avoid overly optimistic planning and incorrect assumptions about the risks and opportunities of new programs?

2. Despite the best-laid plans, external factors can ruin a good strategic plan that was designed to set an organization on a definite course. It is said that the strategic plan should be flexible and adapt to changing social conditions. How would flexibility play out in the following types of NPOs after loss of a funding source that, while not enough to cause layoffs, caused a hiring freeze on positions that were critical to reaching strategic goals as planned?

    •   A rural full-service hospital

    •   A social service agency supporting elder care

    •   A religious institution

    •   A museum

    •   A community-based preschool

EXERCISE

Please revisit the following two parts of this chapter to respond to this exercise: the step-by-step process for developing a strategic plan and the chapter section "Case Analysis: Succeeding in the Strategic Planning Process," which describes how a social service agency, after a down period in its size, developed and implemented a strategic plan that led the agency to new levels of success. Create two columns on a spreadsheet. Label the column on the left side of the spreadsheet "Steps in a Strategic Plan." Label the other column "Case Study Activity." Using Table 3.1 as a framework, analyze the case analysis and identify the activities of the agency that fall under each step in the table. Discuss how and why the activities fit into a particular step. While it might be futile to question the agency's success, it might be fruitful to identify areas where the agency could make improvements in its strategic plan and the planning process. Make some recommendations to the agency that you determine will enhance its success.

INNOVATION AT THE SECTOR BOUNDARIES: STRATEGIC RESTRUCTURING

The traditional strategic planning model focuses on getting organized, developing mission and goals, examining the environment and looking at resources, developing objectives and strategies, developing action plans, implementing them, monitoring, evaluating, and updating. The focus tends to be internal except as it applies to the environment and the need to adjust to it. Today's NPO should be looking at trends that have the potential to work. One of the latest developments in the world of philanthropy is something called "strategic restructuring."[17] While strategic restructuring can be thought of simply as collaboration, it usually leads to long-term legal commitments. In effect, strategic restructuring takes place when two or more organizations form strategic alliances in order to work cooperatively for the benefit of all the organizations involved. The organizations need not all be NPOs. They can come from any sector. For an NPO, an important aspect of strategic restructuring is the extent to which the NPO benefits from the joining of forces with other organizations. The partnership with other organizations is intended to be ongoing and part of a permanent change in the NPO. Thus, it must be part of a strategic plan. Finance and budgeting should be an important aspect of the partnership. One consideration is whether or not funding can be enhanced through a partnership. By collaborating with other organizations, an NPO may put itself in a position to qualify for grants or donations that it could not otherwise have obtained. The gain may also be through expertise lent to an NPO by, for example, a corporate ally that has an interest in the outcomes of the NPO. The financial benefits may include:

- Cost savings such as shared staff, costs of facilities, employee benefits, purchasing

- Economies of scale in the form of access to new markets or clientele, diversity of clients, qualifying for reduced health care premiums, and efficiency

- Revenue enhancements in the form of improved fundraising,

qualification for grant funds that were previously untouchable due to the size of the NPO.[18]

Collaboration should be a consideration for an NPO for strategic reasons. If it fits into the mission and has no negative side effects in terms of core values, it is probably a good idea. Furthermore, if the collaboration enhances the NPO's strategic plan and helps the NPO get to where it wants to be, the collaboration almost becomes a necessity.

When Not to Strategically Restructure

Not all collaborations will succeed. Even if a strategic restructuring results in budgetary enhancement, it is not a good idea to strategically restructure when a partner is not acceptable to a meaningful stakeholder or group of stakeholders. A corporation may benefit more from a strategic restructuring than its nonprofit partner. While there is nothing inherently wrong with this outcome, it might be resented by some important stakeholders. Another concern might arise when a business-sector partner turns out to be doing business with objectionable clientele. Entering into a contract with collaborators is not strategically smart when an NPO's staff either does not have the time or does not possess the expertise to take on new duties that might be necessary to meet the terms of an agreement. It is probably a good idea for an NPO to write an "out clause" into a contract with collaborators.

NOTES

1   P. Brinckerhoff, *Mission Based Management: Leading Your Not-For-Profit in the 21st Century,* 2nd ed. (New York: John Wiley, 2000).

2   Douglas E. Ray, "Strategic Planning for Non-Profit Organizations," *Fund Raising Management* 6 (Aug. 28,1997): 22.

3   Bruce Glasrud, "Advance to the Future or Retreat to the Familiar?" *Nonprofit World* 22 (Nov/Dec 2004): 6.

4   R. A. Bobbe, J. Mendelson, and Y. Schulman, "The Strategic Planning Trap," *Journal of Jewish Communal Service* 76(3): 194–204.

5   Douglas E. Ray, "Strategic Planning for Nonprofit Organizations," *Fund Raising Management* 6 (Aug., 28, 1997): 22.

6   B. Reed and J. Swain, *Public Finance Administration,* 2nd ed. (Thousand Oaks, CA: Sage, 1997).

7   J. Sammer, "Seven Ways to Build Better Budgets," *Business Finance Magazine,* 1997. Online at http://www.businessfinancemag.com/magazine (accessed May 19, 2008).

8   D. Hunger and T. Wheelen, *Essentials of Strategic Management,* 3rd ed. (Eaglewood Cliffs, NJ: Prentice Hall, 2002).

9   Richard Mittenthals, "Don't Give Up on Strategic Planning: 10 Keys to Success," *Nonprofit World* 22, 3: 21–25.

10   G. E. Pinches, "Myopia: Capital Budgeting and Decision Making," *Financial Management* 11 (1982): 6–20.

11   Peter F. Drucker, "What Executives Should Remember," *Harvard Business Review* 84.2 (2006): 144–152.

12   Larry Scanlan, "Budget Reality: It's Up to You," *Healthcare Financial Management* 59 (2005): 78–80.

13   Peter Smergut, "Strategic Planning on a Budget," *Nonprofit World* 23 (2005): 14–17.

14   Edwin P. Moldof, "Strategic planning for nonprofits," *Fund Raising Management* 24 (1993): 29.

15   Richard Mittenthals, "Don't Give Up on Strategic Planning: 10 Keys to Success," *Nonprofit World* 22.3: 21–25.

16   American Heart Association, "AHA Strategic Plan charts a course to a healthy future," AHA News 42 (2006): 1.

17   Amelia Kohm and David La Piana, *Strategic Restructuring: Partnership Options for Nonprofits* (Westport, CT: Greenwood Publishing Group, 2003).

18   James E. Austin, *The Collaboration Challenge: How Nonprofits and Business Succeed Through Strategic Alliances* (New York: The Drucker Foundation, 2000).

CHAPTER 4
Budgeting and Its Complexities

The previous chapter established that an organization's budget should be derived from the goals and objectives of its strategic plan. Budgeting was discussed in that context to underscore the importance of that relationship. Keeping an eye on strategic plans to screen current budgets just makes good sense. Now the discussion turns to budgeting on its own merit. This chapter focuses on the regular budgeting process, its intricacies and its impact on the missions of NPOs. The discussion concentrates on operational budgeting. The chapter begins with budgeting basics by discussing where the budget fits in the finance and budgeting network. As the chapter unfolds it quickly becomes clear that the budget is the most important tool for NPOs. By comparing the nonprofit budgeting process to federal, state, and local budgeting processes, the chapter demonstrates the similarities between nonprofit budgeting and budgeting in the other sectors and the differences that distinguish nonprofit budgeting from budgeting in the other sectors. It is important to do that because of the high incidence of collaborative relationships among the sectors. The important topics involved in budget strategy that are, or can be, applied to real-world situations are discussed in detail.

TOPICS
- The Financial and Fiscal Administration Network: The Budget
- What a Budget Is
- What a Budget Does
- The Budget Process
- Comparing Federal, State, Local, Business, and Nonprofit Budgeting
- Budgetary Decision-Making Models
- Types of Budgets and Budget Evolution
- Budgets and People
- Important Budget Considerations
- Summary
- Discussion Questions
- Exercise: Simple Budget Analysis
- Innovation: Priority-Based Budgeting

THE FINANCIAL AND FISCAL ADMINISTRATION NETWORK: THE BUDGET

The base of the financial and fiscal network is the strategic plan. As shown in Figure 4.1, the budget is the first of the four functions of the Financial and Fiscal Administration Network to be used; without the budget, there is nothing to manage, nothing to account for, and nothing to evaluate. So, the budget should contain the financial story of an NPO. Managers, staff, and members of the governing board in a nonprofit should understand that the budget, created through a periodical (usually annual) budgeting process, encompasses the plans, policies, goals, objectives, and performance measures of the organization.

Figure 4.1: Financial and Fiscal Administration Network: The Budget Function

WHAT A BUDGET IS

All NPOs do not necessarily follow the same rules for budgets. An NPO employee leaving one agency for another might discover that the new employer has a way of approaching budgets that is vastly different than what he or she was used to at the previous NPO.[1] Budgets are thought about in many ways: To some, a budget is a plan; to others it is a policy statement. To some it is an expenditure guidebook, and to others it is a checkbook. And so on. Before the technical definitions are offered, the following metaphors may be helpful in building a basis for the discussion.

It is not uncommon for someone when hearing about a budget to think about pie—pie charts anyway. Most people are used to seeing budgets depicted as pie charts because these types of charts are so good at demonstrating how money is both acquired and used by an organization. As seen in Figures 4.2 and 4.3, pie charts clearly illustrate where an organization gets its revenue and how it intends to spend its money by showing slices of the pie that represent each revenue source (Figure 4.2) or each expenditure (Figure 4.3) and their percentage of the entire pie represented.

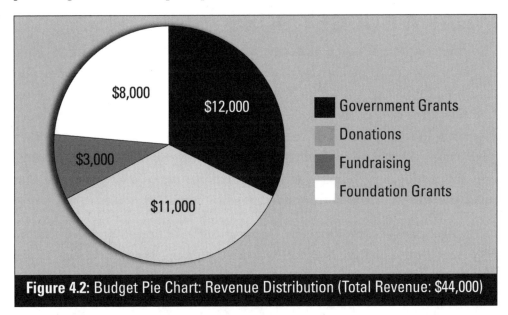

Figure 4.2: Budget Pie Chart: Revenue Distribution (Total Revenue: $44,000)

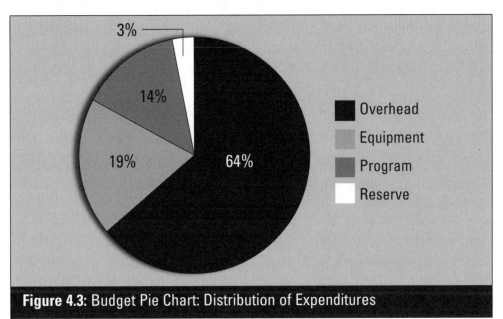

Figure 4.3: Budget Pie Chart: Distribution of Expenditures

The budget can be thought of as a user's manual and should be easy to follow. The format should include a coding scheme that reflects spending and revenue are allocated. A reader should be able to easily identify how money is to be spent by program and line item, and how much is being spent.

WHAT A BUDGET DOES

Most people have a sense of what a budget is. No one would argue that a budget is a spending plan. Individuals and organizations who have a need and a purpose for money know that a budget divides that money up and allocates it among the needs of the organization or individual. A reasonable person or organization knows that their budget is limited by the amount of money they have coming in and that spending the money on the identified needs is similarly limited. So, a spending plan helps maximize use of limited income. But much more can be derived from that spending plan.

Budgets are generally thought of as occurring in a one-year period called the fiscal year. In this text, we refer to that period of time either as the fiscal or the budgetary year. The budget is the start of action at the beginning of the budgetary period, when the board votes and makes the budget the governing policy of an NPO. As managers try to keep their spending within budget during the budgetary period, the budget is the standard for comparing actual spending with planned spending. A budget's strength is that it is still the policy at the end of a fiscal year, when information learned during the year cycles into the next budget. It is also the standard for comparison the rest of the year, when managers try to keep their spending within budget. A budget, according to the Government Finance Officer Association, is defined in the following four parts:

- A policy document that explains both the rationale for policy and the effect it is expected to have

- A financial plan that details not only the operations of a nonprofit but also the capital plan and the plan for debt

- A communication device that provides public relations information and is targeted at investors, bond raters, and others

- An operations guide that explains legal spending limits and performance measures.[2]

A budget is a management tool. The budget that people in an organization have agreed to becomes the organization's user manual. Managers of programs are allocated a certain amount of money to spend on a set of identified activities for a budgetary period, and they value the budget as a means to monitor how the money is being used. The manager's superiors and board members use the budget to monitor how the allocated funds are being used. Many budgets, especially those based on programs, have a performance aspect to them. Managers can measure spending on a program against prescribed goals to determine efficiency and effectiveness. The only way to accomplish performance measurement is against a budget.

Ultimately, however, a budget is a policy statement, the result of compromise in the negotiation process. It is strategic if it is linked with a comprehensive plan. Budgets are constrained by environmental factors that should be understood and examined. Those factors include the following:

- Resources that are affected by economic conditions

- Stakeholder values—their preferences and what they are willing to give up

- Community norms—customs, the amount of change the community is willing to allow

- Competition—for donations, grants, employees, and loyalty

Policy can be measured in many ways, but there is no organizational document that makes a policy platform become more evident than a budget. The programs and activities that an NPO spends money on and the size of the slice of the budget for each program says much about the *ideals* of that organization, the *direction* in which it wants to go, and the *places* it wants to be. If a hospital has decided to allocate an increased portion of the budget to heart technology and associated staff, it is a clear indication that the organization now places more importance on its heart program than it has in the previous time periods. Of course, a reader of the hospital's budget will be able to learn even more by comparing budgets from multiple time periods. This comparison may reveal a trend over a number of years. It might suggest that the heart program had been neglected in previous years compared to other programs, or it might reveal that at some point in time the hospital's leaders recognized that it could establish a niche in its community. A comparison of budgets might also reflect that a grant or a donation from a wealthy person or organization for the heart program had been made and that the heart program's portion of the budget will soon return to normal.

THE BUDGET PROCESS

An NPO budget must first be approved by the executive, and perhaps a board budget committee, before it is sent to the full governing board for adoption. Thus, in this process for an average mid-sized NPO, program directors reporting to an executive submit a wish-list budget to their executive, who then scrutinizes the wish-list budgets in relation to the *big picture*. An executive usually makes the ultimate decision about approving a proposed budget that takes into consideration the wishes of program directors. The approved executive budget is then submitted to the governing board for adoption. Adoption by the board of directors is the process that culminates in the enactment of a budget and makes it the official policy of an NPO. Adoption of a budget by the board should, in essence, make it the NPO's unwavering policy. Allocation is simply the plan for distributing resources to an NPO's various programs. Most NPOs allocate funds on a monthly basis, although it might be appropriate for some NPOs to use an alternative allocation basis if it is more appropriate for meeting the needs of the organization. While the allocation of funds should be defined in the budget, a separate cash flow budget by a manager can provide control if spending problems arise. A monthly *cash flow budget* might result in an even flow of money into a program.[2] The cash flow budget will be discussed in detail in Chapter 9.

Budgeting is not complex in all cases. For some nonprofit agencies the budgeting process is not much more than an exercise in redundancy. The budget annually reflects what the community and the stakeholders expect from the budget. It is not complicated, especially if revenues are reliably stable and obviate the need to search for new programs and new funding sources. The process is simple for the staff, and board approval is not an issue. In these cases, there is no need for a budget's content to convey much about the organization's goals and mission, because they are the same year in and year out. The types of NPOs in which budgeting is a simple process include small organizations, organizations with stable and steady sources of income such as a long-term contracts or grants, and those whose missions are unitary to the point that there will never be a need to add new programs.

For larger, more complex organizations in which budgeting is not an exercise in redundancy, the following general approach is common:

- Compare the budget to the strategic plan.

- Review the previous budgeting period's performance by examining prescribed performance and audited financial reports, if available.

- Adjust the budget process or the strategic plan.

In fact, NPOs should have written polices that describe the budgeting process, including due dates for steps to take and milestones to achieve. After consulting the strategic plan, budget committees and responsible staff should determine what is working and what is not working for the organization, reexamine goals and objectives for the upcoming budget period, and identify strategies in need of adjustment in order to best achieve organizational goals. Then the NPO can look at revenue and spending.

The following is a typical budget process:

1. The staff and board reviews program achievements and fiscal performance over the budget period just ending.

2. Based on the review, new goals and objectives are discussed and agreed upon. These goals and objectives should fit into the NPO's strategic plan.

3. The budget committee consults with relevant staff at all levels to determine program costs. A review is likely to reveal details that executive staff and boards may not be positioned to know.

4. The staff conducts a variance analysis.

5. The staff forecasts all costs and revenues required to achieve objectives.

6. The staff works with the board budget committee to develop spending and funding plans.

7. The executive director and budget committee finalize budget and present it to the board.

8. The full board reviews, revises, and approves the plan for the year.

The Budget Calendar

NPOs should codify a budget calendar and follow it. The steps in the budget calendar are different among NPOs by type of NPO. Some calendars are as simple in small organizations as finding out how much money will be received from an annual fundraiser and then making a spending plan. Most agencies require more sophistication.

The budget calendar emerges from these three steps and reflects various activities. A typical example of a budget process for an agency that receives funding from a local United Way is described here.

February 1	**NPO gets budget package from the United Way (UW) for the fiscal year beginning in January of the next year. NPO begins budget preparation.**
March 1	**NPO finishes next fiscal year budget based on all sources of revenue, including UW allocation and obtains board approval**
May 1	**Hearings held by the UW allocation committee; each participating community NPO makes a case for its funding request**
May 10	**UW committee makes recommendations the UW board**
June 1	**UW notifies agency of funding award**
August 1 to October 1	**UW fundraising drive occurs**
October 15	**NPO determines all funding sources and revises next fiscal year budget**
November 1	**Agency board adopts budget for next fiscal year.**

The budget calendar acts as a guide for meeting internal deadlines as well as those of funding sources.

COMPARING FEDERAL, STATE, LOCAL, BUSINESS, AND NONPROFIT BUDGETING

There is no way to lump all budgeting units into one process and say *this is how budgeting is done.* Each state, city, NPO, and company varies in its approach to budgeting. At the same time, there is a lot of overlap in the process among organizations. Because of the similar nature of the processes, some generalizations can be made. Table 4.1 provides a perspective on the differences of budgeting at various levels of government and at private (business) and nonprofit entities. The table compares the following factors: purpose, actors, authority, features and strategy, budget control, primary revenue sources, spending priorities, interest group pressure, and whether or not the sector engages in capital budgeting. The table shows the similarities and the variety among the various types of organizations in the national economy.

BUDGETARY DECISION-MAKING MODELS

There are a number of ways for an organization to engage in decision making related to its budget. The simplest is to open a checking account. Then, when the organization receives some money, it makes a deposit and starts spending it on needs and wants. While there are small NPOs that use the checking account approach, it is not common. In truth, budgetary decision making should not be taken lightly. Every decision has an opportunity cost. The same decision-making needs that affect the business and public sectors, as presented in Table 4.1, affect the nonprofit sector. Each decision comes with definite risks and potential rewards. The outcome of a decision, not considering pure luck, depends on the approach to decision making. The discussion begins with classical decision making.

	FEDERAL	STATE	LOCAL	BUSINESS	NONPROFIT
Purpose	Contract between President, Congress, and the people.	Strong policy vehicle.	Annual plan for capital and operational demands of citizens.	Plan for maximizing profits.	Plan for reaching mission goals.
Actors	President, agencies, OMB, Congressional committees, CBO, lobbyists.	Governor, agencies, budget office, legislative committees/staffs, subcommittees.	Political or appointed executive, agencies, budget office, council or commission.	Chief financial officer, chief executive officer, owner.	Board, executive director, program directors, fiscal manager, grantees.
Authority	Executive: budget preparation and request; veto and impoundment. Congress: authorization, appropriations, and override.	Executive: budget preparation, item veto. Legislature: adoption, appropriations, and budget override.	Executive: budget preparation and approval. Council/commission: modify and adopt budget, and make appropriations.	Executive levels: approval.	Executive: budget preparation. Board: adopt and approve budget with modifications.
Features and Strategy	"Satisficing," zero-sum game, avoid the worst, repetition, fair share, balance, burden on the President.	Multiple budget bills; tax and expenditure limitations.	Concentrates on revenue enhancement, balancing budget, incrementalism, and limited taxation opportunities.	Allows for understanding the company's financial position. Based on sales, reducing costs, and cash flow.	Concentrates on fundraising, balancing the budget, and getting the job accomplished on an annual basis.
Budget Control	Symbolically agree about balanced budget; limited by entitlements and interest on debt.	Legal balanced budget requirements.	State limits budget authority and balanced budget requirements.	Top level employees; owners.	Legal restrictions; grant restrictions.
Primary Revenue Sources	Income tax, deficit spending.	Income tax, property tax, federal grants, fees, borrowing.	Sales tax, property tax, fees, borrowing.	Product and service sales	Grants, donations.
Spending Priorities	Defense, health/welfare, Social Security, and interest.	Education, health and welfare, job security, highways, prisons, public safety.	Education, roads and transit, housing, public safety.	Profitable and potentially profitable services and products.	Specific programs for clients.
Interest Group Pressure	High: lobbyists and organized constituents.	High: lobbyists and organizations.	Low due to public hearings and other input.	None: consumer-based within a company's markets.	Occasional input by specific interests.
Capital Budgeting	No	Yes	Yes	Yes, in most cases.	In some cases.

Table 4.1: Budget Comparisons: Federal, State, Local, Business, and Nonprofit

Classical Rational Decision Making

In the tradition of classical decision-making theory, making a decision is a rational process. Presented with the critical need to select the best alternative solution to a significant challenge, decision makers are confronted with the need to make the best possible decision. If that decision can maximize an organization's rewards and meets its goals and objectives, there is an incentive to seek out information that will enlighten the decision. In *classical rational decision making*, decision makers must follow a series of purposive steps:

1. Identify and prioritize the goals and objectives that would be fulfilled by making a decision.

2. Identify the alternatives that might help the organization realize those goals and objectives and collect information on the alternatives.

3. Select criteria to use to evaluate each alternative, making sure the criteria are valid, reliable, and applicable to all the alternatives.

4. Apply the criteria and choose the alternative that best satisfies the criteria and attains the objectives.

5. Implement and then evaluate the selected alternative.

Realistic Decision Making

It should be noted that rational decision making works best in worlds that boast large herds of unicorns cared for by leprechauns. In the real world, decision making requires overcoming the obstacles of time, disagreement, and limited dollars. Doing anything less than the steps just listed is something other than rational. When it comes to an important activity like budgeting, life jumps up and applies constraints. Most managers want perfect information, an unabridged list of alternatives, and all the time and money needed to carry out all parts of a strategic plan. Most managers do not get that. Fortunately, while it may not be rational to use a decision-making approach other than the classical rational approach, it is not *irrational* to employ a technique that varies from the rational decision-making steps.

Herbert Simon, a major contributor to management and organization science, coined the terms *bounded rationality* and satisficing.[3] Bounded rationality means that an organization accepts decision processes that use less than what rational decision making calls for because of certain constraints that face practitioners who must make critical decisions. Satisficing means accepting less than maximum outcomes. Simon believed and demonstrated that decision makers understand and accept the existence of political, resource, and time constraints as certainties, and they also understand and accept the existence of other constraints that arise as possibilities that must be dealt with on a case-by-case basis. These constraints are expected. Rational decision making provides a basis as decision makers seek to justify their decisions. Rational techniques for decision making like cost-benefit, cost-effectiveness, and present value analysis can still be applied. But from the beginning of the process, decision makers must understand that the *available* alternatives discussed in rational decision making will not usually exist in the numbers suggested. Not having perfect information actually simplifies the decision-making process. It limits the amount of information decision makers have to deal with and saves time and money resources because decision makers do not need perfect information to make a decision.

TYPES OF BUDGETS AND BUDGET EVOLUTION

It is appropriate to look at where budgeting began and how it has changed in order to understand how budgeting is performed in the nonprofit sector. Performance budgeting, program planning budgeting, and zero-base budgeting did not exist during the early simple days of convenience budgeting. In those early times, generally the turn of the nineteenth into the twentieth century, the budget was truly nothing more than a spending plan. The following is a look backward at the evolution of the budget process.

Performance Budgeting

For many NPOs, budgeting has evolved from a simple pay-as-you-go process to more sophisticated line-item budgeting to a complex system of planning and performance comparisons of multiple funding sources, on which many NPOs depend. The evolution of program budgeting became necessary as NPOs became more complicated and more dependent upon private and government funding agencies that required a separate accounting of the money they were providing. Program budgeting entered the practice of budgeting in the 1950s. Simply defined, program budgeting occurs when each program under the umbrella of an NPO is budgeted separately from other programs under the same umbrella. For an example, consider an early childhood agency with a grant from the state government for a program to assist children with physical needs, and another privately funded grant to identify and work with gifted children. Each program may have a divergent set of goals and different sources of funding but is overseen by the same agency, whose mission is to provide quality early education for all children, including a general population whose programs are funded by donations and tuition.

Performance budgeting ties the outcomes involved in a budget unit to performance measures. According to theory, the budget unit's next annual budget would come under examination as the result of how close it came to meeting its performance goals.

Zero Base Budgeting

The next revolutionary reform in the evolution of budgeting combines line-item, program, and performance budgeting into program and performance budgeting system (PPBS). This very complex budgeting system seeks to get the most out of three approaches to budgeting. Zero-base budgeting (ZBB) was one of the most popular reforms in budgeting over the years. Introduced in the 1970s, ZBB forced agencies to justify not only increases to their budgets, but their very basic annual budget as well. Zero-base budgeting is a particular kind of program and performance budgeting that evaluates all the programs, not just the new ones. It associates the service levels in each program with costs, and then it prioritizes all the options. The highest priorities are funded. If a new program for one NPO program is ranked higher than an old one, the new program may be funded at the expense of the old one. Ideally, then, planning comes from the bottom up as the most efficient and effective programs receive the most attention from the executive staff and board.

ZBB attempts to improve the budget process by engaging in activities that answer two important questions: Are the projects that the NPO is engaged in the most efficient and effective way possible to accomplish the NPO's mission?

If not, should those activities be eliminated, reduced, or otherwise modified in order to concentrate on programs and projects that have received a higher rating in terms of efficiency and effectiveness? In the process of doing ZBB, agencies use the following terms to follow a few basic steps. These are illustrated in the example of a fictitious church trying to budget using ZBB decision packages.

The ZBB Process: A Case Example

Let us begin with a few definitions:

Decision unit is the primary unit whose budget base will be evaluated. Usually this is a program that engages in several activities.

Evaluation is a process that is used to determine a decision unit's efficiency and effectiveness.

Packages are the different levels of funding for each decision unit. There are usually three levels of funding: A minimum level, a maintenance level, and an enhanced level. The minimum level is the basic level of funds that a decision unit will have to have to continue to operate somewhat effectively. This is a cut from the current level of activity and is as low as a unit can go before discontinuing operations altogether. The maintenance level of funding that would keep the decision unit at status quo, and the enhanced level of funding is broken into two increased activity levels, an in-between or intermediate and an enhanced or maximum level of funding.

Rank is the outcome of the evaluation that is conducted by executive staff and a board-created budget committee.

Zero base is the ideal beginning level for each year upon which each program has to justify its budget for the following year.

The ZBB budget process consists of four steps illustrated now.

Step One: Identify decision units. Decision units are the lowest meaningful level at which zero-based budgets can be developed. In most organizations, the unit will be a program. In this analysis for a religious organization, a church, there may be several programs—missions, worship, administration,

---

children and youth, and so on. Each program may have subprograms that comprise meaningful decision units as determined by the church. Meaningfulness will be determined differently by different organizations. When the level of meaningfulness is determined, meaningful decision units must develop individual decision packages for evaluation and ranking. The church's budget decision units are identified in Table 4.2.

MISSIONS MINISTRY	WORSHIP MINISTRY
Asian Program	Altar and Decorations
Mexican Program	Music
Domestic Program	Drama
CHILDREN AND YOUTH MINISTRY	**ADMINISTRATION**
Infants and Toddlers Program	Central Office
Elementary Age Program	Counseling
Junior High Program	Adult Education
Senior High Program	

Table 4.2: Decision or Activity Units

Step Two: Analyze each decision unit in a decision package. Each package will include budgets at four levels. This is demonstrated by examining the Worship Activity as the decision unit, as shown in Table 4.3. The Worship Department puts together the four budget packages shown in the figure.

The Worship Department's justification and rationale for these packages are as follows:

Level One (minimum): Proposes across-the-board cuts in salaries and expenses. This level of funding would have a negative impact on the church.

- The music director's salary is already behind the market level for this position.

- Purchases of new equipment could not be made because all expense funds would have to be dedicated to repair.

- The quality of music would be noticeably lower.

- A part-time musician's salary would have to be cut.

WORSHIP	PACKAGE LEVEL 1	PRIOR YEAR BUDGETED LEVEL 2	PACKAGE LEVEL 2	PACKAGE LEVEL 3
Altar and Decorations	$11,000	$13,500	$17,000	$19,000
Salaries	5,500	5,900	6,400	7,000
Expenses/purchases	5,500	7,600	10,600	12,000
Music	$66,000	$69,500	$73,000	$85,000
Salaries	63,000	65,500	67,000	75,000
Expenses/purchases	3,000	4,500	6,000	10,000
Drama	$6,000	$6,500	$7,000	$7,500
Salaries	3,500	3,500	4,000	4,500
Expenses/purchases	2,500	3,000	3,000	3,000
Total	$83,000	$89,000	$97,000	$112,500
Percent decrease from prior year budgeted.	(-7)	(0)	(+7)	(+26)

Table 4.3: Summary of ZBB Worship Department Packages

- The appearance of the chapel would decline.

- Church member complaints would increase.

- Attendance at all services would decrease.

Level Two (current): Would maintain salaries and expenses at current levels.

- Not giving raises would have the impact of a wage cut because it would put the church behind the market for the salaries.

- Church member complaints would likely increase.

- Attendance at all services would likely decrease.

Level Three (intermediate): Calls for small increases in each program area to increase staff salaries.

- The music program would hire a new part-time musician and

make modest expenditures on replacement and repair of equipment and instruments.

- Requests have been denied in past years, and equipment and instruments are beginning to fail and reduce the quality of the service.

- The new purchases would bring back some of the quality of services lost in recent years.

- There would likely be no impact on complaints or attendance.

Level Four (enhanced): Increases in almost all areas, including hiring two new part-time musicians, giving raises to all part-time workers and the music director, and replacing much of the equipment instead of spending on repairs.

- These enhancements would result in new members attracted by music, drama, and the attractiveness of the chapel.

Step Three: Evaluate and rank all decision packages to develop the appropriations request. In this mode, the senior pastor, working with an administrative board committee, would evaluate the worship unit's individual budget packages alone, using the strategic plan, past performance of the unit, and other criteria like perceived need, perceived preferences of the church members, and perhaps other subjective criteria. Then the worship package will be evaluated by comparing the unit alongside the other decision units to arrive at a ranking of packages. The pastor and board committee would then develop a ranking of one level of service for each decision unit. Laying out the budget alternatives this way gives decision makers a tool to help them with the heavy responsibility of finishing the budget. Note that each decision package beginning with level two, the zero base, would be added to level one, the minimum level. The goal of the budget officer would be to select the first package at a minimum and one or more packages in addition to the first if the budget allows. This gives the NPO budget options for each decision unit.

Step Four: Prepare a detailed operating budget reflecting those decision packages.

The case just presented demonstrates that ZBB is compatible with line-item budgeting in that it is bottom-up. Lower-level managers of programs assemble decision packages for review by higher levels. This bottom-up approach increases the legitimacy of the process for line personnel. The ranking process for the various packages provides management with a technique that allows them to allocate their limited resources by concentrating on key questions. The key for program managers is to focus management's attention on specific important policy issues and discretionary spending. If done correctly, ZBB will identify low-priority programs. By separating the *wheat from the chaff*, it will theoretically improve NPO efficiency and effectiveness. It is a tool to help decision makers recognize where to shift resources.

Advantages of ZBB

The term *zero base budgeting* might be a bit misleading, because the base is actually determined as the previous year's budget. It does not eliminate all funding and build the budget from nothing. Thus, there will never be a budget without any money in it unless a revenue source dries up. What ZBB does is put a high priority on justifying the activities of an NPO's decision unit prior to the next budget period. It keeps people in those budget units both aware of and critically thinking about their missions and activities before every budget period. It also provides a great opportunity to innovate. A decision unit should never stop looking for ways to find new programs that fit into an NPO's strategic plan, nor should it ever stop seeking ways to become more efficient and effective. Zero-based budgeting is intended to motivate these activities to attain results.

Disadvantages of ZBB

The most recognized problems associated with ZBB include the following:

- Bureaucratic resistance to a process that evaluates program effectiveness, which is a requirement of effective administration

- Communication

- Training problems in identifying appropriate decision items program

- Difficulty in measuring workload and performance

The most common criticism of ZBB is that it takes a lot of work and is time-consuming. Program staff who are involved in putting together packages lose the time needed for fulfilling their mission. An NPO has to weigh the costs and benefits of the ZBB process. It is clear that the costs are time and effort. The *potential* benefits are efficiency and effectiveness. If an NPO has some flexibility, then it might try using the ZBB process in years that work schedules of the staff and the board allow.

BUDGETS AND PEOPLE

It has been said tongue-in-cheek by a sage and perceptive budget officer that "this year's budget is worse than last year, but better than next year." This statement by a cynical human being illustrates why it makes sense for staff to begin the budget process earlier rather than later. Humans are involved in the process and will likely have an impact on the smoothness of the budget process. The human aspect of budgeting is politics. It is every human, not only lawyers and professional editors, who gets hold of a document and knows how to make it better. But at some point, and often because of exhaustion with the process, budgets get finalized. While people do act in their self interest, they also make mistakes. It is important to remember that errors and omissions are part of the human condition that cannot be insured against. Sometimes the human touch can be controlled. Sometimes it cannot. To the extent possible, NPOs should organize and standardize the budget process, codify it, provide accurate documentation, and follow a fairly strict calendar during each budget period. Accurate documentation and a reliable schedule will give the board, management, staff, and stakeholders confidence in the budget process.

The Budget and the Board

During times of growth, boards must work through shifting priorities and agendas in a way that supports growth.[4] It is not unusual for a strong and influential executive director of an NPO to have a board that approves budgets because they trust in his or her competence or convincing explanations. This relationship is especially true when a board is timid or does not understand all of the details. This situation could mean that the executive director is hoarding information or that a board may not currently have the knowledge they need to make informed decisions. Such problems are rooted in lack of knowledge but can be overcome, even at the very basic stage, if board members are willing to learn. An executive director needs to instill confidence in the board members' ability to take their positions seriously.

The Budget and Program Staff

At times some leaders and specialists in nonprofit agencies operate under the slogan, "The budget be damned!" There is often disagreement between the program planning and financial management divisions of an NPO because of the different views on economics versus the programmatic mission of an organization. It is wise for program and financial staff to work together with the program director and board members to construct a budget that has a vision of the entire organization's goals, not individual fiefdoms, and that reflects budget limitations. Conflict between the accountants who see the budget process as the lifeblood of the entire operation and the program people who see the budget as an unnecessary evil that offers constraints on their ability to express their talents is not uncommon in NPOs. Everyone has to understand the word *balance*. Compromises are often necessary.

What about new sources of funds? Everyone associated with an NPO has to always look at the mission and open their minds to new ways of implementation that might lead to new streams of funding. We will examine how to look for new sources of funding that fit the mission and strategic plan of an NPO in Chapter 7, which deals with revenues.

IMPORTANT BUDGET CONSIDERATIONS

This section briefly discusses important considerations that should be kept in mind during the budgeting process.

Shortfalls and Rebudgeting

Sometimes the best budgets cannot be met right from the beginning of the budget period. Staff leaders and boards sometimes are forced to change the budget in the middle of the budgetary period. Cutting budgets sometimes can result in improvements in policy processes as well as effective management of a budget crisis. The outcome of a budget crisis may prove to be a blessing in disguise. It can lead to developing a stable and defensible policy position that improves the prospects for future decisions and actions of the NPO. This kind of outcome would also enhance the NPO's ability to deal effectively with difficult policy challenges. The NPO staff and board can take time to reset priorities for allocation of income to match mission and values. Managers are forced to learn and improve their budget management and leadership abilities to deal with the forced reexamination of costs, regulatory requirements, and increased focus on impact and outcomes. Reputation and goodwill can be enhanced if stakeholders can observe the good steps being undertaken to fix problems associated with the budget.

Revenues and Expenditures

Revenues are real dollars used to fund programs. Expenditures decrease those real dollars. These two concepts are forever on a collision course. As the saying goes, you cannot get blood from a turnip. Thus, the starting point for budgeting is the amount of revenue that appears to be available. Many believe that nonprofits benefit most from flexible budgets, which are primarily obtained by emphasizing the importance of understanding revenues in order to forecast activity level and workload. By this philosophy, understanding and identifying revenues would be the greater priority. Expenditures are dependent on revenue. There can be no expenditure without revenue.

Estimated revenues and expenditures should be built around budgets that are planned and controlled. For an NPO, revenue raised for a budget depends on fundraising, stability of income generated, capacity of the institution, demographics, social conditions, community relationships, risk, and legal requirements. Expenditures depend on variables like program necessities, wishes, and current operating expenses, which require future use of net current assets, debt service, and capital outlays.

A primary purpose of budgeting, therefore, is to plan revenues and spending. Almost any rational person can look at a nonprofit agency's needs and divide up the available funds, and spend money in a way that meets those needs. But if one person is focused on spending only, that spending must be balanced with revenues. Expenditures cannot be seriously considered as part of the operation and maintenance budget until the organization knows how much money is available in a budgetary period. The key to a successful relationship between revenues and expenditures is careful planning and realistic projections. This is where a good financial analyst is worth his or her weight in gold.

Trends and Projections

There are many unpredictable factors on a year-to-year basis that have significant impacts on the budget, such as health benefit increases, retirement contribution increases, pending contract negotiations, and inflation. Budgets should include temporary revenue, such as reserves, to get through the hard times.[5] Using the past actual revenues and expenditures to determine what can be spent in the future is logical and legitimate, but is only part of the budget equation. Actual experiences give an NPO a starting point for analysis. The NPO, however, has to look at where those data fit in with current external influences over a budget. Actual figures over a number of fiscal years can be fit into equations that lead to effective estimates about future years. The details of the various methods of projecting and trending will be discussed in Chapters 7 and 9.

Variance Analysis

Sometimes NPOs detect variances between budgeted and actual expenditures. An organization should never allow a continuing deficit to remain from budgetary period to budgetary period. It is important that NPOs achieve an understanding of why departments, program revenues, or spending vary from the approved budget. A periodic variance analysis can help explain the causes of discrepancies. There are innumerable factors that might explain budget variances, including bad forecasting, unanticipated price increases, energy consumption trends, managers' failure to detect unauthorized spending, erroneous assumptions, and so on. Several steps can be taken to analyze variances.

One step is to look at historical experiences. No one should think that past performance will ensure budgetary success or failure. An analysis of past financial data, however, will help managers determine where and when problems have occurred in past periods. By looking at past actual revenues and expenditures, managers can adjust current forecasts. Projections from which funding decisions were based will cycle into the next budgetary period. An NPO has to look at where those projections fit with current internal and external influences over a budget. The budget becomes the standard of comparison for the rest of the year when managers try to keep their budgeted spending within budget figures. Managers can compare programs or departments to see which ones are not participating in good budgeting practices and take necessary corrective actions.

Questions should include: Is poor budget management being practiced? Have there been unexpected cost increases due to price increases? Have there been equipment malfunctions requiring unexpected maintenance or repair?[6] What are the impacts of variances on the organization? On individuals? On clients? On the governing board? Knowing this information allows the NPO to prioritize which areas should be fixed first. For example, a first priority among NPOs will likely be their clients. If they are most affected, then a corrective action plan can be developed. Consistent variance such as overestimating or underestimating revenue or expenditures indicate a material weakness in the budget process. An appropriate response is to rethink budgets to correct the planning process. Flexible budgeting might be an appropriate response to cases where volatility of prices or other external influences cannot be accurately projected. This approach would give an NPO the ability to move money from programs with surpluses to others with shortages. Obviously, this can only be done if the problems are occurring in unrestricted funds.

Different Budgets for Different Organizations

Characteristically, for-profit organizations are more bottom-line and profit-driven than NPOs and can flex their budgeting muscles a little more. A government organization generally has to *try* to spend the people's money wisely. In government, usually, money that is not spent has to be returned to the treasury, which leads to a *spend it or lose it* mentality. NPOs dependent on government grants might, at times, adopt the same mentality. Legally, NPOs cannot show a profit, but they can create reserves from their general fund for use in later periods of time. These excess revenues have to be put in appropriate places. The exception is unused specific-purpose grant money, which must be returned to funding agencies. Despite these differences in how money is generated and spent, each sector can use any of the budgeting methods or processes discussed earlier.

Likewise, there is no single process that will work for all NPOs within the sector. Each of its subsectors—health care, social services, education, religious, arts and culture—might be subject to slight theoretical and practical differences and levels of sophistication as well as other factors involved in budgets, based on organization size.

SUMMARY

If the strategic plan is the seminal concept in finance and fiscal administration, the budget is the operationalization of the strategic plan and the hub of a good financial and fiscal network. It is the center of action at the beginning of the fiscal year when it is made a policy of nonprofit agencies, and at the end of a fiscal year when information learned during the year cycles into the next budget. During the fiscal year, it is the standard for comparison for the rest of the year as managers try to keep their spending within budget. Ultimately, budgets are developed by human beings on behalf of other human beings. Human budgeters are fallible and are prone to preferences and biases. Budgeting processes may vary, but for the most part they are annual and repeating, and they involve prescribed deadlines, follow a step-by-step procedure, are developed by staff members, and are ultimately approved by governing boards. Zero-based budgeting is a useful budgeting process for NPOs because it allows them to reevaluate programs on an annual basis. ZBB allows room for considering adding or eliminating programs. To the extent possible, budget decision making should be rational in nature, with primary criteria for decisions deriving from a strategic plan. NPOs should compare previous years' budgets and look for exceptions and trends to inform decision making. Sometimes undesirable patterns of revenue and revenue usage can be discovered through such variance analysis.

DISCUSSION QUESTIONS

1. Be the Board Member: You are a new board member and the executive director has just presented the budget for the coming year for the board's review and approval. The last few years have been rough, but the economy is getting better. The proposed budget is balanced and shows growth in revenues despite the current climate of declining donations to nonprofit agencies. What are the first three questions you want to ask the executive director about the budget? What are the answers to those questions that would be acceptable to you?

2. A nonprofit CEO writes: "Three years ago, in the midst of the donation reduction that was the after-effect of 9/11, my board rejected my reality budget for their dream budget. They wanted to maintain an aggressive stance instead of cutting back any more than they had to do. Consequently, we had a shortfall that forced us to dip deeply into our reserves. We ended up laying off staff. Last year, my reality budget included hundreds of thousands of dollars of new grant money for which we had agreements with funding agencies. The board, now cautious, undercut some of my budget projections for fear that we might run a shortfall." Consider this CEO's observations factual. Describe what you think of the CEO's performance over this three-year period as well as that of the board. Think about the board-CEO relationship. What should the CEO do to deal with this situation?

EXERCISE: SIMPLE BUDGET ANALYSIS

It is said that nonprofit budgets vary among organizations based on mission, size, culture, preferences, and other factors. Anyone involved in budgeting should never change jobs and expect the same process.[7] Most NPO activities require externally generated financial support and voluntary assistance. Therefore, the development of sound budgets to control and direct the NPO's activities is vital. The budget in Figure 4.3 is for a fictitious nonprofit museum, The Museum of Western Art and History, located in Tombstone, New Hampshire. For the purposes of this exercise, assume the budget in Table 4.4 has been presented to the board by the executive director, who has argued persuasively that the state of the NPO is good. While this seems an odd location to build loyalty for the Wild West–era of the United States, the museum has achieved some success. In the past five years, the museum has attracted a growing number of sponsors, donors, and visitors from the community and beyond, and it has increased activities in a number of areas, especially in the purchase of art. Put yourself on the board of the museum. Look at the information provided. What problems do you recognize? What additional information would you want from the executive director in order to be able to make recommendations to the board members who were not on the budget committee?

MUSEUM OF WESTERN ART AND HISTORY
TOMBSTONE, NEW HAMPSHIRE

REVENUES			
ITEM	BUDGETED 2005	ACTUAL 2006	PROPOSED 2006
Admissions	$96,000	$96,000	$96,000
Gift Shop	8,500	8,500	8,500
Art Class Tuition	11,700	11,700	11,700
Grants	81,000	81,000	81,000
Donations	52,000	52,000	52,000
Sponsorships	39,000	39,000	39,000
Special Events	51,000	51,000	51,000
Private Party Rental	40,000	40,000	40,000
Investment Interest	1,800	1,800	1,800
Total Revenues	$381,000	$381,000	$381,000

Table 4.4: Case Analysis of an Art and History Museum

EXPENDITURES			
ITEM	BUDGETED 2005	ACTUAL 2006	PROPOSED 2006
Salaries	$226,000	$236,000	$231,000
Benefits	38,000	79,010	25,000
Other Personnel Costs	11,000	17,100	7,000
Art Purchases	55,000	57,000	59,000
Volunteer Services	4,800	4,900	5,100
Security	15,000	15,900	17,500
Utilities	11,500	11,100	11,500
Advertising	6,000	5,800	6,200
Operations/Maintenance	3,400	3,400	4,000
Supplies	2,200	2,200	2,500
Exhibit Expenses	9,700	9,400	9,000
Gift Shop	2,850	2,850	9,500
Fundraisers	5,000	4,700	5,000
Capital Purchases	6,800	1,500	4,000
Community Classes	1,250	1,200	1,350
Long-term Investments	2,200	2,050	2,200
Payments on Debt	0	0	1,600
Total Expenditures	**$381,000**	**$389,000**	**$395,100**

PREVIOUS BUDGETS					
YEAR	BUDGETED REVENUE	ACTUAL REVENUE	BUDGETED EXPENDITURES	ACTUAL EXPENDITURES	END-OF-YEAR RESERVES
1999	$364,000	$364,100	$364,000	$364,100	$364,100
2000	366,000	366,500	366,000	366,500	366,500
2001	368,000	367,200	368,000	367,200	367,200
2002	369,000	369,300	369,000	369,300	369,300
2003	370,000	369,900	370,000	369,900	369,900
2004	373,000	374,700	373,000	374,700	374,700
2005	381,000	378,000	381,000	378,000	378,000

INNOVATION: PRIORITY-BASED BUDGETING

As stated earlier, the most common ways of approaching budgeting are the checkbook approach, line-item budgeting, PPBS, and ZBB. There are alternatives. One innovation was introduced by the state of Oregon—priority-based budgeting. This technique is accomplished intuitively by individuals in their personal budgets. Nonprofit officials should consider it as well: NPO boards, staff, and stakeholder determine what they believe are their agencies' mission and core functions before embarking on the annual budgeting process.[9]

To gain control of a budget means the following questions must be answered:

- What is the role of the agency?

- What are the essential services the agency must provide to fulfill its purpose?

- How does the agency know if it is doing a good job?

- What should it cost?

- How will the cuts be prioritized?

Only by carefully considering the proper role of the agency can legislators and governors do a good job protecting individual rights while providing essential services to clients in an efficient, cost-effective manner. This is not an "anti-agency" philosophy; it is just ensuring that what the agency is supposed to do, it will do well. Furthermore, great savings can be obtained if boards and agencies do not spend time determining how a particular function can be performed better, faster, and cheaper if it is not a core function.[10]

With honest and complete answers to these questions, an NPO can develop and implement an effective budget that deals with the priorities of its mission.

With priority-based budgeting, the staff members who implement the budget must be part of the leadership that creates the budget. If only the board decides the financial direction of the agency and the agency runs out of money, the staff will suffer and the director will be blamed. While this method of budgeting may not seem revolutionary, there are risks. Performance budgeting requires well-conceived goals and objectives, quantitative outcome measures, and someone to sort through it all. Even if all this is accomplished, the political process, emerging needs, and windows of opportunity also have to be considered by organizations as they prioritize spending.

NOTES

1   Robert M. Bryan, "The Basics of Budgeting: Your Role in Developing a Meaningful Budget (Board Primer)," *Association Management* (Jan. 1998): 65–67.

2   Murray Dropkin and J. Halpin, *The Budget-Building Book for Nonprofits: A Step-by-Step Guide for Managers and Boards,* 2nd ed. (San Francisco: Jossey Bass, 2007).

3   Herbert Simon, "A Behavioral Model of Rational Choice," *Quarterly Journal of Economics* 69 (1955). Online at http://cowles.econ.yale.edu/P/cp/p00b/p0098.pdf (accessed May 19, 2008).

4   K. Mathiasen, Board Passages: *Three Key Stages in a Nonprofit Board's Life Cycle* (Washington, DC: National Center for Nonprofit Boards, 1998).

5   Steven A. Finkler, *Financial Management for Public, Health, and Not-for-Profit Organizations,* 2nd ed. (Upper Saddle River, NJ: Pearson Prentice Hall, 2005).

6   David A. Palmer, "Budgeting Control and Variance Analysis," 2000. Online at http://www.financial managementdevelopment.com (accessed April 28, 2008).

7   Robert M. Bryan, "The Basics of Budgeting: Your Role in Developing a Meaningful Budget (Board Primer)," *Association Management* (Jan. 1998): 65–67.

8   Bob Miller and L. Harsh, "Say So Long to State Budget Deficits," September 2003. Online at http://www.citizenreviewonline.org (accessed April 28, 2008).

9   Ibid.

CHAPTER 5
Accounting

This chapter examines the effects of accounting on organizations, especially as it affects agencies in the nonprofit sector. Good accounting practices keep any organization running smoothly on a daily basis by maintaining and offering information for reporting on how the business transactions involving money occur and why money is being used in the way that accounting reports show. Accounting is no more or less important than any other financial and fiscal function, but maintaining an accounting of how budgeted dollars are used is critical to the financial health of an NPO. The budget function feeds into the accounting function, which in turn is the basis for budget control. It is the source of information for auditing and evaluation. Finally, it is a major source of decision-making information for managers. The chapter comprehensively explains the components of accounting, including day-to-day operations and reporting at various points during a fiscal year.

TOPICS
- The Finance and Fiscal Administrative Network: Accounting
- The Reasons for Accounting
- The Accounting Function
- The Bases of Accounting
- Funds
- Double-Entry Accounting (DEA)
- Reporting Requirements Unique to NPOs
- The Importance of Documentation
- Summary
- Discussion Questions
- Exercise
- Innovation: Outsourcing, New Staff, Process Redesign, or Technology?

THE FINANCE AND FISCAL ADMINISTRATIVE NETWORK: ACCOUNTING

As shown in Figure 5.1, accounting is a function that is equally as important as the budgeting function and must support the direction set in the strategic plan. Without one of these functions, or with a weakly applied function, the other will have little effectiveness.

An airliner cockpit is one of the most fascinating sights for a person interested in gadgets. Once in a while a passenger boarding an airliner will enter the plane while the cockpit door is open and catch a glimpse of the green, red, and yellow lights flickering, digital readouts everywhere, and even old-fashioned dials and gauges that register volume, speed, altitude, revolu-

Figure 5.1: Financial and Fiscal Network: The Accounting Function

tions per minute, and so on. The pilot and co-pilot make notations not just to check on the condition of the fuselage and engines, but to report to the air traffic tower on status, conditions, and balance. The information from and to the tower allows the controllers to make go/no go, timing, and other decisions leading to the airliner's takeoff. When in the air, the pilot and co-pilot continue to observe and report the readings provided by the cockpit instruments. They also use the information gathered to report later to engineers and mechanics who use the information after the airliner lands at its destination. All this is akin to what accounting information provides. Accountants and managers must monitor the various reports on spending and revenue that are created by the accounting function. Ledgers, balance sheets, statements of revenues and expenses, and *other dials and gauges* provide an NPO with information that can be used to *fly* it to its strategic and operational destinations.

THE REASONS FOR ACCOUNTING

Accounting is the way organizations keep track of their money. If an NPO's accounting function is poorly operated, there will be reduced accountability in that NPO. It is that simple. The accounting function in NPOs must be transparent in the sense of making the books *open*, understandable, and useful to managers and other stakeholders. The result of operating openly can be the establishment of the trust that is essential to good relationships with all stakeholders. The goal of setting up efficient, transparent accounting function is to allow the managers of an organization to make and report on informed choices regarding the direction an organization must take. The accounting function provides the key ingredients in the making of strategic and even tactical managerial decisions.

Accurate budget information is critical to the larger financial management picture of an organization. The budget process feeds into the accounting system. Principle 9 of the generally accepted accounting principles (GAAP) states that an annual budget should be adopted, that the accounting system is the basis for budget control, and that financial statements should show comparisons of budgets from year to year.

THE ACCOUNTING FUNCTION

Accounting comprises the set of procedures that record, classify, and report on the finances of a business, government, NPO, individual, or other entity. The accounting function accomplishes several important purposes, including:

- Describing an organization financially
- Measuring performance and financial status
- Providing information to be used in operational decision making
- Demonstrating efficiency and effectiveness to funding agencies, creditors, members, and other stakeholders

Accounting is much more than simple bookkeeping. The two distinct aspects of an accounting system that interact with the budget and that are discussed in this chapter are:

- Financial reporting, which provides information on budgetary activities to managers, to investors, and to the public

- Operational accounting, that is, the day-to-day activities of a nonprofit agency

All managers and many other staff members in NPOs likely become involved in both of these aspects of accounting. Operational accounting is vital for making sure that the budget, and through it the strategic plan, are complied with and drive the organization in terms of its use of money. In this way, budget and accounting reports provide managers a disciplined way to manage the expenditures for which they are responsible. Essentially, an accounting system should provide internal control over the acquisition and use of revenue. Internal controls can build into accounting functions' effectiveness, efficiency, reliability, and compliance with laws, rules, and regulations. While it does not guarantee anything, internal accounting controls provide some assurance that NPO objectives will be achieved.[1]

A third function of accounting is to provide data that managers can use in decision making. In general, this aspect of the accounting function is referred to as *managerial accounting*. Managerial accounting is not discussed in detail this chapter but is covered in various ways throughout the book. Managerial accounting is more a function of management than the keeping of the books. The topics covered in Chapters 3 and 4, strategic finance and budgeting, for example, rely on information that can only be extracted from an organization's accounting system. Likewise, the chapters that follow this one cover auditing and evaluation, revenue administration and forecasting, expenditure administration, cash and investment management, capital budgeting, and even risk management and business ventures. All these operations are only as good to managers as the quality of information they derive from the other functions, financial reporting, and practical accounting.

Financial Reporting

NPOs are expected to account for the money that flows through their coffers by following generally accepted accounting principles (GAAP). According to InvestorWords.com, GAAP is "a widely accepted set of rules, conventions, standards, and procedures for reporting financial information."[2] GAAP is used throughout all the sectors of the American economy. Also important in assisting and in governing the way finances are reported in the United States is the Financial Accounting Standards Board (FASB), identified by InvestorWords.com as "an independent agency which established GAAP."[3]

The major purpose of financial reports is to provide managers and other stakeholders with an accounting of an entity's financial condition. Reporting is done in a very detailed fashion on an ad hoc or daily, weekly, monthly, or quarterly basis. These are generally produced for managers to use. The comprehensive annual financial report (CAFR) is created annually, and is directed at stakeholders both inside and outside the organization.

Financial Reporting Hierarchy

Figure 5.2 shows the hierarchy of financial reports. The figure is based on GAAP's financial reporting *pyramid*. The word *hierarchy* is a more accurate descriptive term than is the word pyramid. The Financial Reporting Hierarchy shows the hierarchical system of condensing or aggregating financial information for reporting purposes.

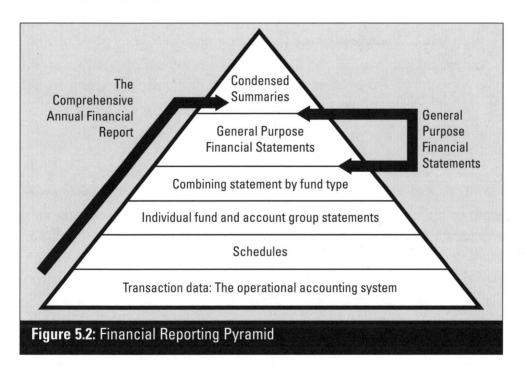

Figure 5.2: Financial Reporting Pyramid

The structure of the hierarchy is quite logical. It starts at the bottom level and builds up to the top. The bottom layer comprises the nitty-gritty detail of operational accounting, the journals and the ledgers that account for the ad hoc, daily, weekly, and monthly transactions and changes in financial condition. As you go up the hierarchy, each level combines the lower level. The fourth level combines all funds by fund type. Near the top are the general-purpose financial statements that present a fairly detailed overview of the combining statements for all funds. The second level from the top contains the essential combined statements that most people recognize as the annual financial report. The top level, the one that most people read and interpret, includes the very high-level tables and graphics, letters, descriptions, and in general, the biggest picture of the comprehensive financial condition of a nonprofit agency.

The financial reports shown in the figure are directed toward several important stakeholders, including:

- Donors

- Funding agencies

- Members

- Clients

- Oversight entities like the Internal Revenue Service

- The board of directors

- Managers

- Media

These reports are the primary source of objective information about a nonprofit entity. It is helpful and important that interim timely information upon which these final reports are based be disseminated to top administrators for management purposes. NPO financial reports differ from a private-sector corporation's financial reports in two ways. First, corporate ownership by stockholders, partners, and proprietors differs from the ownership model of NPOs. Second, in nonprofit financial reports, there tends to be an emphasis on legal compliance. Nonprofits have to prove compliance with the requirements of granting organizations.

In the private sector, the rate of return on investment is a very real and measurable incentive. Investors and creditors require demonstration of positive outcomes. NPOs differ on this particular matter. Private corporations permit immaterial errors, rounding, and omissions. NPOs do not. They account for every penny.

There are a number of types of financial reports that report on an NPO's financial condition. Reports that should be prepared include the following:

- **Popular reports:** Popular reports include charts, graphs, and other high level documents that display the overall condition of the entity (see Figures 5.3, 5.4, and 5.5).

- **General purpose financial statements – simple balance sheet:** The simple balance sheet provides information on liquidity and cash management, equity, and debt management. The balance sheet is generally calculated for each separate program or fund and for all funds together (see Table 5.1).

- **Statement of changes in financial position:** This statement shows the flow of cash for the year (see Table 5.2).

- **Statement of revenues and expenditures and changes in fund balance:** This statement tells the story of whether or not the entity operated efficiently (see Table 5.3).

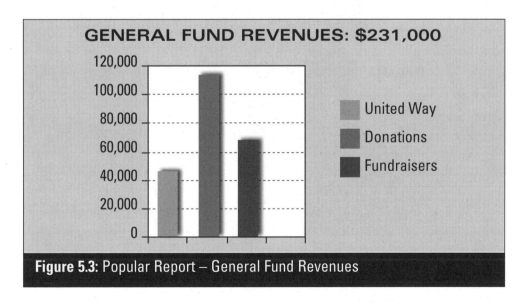

Figure 5.3: Popular Report – General Fund Revenues

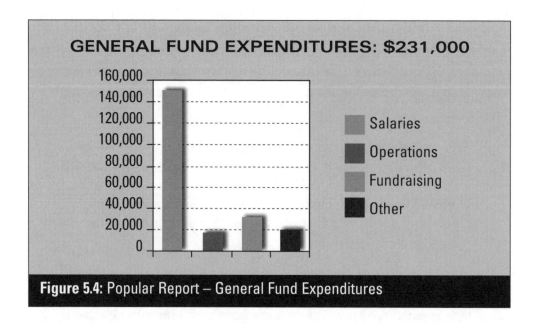

Figure 5.4: Popular Report – General Fund Expenditures

Special General Fund Revenues: $113,000

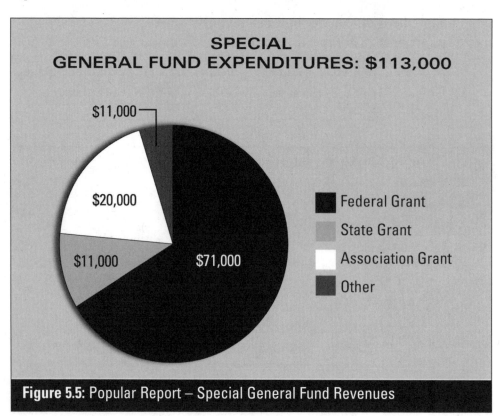

Figure 5.5: Popular Report – Special General Fund Revenues

ASSETS	GENERAL FUND	RESTRICTED ACCOUNTS	TOTAL
Cash and Equivalents	$ 200,000	$ 50,000	$ 250,000
Marketable Securities	9,000	1,000	10,000
Cash Receivables	20,000	2,000	22,000
Fixed Assets	990,000		990,000
Depreciation	(190,000)		(190,000)
Total Assets	$ 1,029,000	$ 53,000	$ 1,082,000

LIABILITIES AND FUND BALANCE	GENERAL FUND	RESTRICTED ACCOUNTS	TOTAL
Accounts Payable	$ 53,000	$ 6,000	$ 59,000
Fund Balance	976,000	47,000	1,023,000
Total Liabilities and Fund Balance	$ 1,029,000	$ 53,000	$ 1,082,000

Table 5.1: Simple Balance Sheet

REVENUES	GENERAL FUND	RESTRICTED FUNDS	TOTAL
Donations	$ 117,000	$	$ 117,000
United Way	45,000		45,000
Fundraising	69,000		69,000
Investment Decisions	2,000	11,000	13,000
Government Grants		53,000	53,000
Total Revenues	$ 233,000	$ 64,000	$ 297,000
EXPENDITURES			
Donations	$ 117,000	$	$ 117,000
United Way	45,000		45,000
Fundraising	69,000		69,000
Investment Decisions	2,000	11,000	13,000
Government Grants		53,000	53,000
Total Revenues	$ 233,000	$ 64,000	$ 297,000

Table 5.2: Statement of Changes in Financial Position

OPERATING REVENUES:	
Charges for services	11,300,000
Miscellaneous	————
Total operating revenues	11,300,000
OPERATING EXPENSES:	
Personal services	3,400,000
Contractual services	350,000
Utilities	750,000
Repairs and maintenance	700,000
Other supplies and expenses	490,000
Insurance claims and expenses	
Depreciation	1,100,000
Total operating expenses	6,790,000
Operating income (loss)	4,510,000
NONOPERATING REVENUES (EXPENSES):	
Interest and investment revenue	450,000
Miscellaneous revenue	
Interest expense	(1,600,000)
Miscellaneous expense	————
Total nonoperating revenue (expenses)	(1,150,000)
Income (loss) before contributions & transfers	3,200,000
Capital contributions	1,600,000
Transfers out	(290,000)
Change in net assets	4,510,000
Total net assets – beginning of period	79,059,015
Total net assets – end of period	83,691,024

Table 5.3: Statement of Revenues, Expenses, and Changes in Fund Balance

Combining and Combined Financial Statements

The financial statements listed in the earlier discussion are the combined or condensed financial statements noted in Figure 5.2, the financial reporting pyramid. Combining financial statements display the financial condition of specific funds such as special revenue funds and debt service funds. References to these financial statements are found on the financial reporting pyramid just below the level of condensed financial statements and just above individual funds. Combined financial statements add together all funds: special revenue funds, debt service funds, and restricted funds. This gives the target readers the opportunity to analyze the entity's overall financial condition by type of account or fund.

A review of any comprehensive annual financial report will demonstrate the function of a combined and combining financial statement. The flow of these financial statements is shown in Figure 5.6.

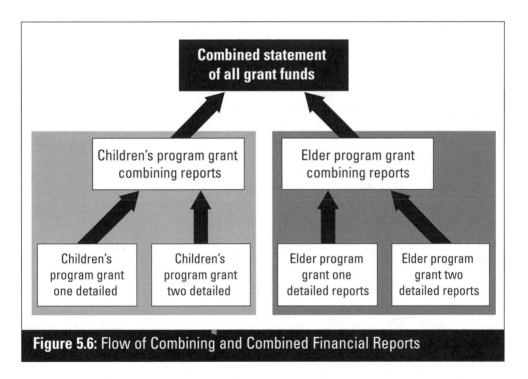

Figure 5.6: Flow of Combining and Combined Financial Reports

Management Analysis of Financial Statements

FASB provides guidance to nonprofits through sections 116 and 117 of its Codification. FASB 117 covers guidelines for financial statements of not-for-profit organizations. The guidance directs that nonprofit financial reports should be audited, have legal force, and contain the real numbers of an organization, not the planned numbers found in the budget. As such, they attempt to provide the true financial position of an organization.[4] Financial reports give managers information for ensuring there are funds available to meet their missions. They are used also to show compliance with government and other grantor agencies.

Managers can use the balance sheet and the other financial statements to make decisions and develop financial strategies. First, as will be discussed in a later section of this chapter, the accounting equation is an accounting concept that requires the value of a fund and an organization's assets to equal its liabilities and fund balance. It is an algebraic equation. If both sides of the equation are not equal, something in the bookkeeping coding or calculations is in error. This knowledge may lead to the discovery of a systematic error that can be corrected. Each year, managers should compare the most current balance sheet to past years and look for changes in assets, liabilities, and fund balance. This analysis should not only look at dollar figures but should also examine the numbers in terms of percentages. For more detail, examine the situation in the simple example shown in Table 5.4.

	2007	PERCENT OF TOTAL ASSETS	2006	PERCENT OF TOTAL ASSETS	YEAR-TO-YEAR DIFFERENCE	PERCENT CHANGE
Current Assets	$110,000	34.3	$100,000	33.8	$10,000	(1.5)
Receivables	10,000	3.2	5,000	1.7	5,000	(88.2)
Fixed Assets	200,000	62.5	190,000	64.4	10,000	3.0
Total Assets	**$320,000**	**100.0**	**$295,000**	**100.0**	**$25,000**	
Payables	$20,000	6.25	$30,000	10.2	($10,000)	63.2
Fund Balance	300,000	93.7	265,000	89.8	35,000	(4.2)
Total Liabilities	**$320,000**	**100.0**	**$295,000**	**100.0**	**$25,000**	

Table 5.4: Management Analysis Case Example

These numbers can also be compared to other documents.[5] For example, the percentages listed in the table can be compared to other nonprofits with similar missions to give a rough measure of industry standards. Looking at comparative information can tell managers valuable information about their own financial position. Statements of revenues and expenses can also provide managers with a tool to compare actual and projected figures shown in the budget.[6] It also provides information on the relative efficiency of operations compared to goals, targets, and limits. The statement of changes in financial position likewise provides managers with information that needs to be interpreted in relation to revenues, expenses, inventory, return on investments, revenue sources, and debt. It answers questions about how resources were used. Individual funds can be monitored through an analysis of combining reports. These reports can be used to stave off financial disaster.[7]

THE BASES OF ACCOUNTING

The accounting basis chosen and used by an NPO is critical to the success of an accounting system. The accounting basis answers the question, "When are revenues and expenditures recognized and reported?" If this information is controlled by the NPO, it moves the NPO toward the ability know its financial status at any given time. There are three bases of accounting from which to select—*cash, accrual,* and *modified accrual.*

The cash basis of accounting, shown in Table 5.7, recognizes revenues only when they are in hand. Expenditures are recognized only when the cash leaves the account and is received by the entity owed the money. There is no recognition of the words *receivable* and *payable* when using the cash basis. This limits the NPO's ability to know its financial status. If the reader can picture his or her own checkbook, the reader will understand cash basis accounting. There is a danger in using the cash basis that goes beyond an old joke about the reaction of the oblivious person who gets a notice of insufficient funds, "There has to be money in my account, I still have checks left." This illustrates the danger that an NPO may fail to recognize incurred expenses that are coming at a later time and may spend cash that should be set aside for those expenses. Likewise, any expenditure that should be made might not be made even though revenues would be com-

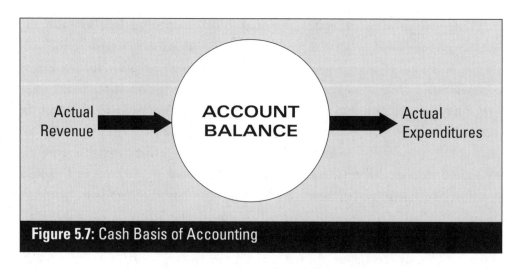

Figure 5.7: Cash Basis of Accounting

ing at a later time. The cash basis format is depicted in Figure 5.7.

Accrual accounting, shown in Table 5.8, recognizes income when it is earned and expenditures when they are incurred. The assumption is made that the income will be appropriately placed in the fund accounts as indicated by the revenue source, and that purchases of goods and services will be paid for even though they may or may not be in hand and no check has been drafted. This allows for better planning of how cash can be used for the benefit of the NPO. It also allows an organization to incur an expense with the understanding that it will be paid when the revenue comes in. The account balance will reflect all expected revenue and expenditures coming due. The accrual format is depicted in Figure 5.8.

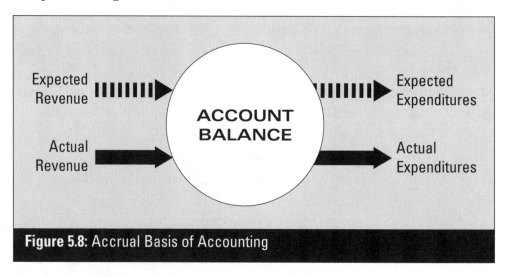

Figure 5.8: Accrual Basis of Accounting

No organization of any size today should be using the cash basis of accounting. That basis does not accurately recognize the financial status of the organization. The cash basis method does not reflect what an NPO is owed and what it owes. Receivables are true revenues and payables are true expenditures. A view of a cash basis account will not reflect receivables and expenditures.

Only accrual and what is called *modified* accrual bases should be used in nonprofit accounting. Both methods recognize receivables and payables. Modified accrual is similar to accrual in that it modifies the true accrual in order to consider the end of a fiscal year. The books of nonprofits are usually closed after the end of a fiscal year. To compensate for late reporting of expenditures or revenues, the accounts of the next fiscal year are modified so that the expenses and revenues not received within one fiscal year are recognized in the next fiscal year.

Most NPOs track revenue and expenses using the accrual basis of accounting. In part, the choice of which basis of accounting is dictated by organization size. Many small NPOs do not have the means or the expertise to engage in using the accrual method. These NPOs use the checkbook method instead, recording revenue when a check or cash is received, and only recording expenses when they are actually paid. Other nonprofits acknowledge and record payroll taxes withheld from employees and large revenue or expense items using the accrual approach. This means recording revenues when they are earned and expenses when obligations are incurred, but otherwise using the cash basis.

Chart of Accounts

An important classification system used in any reasonably sized organization, including NPOs with more than a few dollars and a few people involved, is the chart of accounts. A chart of accounts identifies and lists an organization's accounts that are used to organize and record transactions in its general ledger. Most organizations design their own chart of accounts to reflect their own unique perspective on how financial transactions are recorded. A chart of accounts identifies accounts and transactions by unique account numbers. There are usually two general categories of accounts:

- Balance sheet accounts that capture asset, liability, and fund balance data

- Income statement accounts that capture operating revenues and expenditures

Within the categories of operating revenues and operating expenses, accounts might be further organized by department or division and by program under them. Each of these will have separate accounts with unique identifier codes to help ensure that the right accounts are credited and debited. A chart of accounts is designed according to the size and complexity of the organization.

The way the chart of accounts works is found in the next section in the discussion of fund accounts.[8]

FUNDS

Much of nonprofit accounting is based on fund accounting to a large degree. Most NPOs receive funding from various sources and deposit money into general and specific funds. The general fund usually is used for the general operations of the NPO. Specific funds are restricted by agreement with grantors and donors. Specific funds are used for designated purposes. In general, specific funds are not allowed to be transferred or are not what is called by the wonderful English word, *fungible*, that is, the monies in funds are not intended for use in any other fund, including the general fund.

A fund is a separate fiscal and accounting entity. Thus, money from one fund cannot be moved to another. Portions of the fund, however, may be devoted to general operations of the NPO, and the fund will be appropriately charged. There are several types of funds that an NPO may use. Several common funds include general operating funds and funds set aside for capital purchases and construction of facilities. Large NPOs like hospitals might have proprietary funds that operate to serve the needs of external clients or other internal departments. Fiduciary funds are often created and operated based on trust that the NPO will comply with the stated purposes of the gift or grant, or restricted use funds. These include funds administered by the NPO that are created for specific purposes, including money bequeathed for, as an example, a new service provided by a religious institution, or a pension fund or other benefit. Figure 5.9 demonstrates the flow of revenue through funds.

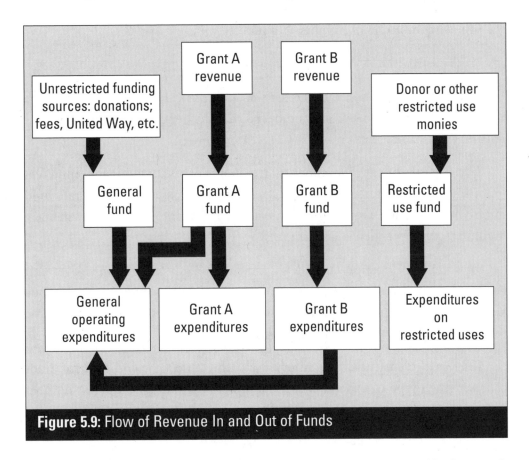

Figure 5.9: Flow of Revenue In and Out of Funds

Funds are separate accounting entities. Transactions on behalf of a specific fund are accounted for using all the daily and monthly accounting produced for a general fund. Year-end financial statements such as balance sheets must be produced for each fund. While these specific funds are independently accounted for, they should be disclosed and reported on by the NPO in its annual financial report.

Identifying Funds and Accounts

GAAP recommends that nonprofit entities organize NPO funds through a meaningful numbering system, the chart of accounts that was discussed earlier. There is no universal or standardized methodology for such a numbering system. Each agency chooses its own fund numbering system. In general, however, the numbering system should identify each source of revenue, should contain a fund-specific number, and should state the authority of those who use the money in the fund and for what the money is to be used. Let's break down the following example of number in a fund numbering system:

03-24-07-1234

03 is the identification number for the adult day care fund created through a grant (each fund has a unique number so that the general fund would be designated 01, a capital fund number 02).

24 is the identification number for the source of revenue—space rental fees (each source of generated revenue has a unique number so that the same fund might have revenue from different sources, for example, an endowment, a grant, fees, or other identifiable source).

07 is the identification number for the day care administration budget unit (each sub-unit that has money appropriated to it in the budget has a unique ID number; this might include other units like the social work department, the recreation department, or other appropriate sub-unit).

1234 is the identification number for the fund's expenditure for floor cleanser (each type of expenditure has a unique ID number; this last number is four digits because of the many different types of purchases that might occur).

Obviously, this numbering system should be maintained on an automated financial system, but should also be written or printed on any hard-copy documents. The numbering system allows for easy tracking by managers, by auditors, and even by boards who have the time to track a nonprofit's accounting system.

Funds vs. Accounts

A large portion of this chapter has been devoted to discussing funds and accounts. It is important to distinguish between a fund and an account. A fund, according to GAAP, is a complete record of an amount of money owned or owed by or to a particular person or entity, or allocated to a particular purpose. A fund is larger than an account. In fund accounting, each fund contains a number of accounts that are consistent with an organization's chart of accounts.

According to the website AccountingCoach.com, an account is a "record in the general ledger that is used to collect and store similar information. For example, an organization will have a cash account in which every transaction involving cash is recorded. A company selling merchandise on credit will record these sales in a Sales account and in an Accounts Receivable account."[9]

Budget Monitoring

The chart of accounts that reflects a numbering system as just discussed assists managers in keeping track of their portion of the budget. Managers should be responsible for monitoring, if not managing, their budgets. Each manager who is responsible for a budget or part of a budget should have a management plan for that budget. The management plan should ensure that expenditures match their purpose and do not diverge from budgeted amounts without proper authorization, that transactions are properly recorded, and that useful reports reach the staff members who use them. This type of management allows those responsible for each portion of the budget to not only easily track the use of funds and identify any problems or missteps, but also to know when to take appropriate action. The vital need for proper authorization becomes just a step in the process of making sure that payment requests, travel reimbursement, payroll, and other allowable expenditures are credited and debited in the appropriate funds. All of these should be accompanied by proper hard-copy or electronic forms that encumber the nonprofit to pay for the good or service in question. The forms reserve or encumber money for specific purposes in compliance with the budget and with funds. When money is encumbered, another form, a voucher, authorizes payment of the money owed for a good or service.

DOUBLE-ENTRY ACCOUNTING (DEA)

Double-entry accounting, also known as the *accounting equation*, is an important concept in accounting. It allows bookkeepers and accountants to create an effective and efficient accounting system that serves an organization's need for accuracy. A discussion of DEA is helpful when discussing accounts and accounting.

There are two types of accounts that show the actual financial position of a fund—real and nominal. There are two types of nominal accounts:

- Revenues

- Expenses

These accounts are called nominal because they change from budget period to budget period.

Real accounts are permanent accounts. That is, they are carried over and reported on from year to year. These real accounts are:

- Assets

- Liabilities

- Equity/fund balance

Assets are what a fund owns or is owed (cash, receivables, buildings, land, equipment, and inventory). Liability accounts represent the debts of a fund. There are two types: current (to be paid in the current fiscal year), and long-term (extending out more than one fiscal year). Equity/fund balance accounts report a fund's financial condition as it changes. Each transaction affects assets, fund balance, and liability accounts.

Double-entry accounting provides a reliable means for recording and monitoring financial transactions. It is from these financial transactions that important financial statements can be developed—income statements, balance sheets, and statements of change in financial condition. DEA ensures that the accounting system is self-balancing. The frequency and complexity of financial transactions mandates daily, monthly, or annual operations in most NPOs. DEA is also called the accounting equation because it is an algebraic formula used to verify that transactions are recorded properly. No matter what area of financial reporting the reader may examine, there are always two sides, and one side of the formula must be equal to the other side. The accounting equation can be seen in ledgers which record revenues and expenditures; journals, which record changes in accounts; the balance sheet; statements of revenues and expenditures; and so on. If any of those financial documents are out of balance, then something is wrong and the only solution is to review the accounts and discover the erroneous entry. If they do not balance, something is amiss in the accounting department.

The basic accounting equation is:

Assets = Liabilities and Equity/Fund Balance

The following example from AccountingCoach.com demonstrates how entries into a double-entry account occur:

A nonprofit that "pays the rent for the month credits rent expense and debits cash;" the former is paid for out of the latter. Both are asset accounts. If an NPO provides a service and gives the client receiving the service 30 days to pay for the service, the NPO's revenue account, an asset account and accounts receivable, and a liability account, are affected. A single transaction can actually result require action in even more than two separate accounts. "An example of a transaction that involves three accounts is a company's loan payment to its bank of $300. This transaction will involve the following accounts: cash, notes payable, and interest expense."[10]

Debits and Credits

Two often baffling concepts, *debits* and *credits*, are historically five hundred years old. They were used to describe a double-entry accounting system much in the same form that it is found today.[11] As the following demonstrates, debits and credit rules are rather simple.

Under the *double-entry system*, every business transaction is recorded in at least two accounts. One account will receive a "debit" entry, meaning the amount will be entered on the *left* side of that account. Another account will receive a "credit" entry, meaning the amount will be entered on the *right* side of that account. The initial challenge with double entry is to know which account should be debited and which account should be credited.[12]

The use of these concepts is explained now.

Transaction Data: Journals and Ledgers

Note that in Figure 5.2 the base of the Financial Reporting Pyramid consists of operational transactions. These are the day-to-day transactions that are accounted for in a fund. Each fund includes individual and specific journals and ledgers. Journals provide a place to record all detailed financial transactions of an NPO. As seen in the general journal entry examples, each transaction is recorded by date, and each receives an individual transaction number and document number (Table 5.5). Furthermore, each transaction is assigned to the proper account and entered either as a debit or a credit. Note that the journal is not self-balancing, but identifies each transaction as either a debit or credit. It provides information for the ledger, which is a self-balancing.

DATE	TRANSACTION NO.	DOCUMENT NO.	ACCOUNT	DEBIT	CREDIT
1/1/02	1234	Income received	02-246-2468		$50,000
1/2/02	1235	Voucher 987	03-188-1888	$20,000	
		Warrant 13579	03-188-1888		$20,000
1/3/02	1236	Voucher 988	04-040-9999	$2,400	
		Warrant 13586	04-040-9999		$2,400
1/4/02	1237	Voucher 999	05-040-0001	$500	
		Warrant 13599	05-040-0001		$500
1/5/02	1238	Income received	02-246-2469		$5,000
1/30/02	1333	Voucher 1234	01-023-1111	$4,000	
		Warrant 1234	01-023-1111		$4,000

Table 5.5: Journal Entries Example

Note that no balances are reported in the journal.

Ledgers are the transactional documents that record and report on changes in accounts that are recorded in the journal. The information entered in the ledger allows calculation of an organization's balance sheet. Ledgers can be in either of two formats: T-accounts or ledger accounts. Table 5.6 shows a ledger account entry that reflects the transactions from the journal example in Table 5.5. Every transaction is recorded by entries in at least two accounts as shown in the example. Each entry tracks the account's balance.

TRANSACTIONS	ACCOUNT	DEBIT	CREDIT	BALANCE	ACCOUNT	DEBIT	CREDIT	BALANCE
1234	Cash		$50,000	$50,000	Equity	$50,000		$50,000
1235	Cash	$20,000		30,000	Computers		20,000	30,000
1236	Cash	2,400		27,600	Rent		2,400	27,600
1237	Stationery		500	28,100	Acct. Payable	500		28,100
1238	Cash		5,000	33,100	Equity	5,000		33,100
1239	Cash	4,000		29,100	Equity		4,000	29,100

Table 5.6: Ledger Entries Example

How Debits and Credits Affect the Balance Sheet

The balance sheet is a year-end financial report that sums the transactions in a fund or account that take place over a year's time. Look at the fund balance sheet in Exhibit 5.1. The purpose of the exhibit is to demonstrate how transactions affect the balance sheet as transactions in a ledger occur. Note how both sides of the equation are affected by the following transactions, but the equation stays in balance.

Transaction 1: $50,000 is budgeted to start up a teacher support area of a nonprofit library.

Transaction 2: $20,000 is spent on new computers.

Transaction 3: $2,400 is spent on the rent for the upcoming month.

Transaction 4: $500 worth of stationery is ordered. This asset will be zeroed out when the payment is made.

Transaction 5: $5,000 additional is allocated to the Office Pool Section.

Transaction 6: $4,000 is spent on payroll.

	PREPAID CASH	RENT	STATIONARY	EQUIPMENT	ACCOUNTS PAYABLE	EQUITY
Transaction 1	$50,000					$50,000
Transaction 2	($20,000)					
Transaction 3	($2,400)	$2,400		$20,000		$2,400
Transaction 4			$500		$500	
Transaction 5	$5,000					$5,000
Transaction 6	($4,000)					($4,000)
Subtotal	$28,600	$2,400	$500	$20,000	$500	$51,000
TOTAL	$51,500				$51,500	

Exhibit 5.1: Effects of Transactions on Balance Sheet

Transaction 1 credits cash and debits equity. Balance on both sides of the equation is $50,000.

Transaction 2 debits cash and credits equipment. The balance on both sides of the equation is unchanged at $50,000 because the expenditure on equipment has a value of $20,000 as an asset at this time. There is no change in liability or fund equity.

Transaction 3 debits cash and credits prepaid rent. The balance on both sides of the equation is unchanged because the expenditure on prepaid rent has a value of $2,400 at this time.

Transaction 4 credits stationery and debits accounts payable. This is a debt that changes the balance.

Transaction 5 credits cash and debits equity. It is an addition to cash that changes the balance of the equation.

Transaction 6 debits cash and credits equity. The expenditure changes the balance of the equation.

REPORTING REQUIREMENTS UNIQUE TO NPOS

Because of their unique nature, NPOs are obligated to report contributions if they qualify under section 501(c)(3) of the IRS and if the NPO receives contributions that the donors may claim as deductible from their income tax. The IRS has established procedures for NPOs to follow. More than one type of contribution is subject to this requirement. Examples are the following:

- Pledges are promises to give. FASB 116 requires that "legally enforceable, unconditional pledges be recorded in the accounting records. An unconditional pledge is one which is not contingent on some uncertain future event, such as a matching grant from another donor."

- In-kind contributions come in the form of donated materials and services. NPOs must report these in financial statements. Volunteer time, for example, must be reported when the volunteer time results in the creation or enhancement of nonfinancial assets, such as volunteer labor to renovate a child care center, or when the services volunteered are specialized skills, such as those provided by accountants, nurses, electricians, teachers, or other professionals and craftsmen.[13]

NPOs are also obligated to report on the allocation of some expenses.

Nonprofits are required to report their expenses by what is known as their functional expense classifications. The two primary functional expense classifications are program services and supporting activities. Supporting activities typically include management and general activities, fundraising, and membership development. Practices vary widely from organization to organization in the nonprofit sector as to how expenses are categorized by functional areas.[14]

THE IMPORTANCE OF DOCUMENTATION

An important decision any NPO must make is how to document financial information to provide the organization with knowledge needed to meet financial requirements. Proper accounting documentation has a unique and valuable contribution to an organization's success. It would be well for an NPO to invest the most possible resources into this vital utility. A mere 41 percent of 860 nonprofit organizations surveyed published an accounting policies and procedures manual.[15] Documentation is vital to an NPO, and the better the organization of accounting information, the better suited the NPO will be to provide information to various stakeholders, including auditors. Documentation ultimately is a responsibility managers have; they must provide critical staff members with information about when and how to do bookkeeping and accounting. Policy and procedure models reassure an NPO that accounting requirements can be accomplished, and in a proper manner.[16]

Having poorly documented systems can bring an organization down. Some NPOs have excellent documenting systems, and others have very poor documenting systems. The key to having an excellent documenting system is through providing education to new employees. If an employee orientation schedule includes working with documentation, the new employee will have a better understanding of what is going on in the organization. Cross-training new and old employees to job standards and job expectations can be helpful as well. Another solution in getting a better handle on this problem is for NPOs to cross-train their employees in understanding and working with various system applications so that the staff does not have to always rely on senior members to get their jobs done.

SUMMARY

This chapter enumerated the reasons for engaging in accounting. Covered were not only the functions including accountability, financial reporting, accounting bases, funds, and operational accounting, but also key concepts of accounting, including quality, accuracy, and accountability. NPOs should never let quality lapse in accounting. Nowhere in the practice of NPO management is accuracy, quality, and accountability more of a necessity. An accounting system provides all the monetary information an NPO will need if these concepts are followed. Such information can be used by managers and boards to make important decisions regarding mission attainment. Most NPOs use fund accounting. This method puts revenue into separate caches that have specified uses. NPOs that receive foundation grants, federal funds, and money from state and local governments usually must follow fund accounting's practices.

DISCUSSION QUESTIONS

1. Some NPOs operate with inadequate computers and financial software. Consequently, it can become difficult to retrieve and manipulate useful data. The modern world demands the maximum use of technology. For NPOs, many times managers do not know what they want from their accounting function. These two observations point to a lack of both technology and expertise. Discuss these problems. Come up with appropriate solutions that different types of NPOs might be able to apply.

2. Accounting provides managers with tools for achieving efficiency, effectiveness, and accountability. Operational accounting and financial reporting have very different functions. Yet day-to-day operations and annual statements of financial position are very much related. It has been said that an organization's financial reporting is only as good as its operational accounting. Distinguish between operational accounting and financial reporting. Identify areas where the two functions are integrated and explain why one of these functions is only as good as the other.

EXERCISE

A nonprofit neighborhood health facility, GPS, has been granted funds by the city it serves, Lucilleville, under a contract to build and operate a therapeutic swimming pool. The agreement allowed GPS to set up a separate enterprise from its other operations and account for financial transactions in a special enterprise fund. Using the following six-month summary of transactions, post each transaction under the appropriate accounts listed. Show the final balance after all transactions have occurred. Finally, offer an explanation of what has transpired.

TRANSACTIONS	CASH +	SWIMMING POOL +	LAND =	ACCOUNTS PAYABLE +	EQUITY
1. Lucilleville allocates $750,000 to develop, open, and operate swimming pool.					
2. GPS purchases property for pool for $500,000.					
3. The pool is constructed for $600,000. GPS pays $300,000 of the total.					
4. First six-month gross receipts total $160,000.					
5. Salaries paid during same period total $100,000.					
6. Utilities paid during same period total $55,000.					

HINT: Transaction 3 requires three entries.

INNOVATION: OUTSOURCING, NEW STAFF, PROCESS REDESIGN, OR TECHNOLOGY?

Both technology and processes in all three major sectors of the economy are studied and evaluated, in order to find ways to improve how organizations operate their financial systems. Like a slow-moving stream, technology and processes are forever changing. Some organizations keep up. Others do not. This section is not about the latest in computer hardware and software. It is about organizational strategies for maintaining an appropriate pace for changing financial and budgeting technology and processes. It recognizes that common barriers to efficiency identified in the following section exist.

Common Barriers to Efficiency

Many accounting systems are overrun by paper flow and a chart of accounts that don't provide the information management needs or external reporting requires.

System knowledge is often solely in the heads of long-time staff members. When they are not available, new employees can't function efficiently, and others can't get needed information.

A lot of accounting department work is clerical and adds little value. A classic example is excessive review of travel expense reports.

Accounting departments often waste time waiting for employees to turn in expense reports before closing accounting periods.

Many organizations have difficulty extracting data from their general ledgers or other systems for needed reports, requiring additional time to create spreadsheets.[17]

Some nonprofits still operate with technologically disadvantaged systems that cannot transfer data easily, and their reporting capabilities are poor. Every institution needs to investigate the technological option, because it is the way to overcome the paperwork mess. If good time is spent educating workers, and specialized technicians with viable logistics are in place, it will help reduce some of the disadvantages of upgrading. Changes in the nonprofit economy leading toward adoption of new technologies suggest the need for a warning to every NPO to reinvent itself to the extent that it is able. And even in stating this, it is still possible that new technology might not be needed for some NPOs. Perhaps redesigning processes that use technology is a more appropriate strategy, or the best solution might be for the NPO to outsource most of its accounting functions. The following decision flowchart is provided to lead NPOs to the right decision.

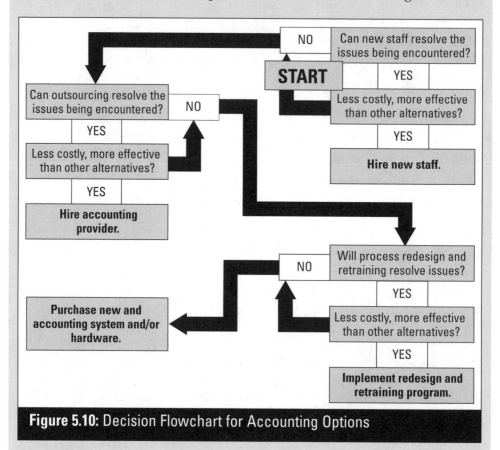

Figure 5.10: Decision Flowchart for Accounting Options

The Outsourcing Option

Instead of having agency staff operating an in-house financial system, some NPOs may find it less costly and sufficiently effective to outsource accounting functions. An NPO with a $1 million budget can sometimes pay less than one percent of its budget for outside accounting services. That is far less than it would have to pay for a person on staff to conduct operational accounting services and financial reporting. Training staff is also important in areas where they interact with an outside contractor. As with most business transactions, "garbage in, garbage out" is a fact of life. If staff members are not putting revenues and spending activities on the proper line, the financial picture of the agency will not be accurate. The relationship with an outsourced accounting firm, like any other important contractor, should be beneficial to both parties. Therefore, it is important to have a good professional relationship with that contractor.

While the outsourcing option may be less expensive than other options, an NPO must consider to what extent the contractor is effective and efficient. It must answer questions about the need for financial services to produce the best results. No contractor can know the needs of an organization more than internal accounting staff can. Therefore, consideration should be given to both outsourcing and in-house staffing of accounting functions.

The Hiring Option

Efficiency is not necessarily found in a machine; much of it can be found in people, and until people are held accountable for their jobs and the responsibilities for reporting that those jobs entail, no amount of technological upgrades will solve a problem of inefficiency. Hiring new staff with appropriate accounting expertise can improve accounting processes, help staff make important decisions for the organization, and help staff interpret and present financial statistics that serve managers and other staff members. Hiring new accounting staff may be much more expensive than other options. The question to be answered is whether or not the new staff option provides more effectiveness and efficiency to the NPO.

The Internal Process Redesign Option

As stated in the previous section, efficiency is not necessarily found in a machine; it is what people are capable of doing with hardware and software. Ultimately, no amount of technological upgrades will solve the problem of inefficiency if staff members responsible for financial reporting do not properly use the software and hardware they are provided with. Efficiency does not always mean getting something you know you are going to need at the last minute; it means, instead, doing the work in a timely manner to ensure that you have what you need when you need it—before you enter crisis mode. Even NPOs that are technologically disadvantaged can manage to perform efficiently with a pen, an accounting pad, and the right input from others. Many people fear technology and refuse to let go of the paper. In several nonprofit settings, the authors have observed either too much information (quarterly records of all agency transactions) or too little information (because expenditures were rolled into line items with no program breakdowns).

These issues point to the possibility that problems of inefficiency and ineffectiveness are due to poor processes. If that is true, then staff training and thoughtful redesign of the accounting system can overcome the problems. Taking such actions might be the best option for a nonprofit agency, especially if it is less costly than the other options.

The Technological Option

Computer software and hardware may contribute to successful NPO accounting more than any other component of the financial and fiscal network. Computers have an increasing capacity to support all of the tasks involved in operating an NPO, and failure to take advantage of this technology means that the function is being done at a greater expenditure of human effort than necessary or is being done inadequately, or both. That said, adequate technology does not have to mean the most current. Last year's computers using one or two earlier versions of the current software releases can still support very sophisticated accounting applications at dramatically lower costs. NPOs often still conduct accounting functions in a darkened mist, and many times the problem with computer applications is that managers do not know what they want from the accounting system and they get more than they need—or less.

Even if an NPO's computer hardware is an antiquated (three years or older by modern standards) computer system, the software upgrades are available online or in retail stores. Operating systems have not changed so dramatically that they prevent the use of older software. Many times, old accounting software is still supported by manufacturers. In addition, any good IT manager worth his or her salary can adapt an existing system in a fairly quick time frame, or knows how to accomplish outsourcing to an IT firm. Accounting functions have not changed in decades, accounting departments or divisions have not changed their needs overnight, and those doing their accounting are usually fairly capable. It's clear that there is no excuse for failing to obtain accurate reports in a timely manner.

If a decision is made to purchase software and/or hardware, there are some important considerations. First, how much can the budget be adjusted for a major purchase, including consultative and training activities that may be needed? Will new staff be needed? Another issue is determining what features of the hardware and software are needed to best serve the internal control and operation of the NPO.

NOTES

1   The Committee of Sponsoring Organizations of the Treadway Commission, "COSO Definition of Internal Control," 2005. Online at http://www.coso.org/key.htm (accessed April 28, 2008).

2   InvestorWords.com. Online at http://www.investorwords.com (accessed May 19, 2008).

3   Ibid.

4   Herrington J. Bryce, *Financial and Strategic Management for Nonprofit Organizations* (San Francisco: Jossey-Bass, 2000).

5   XiaoHu Wang, *Financial Management in the Public Sector: Tools, Applications, and Cases* (San Francisco: M. E. Sharpe, 2006).

6   Ibid.

7   Ibid.

8   AccountingCoach.com, "Explanation of the Topic... Chart of Accounts," 2008. Online at http://www.accountingcoach.com (accessed April 28, 2008).

9   Ibid.

10 AccountingCoach.com, "Explanation of Debits and Credits," 2008. Online at http://www.accounting coach.com (accessed April 22, 2008).

11 Ibid.

12 Ibid.

13 Alliance for Nonprofit Management, "Frequently Asked Questions," 2004. Online at http://www.allianceonline.org/faqs.html (accessed April 28, 2008).

14   Ibid.

15   Grant Thornton, LLP, *National Board Governance Survey for Not-for-Profit Organizations.* Online at
     http://www.grantthornton.com (accessed April 22, 2008).

16   Accountants for the Public Interest, *What a Difference Nonprofits Make: A Guide to Accounting
     Procedures,* 1990. Online at http://www.nysscpa.org/cpajournal (accessed April 21, 2008).

17   Kern-DeWenter-Viere, "Common Barriers to Efficiency." Online at http://www.kdv.com (accessed
     April 22, 2008).

CHAPTER 6
Evaluating Finances and Assessing Financial Conditions

Checks and balances are vital for NPOs. "Arrangements to certify that an organization's management systems meet standards of good practice are an increasingly prominent feature in the environment of public and private nonprofits."[1] In this chapter, the focus is on the evaluation of financial activities, primarily financial audits and reviews, from several different perspectives. The discussion covers the theoretical and practical values involved in establishing trust with stakeholders like board members, clients, patrons, and funding agencies through regular examinations of financial documents. The chapter explains the reasons auditing is a requirement in most nonprofit organizations that ensures trust, accuracy, and risk reduction. While this chapter focuses mainly on audits, it also discusses the assessment of financial condition, analytical examinations of the economy, and the efficiency and effectiveness of a program or an organization. These attributes contribute to an organization's success in much the same way as do financial audits. Finally, the chapter delves into the use of indicators that allow the NPO to assess its financial condition in order to assist it in strategic planning.

TOPICS

- The Financial and Fiscal Administration Network: Financial Evaluation
- The Purposes and Reasons for Monitoring NPO Finances
- Types of Audits
- The Independent Audit Process
- Preparing for an Independent Audit
- How to Increase the Success of an Audit
- The Auditing Profession
- Assessing Financial Condition
- Financial Ratios
- Summary
- Discussion Questions
- Exercises
- Innovation: Innovation Audits

THE FINANCIAL AND FISCAL ADMINISTRATION NETWORK: FINANCIAL EVALUATION

NPOs must be acutely aware of their financial condition. This knowledge is important because it keeps organizations from hiding their heads in the sand. The discussion of assessing financial condition covers the use of financial ratios that paint an NPO's financial picture. Financial ratios may be applied to pledges and contributions, grants and endowments, expenditures and commitments, and responsiveness to the results of an audit.

Early in the 1990s, United Way of America (UWA) experienced the anguish of a financial scandal when a top executive used charitable funds for his own benefit. To the dismay of United Ways across the United States, the scandal was covered by all sectors of the media. The malfeasance was discovered when an audit revealed the fiscal irresponsibility of the organization's president, William Aramony. Aramony was convicted of using the organization's funds to procure jets and vacation homes, as well as other excesses. In addition, the audit found that the UWA board was aware of Aramony's excesses. His travel and expense records were periodically made available for board review. In addition, the board had explicitly approved the three for-profit spin-offs that were under Aramony's control.[2] This incident underscores the importance of regular and credible auditing.

Auditing is an important part of the monitoring mechanism that holds agents accountable to budgets, to laws regarding fund accounting, to the board, and to all other stakeholders. Moreover, auditing provides management with self-correctable information about the financial status of the organization. The audit and review findings, exceptions, and evaluation reports tell managers what they need to do in order to be operating at full impact.

Auditing has to be independent. Auditing can be an ongoing internal process that keeps an NPO prepared for an external independent audit. Many organizations have internal auditing operations. Others do not have staff available for internal auditing. Internal audits do not replace independent audits, but they do hold the organization's feet to the fire on an everyday basis. Performance in response to an audit, whether internal or external, is a key part of the integrated financial and fiscal network (see Figure 6.1).

The evaluation function obviously links to accounting because the information contained in journals, ledgers, balance sheets, and other financial reports provides the financial information used in audits, reviews, and evaluations. Audits examine the applicability and effectiveness of processes used by managers. The evaluation function links naturally to the budget, both of the fiscal year an NPO is in when the audit is completed

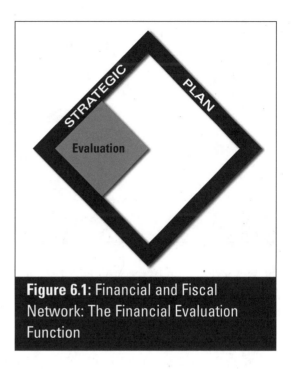

Figure 6.1: Financial and Fiscal Network: The Financial Evaluation Function

and to the NPO's next fiscal year budget. Some changes recommended in an audit can be made immediately, while others may be only implemented during the next budgetary period. Finally, some audit findings may require changes in the flexible strategic plan. For example, an audit might reveal that an error in a payment formula caused an NPO to overpay for certain critical services. When corrected, the agency might be able to fund a new program two years earlier than anticipated and might be able to move the long-term horizon a little closer. Thus, the strategic plan can also get revised to reflect new circumstances.

THE PURPOSES AND REASONS FOR MONITORING NPO FINANCES

The purpose of auditing is summarized in Figure 6.2.

If the reader's spouse, partner, a good friend, or relative pointed out some personal flaw or defect that the reader may possess, or some odd or unacceptable behavior that the reader exhibits, would the reader respond with appreciation? That is the job and the fate of an auditor, to inform an organization of its financial and operational flaws and defects—its odd and unacceptable

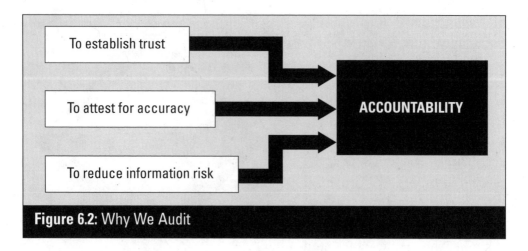

Figure 6.2: Why We Audit

behavior. It is rarely recognized that auditors contribute greatly to an NPO's success. Audits are viewed by some people as threats. By those willing to make use of constructive criticism, audits are viewed as breaths of fresh air. Of course, when you are in the middle of an audit and the auditor is asking questions about how invoices are filled out and filed, the auditor can seem to be quite oppressive. This is an unfortunate view, because auditing has great value to an organization as a provider of course corrections or a confirmer of good news about an NPO's financial status.

Auditing should be thought of as a positive economic and management experience. Having auditors around is uncomfortable, because they do measure the rightness or wrongness of the efforts of individuals and organizations. Rather than monsters, it might help to consider auditors as fence-riding cowboys checking barbed wire fences for broken sections through which cattle might escape to the open range. If they find a break in the fence, they can fix it before any cattle get out. Likewise, a good audit can find problems that can be fixed before the NPO gets crippled or lost.

Being fiscally sound does not mean simply operating in the black. It also means being able to provide an accurate financial picture of the organization at all times. Auditing is a financial evaluation processes that helps NPOs make sure that their financial information is accurate. The FASB, which was discussed in Chapter 5, offers to all organizations, including NPOs, guidance in verifying financial information that stakeholders of organizations examine to hold NPOs and all organizations accountable for their activities.

Responsibility and trust should be part of the nature of NPO accounting because of the fiduciary obligations to clients and stakeholders. While accounting provides the day-to-day data used by organizations to track spending and investing, auditing provides guarantees that those activities are performed responsibly. Audits are important to many granting agencies that require a copy of an audit and a Form 990 from NPOs submitting proposals for funding. Thus, auditing is one of the best means that organizations have at their disposal to establish trust. It is a legal issue as well; many states mandate that nonprofits be audited and any NPO that receives a grant, in most cases, will be subject to a periodic audit. These are just some of the reasons for auditing. There are others.

Bondholders, government, and foundation grant funding agencies are most concerned with the outcomes of audits. Others who have an interest in the financial information of an NPO include contributors to the NPO, regulatory agencies, beneficiaries of the services rendered by the NPO, employees, creditors, and local chapters of a national organization like the YMCA.

What an Audit Does for an Organization

Simply stated, an audit tells the reader whether the financial information that management has reported to the auditors properly portrays the financial health of the organization as of a given date (typically it's year-end, although audits should also report substantial subsequent events). So, assuming an "unqualified" audit opinion (meaning no substantial problems), the reader can take some comfort that financial information presented by management can be relied upon.[3]

The financial and operational audit is intended to underpin good accounting and good budgeting subsystems. It determines where obligations and expenditures were adequately reported. A financial audit also assesses the adequacy of budgeting and auditing procedures. A good accounting subsystem must precede a good auditing subsystem. Otherwise, audits will only point out the complete inadequacy of an NPO's accounting function, leaving it unable to establish a pattern of accountability.

Audits are important evaluation mechanisms that help to ensure accountability and to evaluate whether or not the organization is achieving its goals and objectives effectively and efficiently. Audits provide managers with information that helps to improve operations, and they have the potential to "uncover operational deficiencies and determine whether [the organization] has been effective in accomplishing its goals." [4]

Nonprofit organizations whose performance is subject to a periodic audit may realize better accountability, productivity, efficiency, and effectiveness than those that do not receive audits. A governing board can get information from an audit that it cannot get anywhere else. In practice, the value of auditing can be assessed to the extent that problems are discovered and are corrected by the NPO being evaluated.

The audit, having determined the conditions of the accounting and performance management functions, provides information back into the budgeting function. Two different types of audits provide feedback to the budgeting system: financial compliance and performance management audits. The financial compliance audit determines whether financial transactions have been properly reported and classified, whether internal controls are sufficient, and whether or not legal requirements of spending are in order. Auditors, in this case accountants, scour financial statements to see if they fairly present the financial position, the results of operations and cash flows, and the changes in financial position. Financial compliance audits can also examine compliance with laws and regulations for those transactions. Auditors can use a well-fashioned budget for this purpose.

Even though we usually think of an audit as being financial, a performance management audit determines how well programs meet their performance objectives—what actually happened as a result of budgetary expenditures. These audits can examine the economy and efficiency of the expenditures to determine the cause of any inefficient and uneconomic practices. Performance management audits can also examine particular programs to establish the extent to which programs reach objectives and comply with regulations and laws, and with funding agencies requirements.

Many local and regional nonprofits that are members of national organizations that accredit the local organization (e.g., Big Brothers Big Sisters, Boys and Girls Club, YWCA) are subject to compliance auditing conducted by the national agency. Some national agencies require local agencies to send their annual audits to national agencies. Periodically, a local agency will be audited for sound management and compliance with the national agency's standards and policies. This may take the form of an internal audit with a written report to the accrediting agency or it may take the form of an internal audit followed by a national representative visiting the local agency. In the best-case scenario, such a visit will be followed by advice from the national organization on areas in the agency that are found to be weak or areas for which employees need training in order to improve. This technique helps national agencies to keep their thumbs on the heartbeat of their local agencies.

The Economic Value of Audits

There are theoretical explanations of the value of auditing of the financial activities of organizations. They explain why and how auditors add value to organizations in terms of certifying and monitoring the financial activities.[5] These explanations include agency theory, the economic good hypothesis, and the insurance hypothesis. Under the tenets of *agency theory,* appointed officials are agents of boards of directors who hold the authority under which an NPO operates. Theoretically, agents are expected to act in a self-serving manner on behalf of their organization. Having someone to explain financial problems if the media picks up on fraud or malfeasance is of value to the NPO. The *economic good hypothesis* explains that auditing is a desirable economic activity for which there is a demand and supply for auditing, and a market clearing price as well. Organizations like NPOs that need to be audited periodically have to "buy" auditing services. Finally, the *insurance hypothesis* puts the auditor in a position of guaranteeing the results of an audit. In the corporate sector, the auditor and the client are often sued by stockholders when the client may be in deep financial trouble because of failure of auditors to find errors or malpractice. The auditor's "deep pockets" and malpractice insurance ensure that damages caused by the auditor get paid.

TYPES OF AUDITS

According to generally accepted accounting principles (GAAP), financial audits include tests of the financial statement and other related statements.

Two types of audits, *internal* and *independent,* seek to answer the following fundamental questions:

- Do the financial statements present an NPO's financial position fairly?

- Do results of operations and cash flows conform to GAAP?

- Are financial statements prepared in conformance with bases of accounting as discussed in auditing standards issued by the American Institute of Certified Public Accountants (AICPA)? Does financial information as presented comply with criteria established prior to the audit?

- Has the entity adhered to specific financial compliance requirements?

- Have internal financial reporting controls been designed to be consistent with assets and are control objectives being met?[6]

Internal Audits

The Nonprofit Resource Center found in a survey that most NPOs do not have an internal audit system in place.[7] This is unfortunate, because internal auditing provides good management-oriented information that is useful in keeping an NPO's finances in line between independent audits. For smaller NPOs, utilizing internal auditing may be limited by tight resources and lack of expertise. But even a reduced version of internal auditing is helpful because of the importance of financial and accounting matters. The process of internal auditing can vary in intensity. It is essentially identical to independent auditing, though less formal. The internal auditor will select files and account information and test them for accuracy. If deficiencies are found, the offending section of the agency will be notified and a fix will be required. Internal audits are intended to be value-added and designed to improve an organization's operations. Internal auditing helps because it is a systematic, disciplined approach to risk that monitors management, control, and governance processes. It should be ongoing. The idea of internal auditing is to ensure that internal control is suitably designed and implemented in order to help an organization achieve its objectives efficiently, effectively, and accurately.

Independent Audits

By definition, independent auditors are external to organizations. An independent auditing firm is hired to ensure that a company, a government agency, or an NPO maintains its financial records in an accurate and timely manner. Even though the auditor can take on the look and feel of Freddy in the old movie *Nightmare on Elm Street,* in the end it is helpful both to the organization being audited and to its stakeholders.

The A-133 Single Audit Act: Audits of States, Local Governments, and Nonprofit Organizations

An audit process that NPOs may be concerned with is the federal A-133 single audit. An A-133 audit monitors and tracks agency revenue from federal sources. Any audit conducted on an NPO that has received federal funds must include an audit of those federal funds under the conditions of the Single Audit Act, with one important exception. Nonprofits that receive less than $500,000 in federal funds are not required to conduct an A-133 audit. According to E. K. Keating et al, "Each A-133 audit consists of a traditional audit conducted by a licensed certified public accountant, an assessment of the internal control structure, and procedures that assess the use of federal funds and compliance with certain laws and regulations."[8] Because of the federal government's concern with compliance with federal grant conditions, the A-133 audit adds to the cost of an independent audit.

THE INDEPENDENT AUDIT PROCESS

There are so many different types of NPOs that there is no way to capture all of them and apply one independent audit process. And every audit project presents unique challenges. Still, most audits have similarities that are discussed in this chapter. While it is professionally desirable for auditors to avoid disrupting and diverting the NPO's work routine, NPO involvement in the audit process is required, because questions continually arise that only the NPO can answer.

The outcome of an independent audit is the auditor's report and the management letter that contains the auditor's opinion.

The audit opinion itself does not address the systems or procedures at an organization that helped to create the figures subject to the audit, nor does it provide any form of assurance on the systems or procedures used by the NPO. No one outside the organization and its board should rely on an organization's financial statement audit opinion to gauge the efficiency and effectiveness of an organization's internal reporting mechanisms.[9]

The independent auditor gives an either unqualified or qualified opinion of the financial management of the organization. An unqualified opinion is given when the auditor believes that the organization has followed the rules and that the financial records reflect an accurate picture of the organization's finances. A qualified opinion is one that expresses one reservation or more about some part of the organization's financial condition because of unavailable financial records or a deficit in a financial report. One must keep in mind, however, that even if an independent auditor gives an unqualified opinion, it does not mean that there are not problems within the organization's financial system.

After the NPO contracts with an independent auditor or auditing firm, the auditing process begins with the auditor and the NPO collaborating to plan the audit project. When the planning is finished, implementing the contract and the auditing plan generally follows the process components discussed in this section.

Engagement Letter

An executive of the auditor's company sends an engagement letter to the NPO management that contains the audit's objectives according to the audit company's understanding. When both parties agree on the objectives, the audit process is scheduled. A sample letter is shown in Exhibit 6.1.

Entrance Conference

The entrance conference is a formal meeting to explain the audit's nature and scope. The auditor collects relevant and important information from the NPO about the organization and its financial and fiscal network. Staff members who can provide information about programs, human resources, physical plants, equipment, funding and spending strategies, and other information useful to the auditor should be included in this meeting. Generally, one senior NPO officer will work directly with the auditing team. This person will be

AUDITS R US, Inc.
Ste. 54
METROPOLIS

Mr. Clark W. Kent, Executive Director
Superhero Preservation Society
123 American Way
Metropolis, IL 62960

Dear Mr. Kent:

The purpose of this letter is to confirm our understanding of the audit of the Superhero Preservation Society's (SPS) financial statements for the fiscal year 2007, which ended on December 31, 2007. We will examine the agency's balance sheet, statements of income, and changes in financial position as well as accompanying notes and schedules.

The audit will be conducted in accordance with generally accepted accounting principles for testing the financial records of nonprofit agencies. We will apply other accepted auditing practices.

Our audit staff will test evidence that is intended to support relevant financial statements.

In addition, we will evaluate the propriety and appearance of the financial statements and notes to the statements.

The SPS will provide relevant documents identified in the attachment by the due dates indicated also in the attachment.

If this engagement agrees with your understanding, please sign in the appropriate space below.

Sincerely,
Lex Luthor, Partner
Audits R Us, Inc.

_____   _____
Clark W. Kent   Date

Exhibit 6.1: Sample Engagement Letter

responsible for assisting and communicating with the auditor. All participants should understand that the audit is conducted in accordance with generally accepted auditing standards.

Preliminary Review

The auditor reviews the NPO's internal controls and internal financial analysis to determine areas that will be reviewed and tested. It then collects information about the NPO and learns how it operates by examining the information collected. The auditor will review the NPO's internal control structure to determine potential problem areas in the organization and design tests to determine the potential risks. Some of these tests should examine the NPO's compliance with laws and regulations.

Audit Program

This is the plan the auditors will follow. The audit program should demonstrate a good understanding of the NPO's internal control structure. The audit program outlines the plan for field work that the auditor will use to determine the efficacy of the accounting and transactional documentation of the NPO that is being examined. As long as the audit program does not violate the terms and purposes of the audit, the auditor should not reveal any privileged information.

Field Work

Field work is at the heart of the audit. Auditors gather evidence for measuring the efficacy of an NPO's financial operations. Field work subtasks focus on accounting transaction testing. Evidence comes from observations, testing, and inspection and is used to develop audit conclusions. Every financial control and transactional aspect of the audit program is tested, usually by using rigorous sampling. During this stage, the auditor usually communicates with the NPO's staff that are involved in the audit, the very people who handle program transactions on a daily basis, and management is apprised of progress and interim findings. From the information examined, auditors will compile their significant findings and begin the analysis, interpretation, and conclusions that will be reported to the NPO.

Meeting with Management: Audit Results

The audit executive and key auditing staff members discuss final results with NPO management. A draft audit report might be offered at this stage. The draft audit report contains findings, including audit exceptions and recommendations that discuss the auditor's rationale. The draft audit report is given to management for review. Managers have the right to examine the report and ask for changes in it. Changes may or may not be agreed to and are based on discussions between the auditors and NPO management. Interim or working reports are similar to notes. They provide the auditor with vital documentation to support their findings. The reports state the major conclusions of the audit and show how the auditor arrives at those conclusions.

Final Audit Report

The final audit report includes findings, recommendations, and management's responses to the conclusions and recommendations. The audit report is the principal product that is presented to the NPO at the end of the audit. Opinions, findings, and recommendations that discuss the auditor's rationale are posted to the audit report. When satisfied with the audit report, the auditor will present the document to senior NPO staff. NPOs should expect their auditors to report on the results of the tests they perform in writing. It is important to make sure that the auditor submits a management letter to accompany its opinion.

The audit's usefulness to management and the board is severely curtailed if it is not accompanied by a detailed management letter and a meeting with the appropriate board oversight committee (preferably the finance committee, but if not, then the board of directors itself) to discuss the audit process and audit findings (including the processes that were needed to adjust the financial statements). While the auditor can communicate these management letter findings either orally or in writing, the board should insist that the communication be in writing.[10] Exhibit 6.2 shows a sample final management letter.

Exit Conference and Final Report

The exit conference and final report is a meeting held between the principal auditors who were involved in the NPO audit and the senior managers of the NPO. The purpose is to explain the report, to answer questions from the NPOs senior management, and to clear up misunderstandings or disagreements. If differences between the NPO and the auditor cannot be resolved, the NPO may decide to include their rebuttal on problematic issues in the report.

AUDITS R US, Inc.
Ste. 54
METROPOLIS

Mr. Clark W. Kent, Executive Director
Superhero Preservation Society
123 American Way
Metropolis, IL 62960

Dear Mr. Kent:

We have audited the financial statements of the Superhero Preservation Society's
(SPS) activities. The purpose of this letter is to present our findings of the audit of
your financial statements for the fiscal year 2007, which ended on December 31,
2007. We examined the agency's balance sheet, statements of income, and changes
in financial position as well as accompanying notes and schedules. The audit
was conducted in accordance with generally accepted accounting principles for
testing the financial records of nonprofit agencies. No matters of noncompliance
or misstatement were found in any component of this audit.

In planning and performing our audit, we considered SPS' internal control over
financial reporting in order to determine our audit procedures for expressing our
opinions on the financial statements. In doing so, we determined, in our opinion,
no material weaknesses in SPS' internal controls over financial reporting.

To determine compliance with relevant laws, regulations, contracts, and grant
agreements, we conducted tests of such compliance. Noncompliance could result in
material misstatements of financial condition. In doing so, we found no matters of
such noncompliance required to be reported under nonprofit auditing standards.

Sincerely,
Lex Luthor, Partner
Audits R Us, Inc.

_____   _____
Clark W. Kent   Date

Exhibit 6.2: Sample Final Management Letter

The final report is generally not released to the public by the auditor.
Disclosure of the audit report is the NPO's responsibility.

Implementing Changes

Auditors seldom have additional responsibilities regarding the NPO's audit unless called on to provide information and explanations. The NPO has the singular responsibility for implementing recommendations reported by the auditor. The NPO should implement the recommendations as soon as possible after accepting the audit from the auditor. Unimplemented recommendations will be the subject of future audits.

PREPARING FOR AN INDEPENDENT AUDIT

Rather than go blindly into an impending audit, NPOs need to take an honest, realistic, and proactive approach to the day that the auditor arrives to inspect the books. There are some steps an NPO can take to be prepared. The auditor, in fact, is usually very helpful in that regard. For example, auditors will ask an NPO to provide confirmation letters in advance of the audit to verify the amount of money that the NPO owes creditors and funding agencies. The auditor will receive these letters directly from the entities to whom letters have been mailed.

The auditor will also want to gather information regarding financial activities. This is done either through questionnaires or by interviewing staff members who are involved in the internal control of the NPO's financial transactions. In addition, the auditor will likely request identification of individuals and entities who either provide revenue to the NPO or who are owed by the NPO. The auditor will also need documentation on financial assets, including the following:

- Property
- Equipment
- Payables
- Debts
- Donations
- Grants
- In-kind contributions

- Donated material

- Fundraising events

- Tuition

- Fees

- Registrations

- Contracts

- Inventory

- Payroll

- Vacation and sick leave records

- Tax-related documents

- Other expenses

The auditor may also request the following:

- Board minutes signed by the board secretary

- Leases

- Bank statements

- Receipts and invoices

- Journals

- Ledgers

- Budgets

- All grant contracts and reports

Any related parties should be disclosed as well. Having these types of documents ready for the auditor will also save the NPO money because it is less costly for the NPO staff to gather the materials than it is for the auditor staff, which likely includes high-cost accountants. While there are opportunities for committing errors in an audit, NPOs can minimize the errors by keeping track of key documents that will be required by the auditor.[11]

HOW TO INCREASE THE SUCCESS OF AN AUDIT

Much of the auditing process can become routine if the NPO creates an active and effective audit or finance committee that appoints one person with considerable knowledge of the NPO's finances to act as audit coordinator. The audit or finance committee can be a sub-function of a more comprehensive finance committee.[12] Given the importance of a financial audit, the NPO's executive director and financial director should be involved in this internal preparation process. The purpose of an audit committee, according to J. West and E. Berman, is to assist the management in "overseeing and monitoring the financial accounting as a way to review and improve standards and procedures for financial accountability."[13] Unfortunately, audit committees are rare.[14] Grant Thornton, LLP, found that only about half of NPOs surveyed put an audit committee charter into action.[15]

There are several tasks that an audit committee may perform, such as the collection of information to investigate ethical problems that are related to the finances of an organization, or the audit committee may need to review the relationship between the organization and the external auditor.[16] If an ethical issue arises, the committee is responsible for the investigation, which removes the managers and auditors from a potential problem and allows for a more objective perspective of the issue.

The most important factor in determining the success of the audit committee is the people involved in the committee. The members of the committee must understand the needs and objectives of the organization, and at least one of the members must have knowledge of financial reporting and auditing.[17] Members of the committee need to remain aware of any changes in accounting rules to ensure that the agency remains in compliance with auditing standards.[18]

All evidence that an auditor gathers should be reviewed by the NPO management with what S. Whitehouse calls "an increased focus on professional skepticism."[19] Auditors must be sure that the organization is in compliance with the generally accepted accounting principles (GAAP) by doing their work in accordance with the generally accepted auditing standards (GAAS).

The NPO needs to establish a control policy in a controlled environment that can help ensure successful auditing. A good approach to financial protection for an NPO is to have a control system in place to increase the success of audits.[20] A good control system will accomplish the following objectives:

- Instill ethics, integrity, and a commitment to competence.
- Establish control activities through formal policies.
- Perform risk assessments.
- Communicate financial information to all stakeholders.
- Reevaluate the audit approach on a yearly basis.[21]

A controlled environment is an important part of the organizational culture. To provide employees with certain standards that they need to adhere to decreases the chances of fraudulent or incompetent activities. By establishing a healthy environment that is intolerant of negative exceptions, an NPO increases its chance of success.

THE AUDITING PROFESSION

Auditors, quite simply, carry out the function of auditing. The word audit has traditionally been associated with other terms like trust and honesty. This concept of being viewed as honest or giving the appearance of honesty becomes suspect from time to time when scandals occur that somehow involve auditors. Independent auditors are less likely to be accused of bias in that they are not subject to the whims of the organization's management. Independent auditors are also not connected to a company through other relationships such family or employment through a sub-contractor.

There are two types of independence: *independence in appearance* and *independence in fact*. Independence in appearance refers to the physical nature of the auditor/client relationship. The auditor is not part of the client's employee base and is therefore perceived as independent by investors, consumers, and stockholders. Independence in fact is more difficult to assess because it is considered a mental state.[22] Independence in fact relies on the morals, ethics, and character of an individual auditor. Auditors are agents of their own companies.

In 2003, David Walker, then Comptroller General of the United States, said:

> *"Our profession, the performance and accountability profession, currently faces a 'crisis of confidence' that must be addressed not only for the good of our profession but also for the good of our country and the nation's capital markets. We are not, however, the only ones who are under the microscope, as recent events in the private sector have made clear. Restoring public trust and confidence in a manner that can be sustained over the long term will require concerted actions by various parties in order to address some very real systemic weaknesses plaguing our current corporate governance, accountability, and related systems."*

Unfortunately, the relationship between auditor and client is not always managed correctly. An NPO's trustworthiness can be at risk if auditors are inclined to overlook critical areas of the operation and accounting practices that should be addressed. In addition, in such a circumstance it becomes difficult for both parties to maintain a high degree of integrity, objectivity, and independence. Familiarity, discounting, and escalation are the three aspects of human nature that can magnify unconscious biases.[23] The more familiar an auditor becomes with an organization, the more biased his or her judgments may become. Although it is beneficial for an auditor to become familiar with the company he or she is auditing, the longer the auditor works with the organization and the more enmeshed the auditor becomes, the more difficult it is for the auditor to separate himself or herself from the organization.[24]

As a result of legal and ethical problems involving several organizations in the late 1990s and early 2000s, Congress passed the Sarbanes-Oxley Act of 2002 (SOX). The law is targeted at auditing/accounting firms and the way they evaluate corporate financial governance, financial disclosure, and the practice of public accounting practices.

Although SOX primarily responded to the financial scandals in the private sector (the former Enron Corporation, WorldCom, and others), it has had an impact on NPOs. The scandals involved unreported financial activities that were missed by independent auditors such as Arthur Andersen. While Andersen, in the case of its Enron audit, was ultimately cleared of wrongdoing, its tainted image brought it to collapse, and SOX changed the atmosphere of accounting within all organizations in all sectors. It is now far more important for organizations and management to be accountable for how money is spent in the organization than it was before the financial scandals. Because many nonprofit organizations rely on public monies for much of their funding, those within management need to be accountable for the way the money is spent.

Only two provisions of SOX actually apply to NPOs. Both provisions involve whistle-blower protections and document destruction. The Internal Revenue Service does not mandate that NPOs prove their status annually, but it does require Form 990 to present data that can give government oversight agencies the required information to enforce the laws that distinguish non-profits from other sectors. NPOs have been granted special privileges that come with special obligations. The Form 990 helps monitor NPO spending to prevent their doing anything that might cause them to lose their charitable and tax-exempt status. It also collects information about NPOs' financial condition that enables a reader to discern financial strength or weakness, spending priorities, and sources of income.[25] And even though NPOs were not required to comply with the legislation, 48 percent of NPOs altered their operational practices to conform to SOX.[26]

The scandals underscored the importance of the auditing function. The changes to the auditing profession include requiring auditors to disclose their independence from the firm being audited. Disclosure addresses the principal-agent problem, which assumes that audit managers can have interests that constitute a conflict of interest with the organization being audited.[27] Another important provision in SOX establishes limits to the auditing firm's additional business activities with the organization it is auditing.

ASSESSING FINANCIAL CONDITION

An auditing maxim says that you get what you inspect, not what you expect. Measuring certain outcomes to obtain information on how well the organization is doing compared to itself in previous years, to other similar agencies, and to industry standards is another way of ensuring integrity in an NPO. Measurement of financial data gives reference points. A useful way of measuring financial data is to use ratios that depict the relationship between financial variables. These relationships can then be used to compare the organization to standards in the industry or to organizational ratios from past years. Then this information can be used to establish financial goals. Exceptions from the standards can be readily seen. Examinations of revenues, expenditures, operating position, debt service, unfunded liabilities, reserves, and investment policies keeps an NPO informed. Exhibit 6.3 is a typical checklist that can be used to collect data that measures status.

Analyzing an NPO's revenue structure will help identify the types of data that can be used in maintaining a good financial status. The data can be used to monitor the status of the revenue base, procedures and policies, relative dependence on revenue sources, adequacy of fees, efficacy of cost controls, and efficiency of collection procedures. The measures are the following:

- Revenue per client, to provide quick information on productivity of fundraising efforts or pricing.

- Revenue base monitoring, to help the NPO detect problems early so that solutions may be found in a timely manner.

- Board policies affecting revenue yields should be periodically examined to make sure there are no negative effects occurring, such as violating rules and regulations.

- Agencies that have relative dependence on obsolete or external revenue sources prevent the agency from fully realizing its mission potential. The environment should be scanned for potential new revenue sources.

- Fees that do not cover the cost of services need to be monitored to signal negative effects.

- Revenue estimating practices that don't exist or are inadequate need to be caught and corrected early.

- Revenue collection and administration that is inefficient presents problems for NPOs that tend to operate on tight budgets.

INDICATOR	EVALUATION*	DESCRIPTION/EXPLANATION/COMMENTS
Revenues per client		
Board procedures affecting yields		
Dependence on external sources		
Fee for service compared to cost for service		
Revenue estimating procedure		
Revenue collection procedures		
Expenditures per client		
Expenditure growth		
Increase in fixed costs		
Budgetary controls		
Personnel productivity		
Program growth per expenditures		
Cash management procedures		
Expenditure procedures		
Reliance on long-term debt		
Use of debt for current operations		

* Evaluation codes: + = good: - = needs immediate attention: ~ = can be postponed

Exhibit 6.3: Financial Indicator Checklist

INDICATOR	EVALUATION*	DESCRIPTION/EXPLANATION/COMMENTS
Debt available for use		
Condition of buildings/grounds		
Condition of major equipment		
Utility costs		
Compliance with code		
Change in population size		
Average household income		
Average household size		
Average age		
Other		
Increase in pension liability		
Speed of increase		
Amount unfunded		
Revenue to benefit growth ratio		
Growth in unused leave		
Policies consistent with affordability		
Health care costs		

Exhibit 6.3: Financial Indicator Checklist (Cont.)

Analyzing an expenditure profile can reveal some important information for managers. The data collected can be used to track expenditure growth, changes in fixed costs, budget monitoring, productivity issues, and the effects of new programs. The data measures include the following:

- Expenditures per client yields a ratio that can easily be compared to past time periods and to other similar agencies using Form 990.

- Expenditures growth as compared to revenue growth can reveal problem areas in expenditure control.

- Fixed costs increases are important because fixed costs (such as liability insurance and facility rent in the short run), unlike variable costs, are not subject to the control of the NPO.

- Budgetary controls need to be recognized and managed (indicators of procedural breakdowns are a major concern).

- Personnel productivity indicators compare output among employees and of the same employee over time.

- Expenditure growth in programs need to be recognized and controlled.

Operating position analysis refers to examining an organization's ability to balance books on a current basis, including reserves, contingencies, and liquid assets. Debt structure analysis can reveal the following:

- Inadequacies in cash management procedures, such as not investing surplus funds or making poor estimates of expenditures so as to cause surprises during the fiscal year.

- Inadequacies in expenditure procedures in which not enough attention is paid to who spends money, who receives goods and services, and so on.

- Relative reliance on long-term debt to the point that debt is beginning to become too large a part of the NPO's overall budget.

- Use of short-term debt to fund current operations without a plan that guarantees the ability to repay the short-term debt within the fiscal year.

- Lack of a policy on restricted and practical amount of additional debt available to be used, which can weaken control.

The condition of facilities and costly equipment is vital to many nonprofits. While many NPOs in the social service sector may rent their office space, hospitals, colleges and universities, recreational NPOs, museums, theatres, and other NPOs invest in capital facilities. They have to be concerned with maintenance of those capital items and monitor the following:

- Condition of the buildings and grounds as an early warning system for repair and replacement

- Condition of major equipment

- Utilities costs to make sure they are not out of the ordinary or the expected

- Compliance with codes and regulations to avoid legal and regulatory problems

NPOs must pay attention to demographics and resources within their communities. As these factors change, NPOs may need to adapt, expand, or otherwise change their missions. Demographics and resources include such factors as:

- Community population, both in terms of size and mix of characteristics

- Average household income, to be able to anticipate what the relative contribution the NPO might rely on

- Property values, which indicate the impact on the community in terms of affordability of housing and the size of property taxes

- Age of the population, which is usually important to all subsectors of the nonprofit economy

- Other factors dependent on individual characteristics of the NPO

Unfunded liabilities are those incurred but not yet covered with set-aside funds (pensions and employee leave). An analysis can provide information like the following:

- Stability of pension liability

- Relative speed of changes in liability

- Percentage that is unfunded

- Success at keeping contributions and investment earnings on a pace with growth in benefits

- Magnitude of unused vacation and sick leave

- Consistency of NPO's vacation and sick leave policies with the NPO's ability to pay

- Difficulty of NPO to keep up with market health insurance costs

To determine its financial condition, an NPO needs to evaluate its financial records and its financial position. Inadequate financial records will lead to an inadequate analysis of financial condition. The NPO must examine cash balances and reserves for their adequacy; investment and reserve policies for their compliance and effectiveness; accounting practices for their ability to provide monetary control; budget processes for their ability to plan and guide fundraising and spending; internal financial review processes to monitor financial decision making; and audit information to guarantee that audit exceptions are corrected.

By keeping good accounting records, an NPO puts itself in a good position to understand its financial condition. General ledgers contain balances such as cash, investments, accounts receivable, and accounts payable. Net assets provide information that can be used to calculate financial condition indicators. Examining the schedules in detail and comparing totals with the standards tells the NPO how well it is doing in comparison within its subsector and how much progress it is making toward financial health. Based on this information, an NPO can assess whether the financial records support the organization's financial goals. An NPO can evaluate its short-term financial position and its ability to meet its immediate needs by looking at several financial factors, including the amount of cash on hand, accounts receivable, and cash liabilities.

Finally, when contemplating how to best use the information discussed earlier, some additional nonfinancial but related factors need to be discussed in context. An examination of demographic and economic characteristics can identify a decline in the revenue base, a need to shift client customer service priorities, or a need to shift policies because of a loss of donor or client interest.

FINANCIAL RATIOS

For-profit sector managerial accountants have developed numerous ratios to assess company's financial condition. Many of these ratios, because of the profit-making characteristics of the private sector, may not be useful to most NPOs. The financial ratios shown in Exhibit 6.4, however, might prove useful in assessing the financial condition in any sector. While there are many that could be considered, three are offered as examples.

Financial indicators, expressed as a ratio or trend, facilitate comparisons with other nonprofit entities and provide an illustration of the entity's activity in recent years. The idea is that you not only keep up with the day-to-day operations, but you also look for clues to the position in the market and look for long-term as well as short-term measures. Without good assessment information, there cannot be effective planning. Organizations can really get bogged down in a tradition of not knowing their financial condition. Being fiscally sound, however, is not only operating in the black, but also being able to provide an accurate financial picture of the organization at all times.

These ratios can be used in strategic planning, because deficiencies and discrepancies can be fixed and then translated into goals and objectives based on comparisons with other similar agencies. Information about similar NPOs can be obtained by analyzing Form 990 financial information. Excellent additional information on ratios can be obtained from a copy of the *Operating Ratio Report* published by the American Society of Agency Executives (ASAE). Contact information for the Society is:

ASAE & The Center for Association Leadership
1575 I Street, NW
Washington, DC 20005

Main telephone number: 202-626-2723

Current Ratio: Current assets divided by current liabilities.

If current assets (cash on hand, checking, CDs, receivable, inventory, marketable securities) are $100,000, and current liabilities are $50,000, then the current ratio is:

$100,000 % $50,000 = 2

Interpretation: Current assets are twice that of current liabilities.

Acid Test Ratio: Current assets less inventories divided by current liabilities.

Cash, marketable securities, accounts receivable divided by current liabilities are $80,000. Marketable securities and accounts receivable are $80,000. Current liabilities are $50,000. Then the current ratio is:

$80,000 % $50,000 = 1.6

Interpretation: Current assets less inventory are 1.6 times that of current debt. Compare to other similar NPOs.

Current Debt Ratio: Current cash and equivalents divided by notes payable and bonded indebtedness.

Cash and marketable securities = $70,000. Marketable securities and accounts receivable are $70,000. Current debt is $20,000. Then the current ratio is:

$70,000 % $20,000 = 3.5

Interpretation: Cash flow is 3.5 times that of current debt. Compare to similar NPOs.

Exhibit 6.4: Financial Ratios

SUMMARY

This chapter is challenging. The topics under evaluation—auditing and assessing—involve new ways of thinking about the nature and activities involved in the financial and fiscal network and how they affect an organization and, in the case of NPOs, the diverse clients they serve. Auditing is a truth detector. This topic is an important one whose significance is often overlooked. Auditors are misunderstood, abused, shunned, and disliked for the wrong reasons. But they can do something that few of us can. They can overcome our prejudices. They can establish trust.

The other topic of this chapter is important to organizations with a concern for how well they are doing financially. That should cover every organization in every sector of the economy. And it should cover all economies and all families. When considering financial condition, it is important to look at not just the obvious factors that affect financial condition, like revenues, expenditures, payables, and receivables. Other information like demographic trends, company profiles, economic trends, political trends, and community and organization factors should also be taken into account.

DISCUSSION QUESTIONS

1. What is the role of the independent auditor in the financial reporting process? What are the reasons it is important for the public to view the auditor as independent from the organization undergoing an audit? The consulting/auditing issue in particular involves arguments about whether or not the auditor's knowledge of the client's business might make the auditor the most effective consultant. Does the performance of consulting work improve the auditor's knowledge of the business and therefore make it more effective on the audit, or is the auditor so aligned with NPO management that it might form biased judgments during the audit?

2. Considering the discussion in the chapter and in the readings related to assessing financial condition in NPOs, evaluate and explain how and how well your organization tracks and assesses its financial condition. If they do not, explain why they do not and suggest some appropriate measures and how those measures would be calculated. If you are not currently with an organization, use one with which you are familiar.

EXERCISES

1. Go on the Internet and find a nonprofit's audited annual report or acquire one from a local NPO. Read the auditor's management letter and consider the findings presented. Write a one-page analysis of the findings that discusses the management letter, the audit report, and the condition of opinions (qualified or unqualified).

2. The Knotfer Prophet Agency (KPA) finds the five years of data shown in the following table.

	YEAR ONE	YEAR TWO	YEAR THREE	YEAR FOUR	YEAR FIVE
Revenue per client	$321	$318	$329	$329	$328
Fees for activities as a percentage of program cost	.89	1.00	1.01	.95	.98
Expenditures per client	$321	$321	$333	$334	$334
Clients as a percentage of population	.01387	.01389	.01420	.01555	.01559

Evaluate KPA's condition based on the factors given. Consider observable trends and their meaning. To compare, in some cases, it is best to convert dollar figures to percentages.

INNOVATION: INNOVATION AUDITS

Businesses must continually look for the edge that will let them achieve a greater market share, increase the bottom line, or increase the wealth of their owners. These activities may seem foreign to the nonprofit sector, but in fact there are competitive benchmarks that can be routinely audited and that may help an NPO grow and generate more revenue as well as lead to financial stability. An innovation audit is one method for an NPO to accomplish these things. Businesses are hiring consultants to conduct audits of their practices and activities to determine how up-to-date they are. One of the main features of an innovation audit is to look for innovative ways to improve the financial management practices, with the goal of creating value for the company. Those in charge of finances are in a position to keep an organization informed of how to improve decision making by making innovation a prime goal.[28] An innovative organization will make innovation itself part of its culture.

NOTES

1   R. Paton and J. Foot, "Nonprofits' use of Awards to Improve and Demonstrate Performance: Valuable Discipline or Burdensome Formalities?" *Voluntas* 11 (2000): 329–353.

2   D. Shenk, "Board Stiffs," *Washington Monthly* 24 (1992): 9–14. Online at http://www.questia.com (accessed April 22, 2008).

3   "Making the Best Use of the Auditing Process," *The Nonprofit Quarterly* 12 (2005): Special Issue.

4   B. Reed and J. Swain, *Public Finance Administration* (Thousand Oaks, CA: Sage Publications, 1997).

5   S. Y. Rauterkus and K. Song, "Auditor's Reputation, Equity Offerings, and Firm Size: The Case of Arthur Andersen," *AFA 2004 San Diego Meetings* (2004): 121.

6   ACE Electoral Knowledge Network, "Types of Audit: U.S. Auditing Standard." Online at http://ace project.org/ (accessed April 22, 2008).

7   Nonprofit Resource Center, "Internal Audit Services," 2008. Online at http://www.nonprofitresource.com/auditsvcs/index.cfm (accessed July 29, 2006).

8   E. K. Keating, M. Fischer, T. P. Gordon, and J. Greenlee, "The Single Audit Act: How Compliant Are Nonprofit Organizations?" *Journal of Public Budgeting, Accounting & Financial Management* 17 (2005): 285–309.

9   "Making the Best Use of the Auditing Process," *The Nonprofit Quarterly* 12 (2005): Special Issue.

10 Ibid.

11 J. A. Servage, "Policy and Governance," *Internal Auditor* (Aug. 2006): 83–87.

12 Richard Larkin, *Sarbanes-Oxley and Nonprofits, BDO Seidman Nonprofit Alert.* Online at http://www.bdo.com (accessed May 12, 2008).

13 J. West and E. Berman, "Audit Committees and Accountability in Local Government: A National Survey," *Public Administration Review* 26 (2003): 329–363.

14 Ibid.

15 Grant Thornton, LLP, *National Board Governance Survey for Not-for-Profit Organizations,* 2005. Online at http://www.grantthornton.com (accessed April 22, 2008).

16 J. West and E. Berman, "Audit Committees and Accountability in Local Government: A National Survey," *Public Administration Review* 26 (2003): 329–363.

17 Ibid.

18 S. Whitehouse, "The Sarbanes-Oxley Act and Nonprofits: But I Thought That Didn't Apply to Us?" *Nonprofit World* 22 (2004, Sept./Oct.): 10–15.

19 Ibid.

20 Frank Grippo and Joel Siegel, "Untangling the Audit Confusion Society for Nonprofit Organizations," *Nonprofit World* 21.3 (2003). Online at http://www.snpo.org/publications (accessed April 22, 2008).

21 Ibid.

22 M. Nelson, "Ameliorating Conflicts of Interest in Auditing: Effects of Recent Reforms on Auditors and Their Clients," *Academy of Management Review* 31 (2006): 30–42.

23 Max Bazerman, George Lowenstein, and Don A. Moore, "Why Good Accountants Do Bad Auditing," *Harvard Business Review* 80 (2002): 96–103.

24 Ibid.

25   P. Swords, "Inside Form 990," The Grantsmanship Center, 2003. Online at http://www.tgci.com (accessed April 22, 2008).

26   G. Williams, "Accountability Law Spurs Charities to Make Changes," *Chronicle of Philanthropy* 17 (2004): 4.

27   J. W. Thompson and G. Lange, "The Sarbanes-Oxley Act and the Changing Responsibilities of Auditors," *Review of Business* 24 (2003): 8–12.

28   Sarjay.com, "Innovation Audit," 2007. Online at http://wiki.sarjay.com

CHAPTER 7
Revenues, Revenue Management, and Forecasting

This chapter discusses revenues, the vital nourishment of an NPO. The discussion begins with a look at the philosophy of philanthropy and giving. The chapter discusses various sources of revenue, including fundraising, tax management, grants, and others, and it describes and analyzes the legal and contractual limits to fundraising. Tax credits are an important topic that is also covered. Finally, the chapter talks about revenue management strategies that organizations should employ.

TOPICS

- The Financial and Fiscal Administrative Network: Revenue Management
- The Importance of Philanthropy
- Nonprofit Funding Sources
- Legal Limitations on Fundraising
- Trends and New Ideas in Revenue Sources
- Revenue Administration
- Determining Prices
- Forecasting Revenue
- Tax Credit Policy
- Summary
- Discussion Questions
- Exercise
- Innovation: Branding

THE FINANCIAL AND FISCAL ADMINISTRATIVE NETWORK: REVENUE MANAGEMENT

"Show me the money," the passionate demand from the movie *Jerry Maguire,* could be the catchphrase for many organizations in the nonprofit sector. NPOs raise funds from multiple sources in the hope of maximizing the achievement of their mission goals and objectives. After the mission and its goals, nothing in a strategic plan is more important than the management of revenues. Managing revenues means forecasting revenue sources and acquiring money, the lifeblood of any organization. Figure 7.1 shows the final component of the Financial and Fiscal Network, management. The rest of the book involves discussions of NPO management responsibilities.

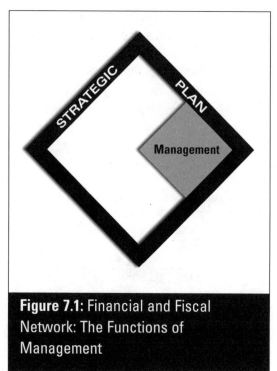

Figure 7.1: Financial and Fiscal Network: The Functions of Management

THE IMPORTANCE OF PHILANTHROPY

The nonprofit sector is built on and continuously relies upon philanthropy. To be philanthropic is to volunteer one's goods, time, effort, or goodwill to support a humanitarian cause. All of these activities translate into a value and provide life and energy to NPOs. While the primary motivations for philanthropy may be altruism, there are other reasons that, while perhaps less heart-warming, lead to volunteerism and financial support. It is the financial support that this chapter examines.

NONPROFIT FUNDING SOURCES

Individual Americans privately contribute over $130 billion to nonprofits annually; overall, these organizations receive $665 billion dollars in revenue, some 7.1 percent of national income. NPOs obtain their funds from a variety of sources. Most NPOs have basic and familiar sources of revenue. For many, the usual sources do not provide enough funding to ensure that organizations achieve their mission. Therefore, most NPOs have to view finding additional and reliable sources of revenue a necessary activity. An overview of nonprofit revenue categories appears in Table 7.1.

REVENUE TYPE	EDUCATION/ RESEARCH	SOCIAL SERVICES/ LEGAL	RELIGIOUS	ARTS & CULTURE	HEALTH SERVICES
Donations	■	◆	◆	■	■
Government Grants	◆	◆	●	■	■
Foundation Grants	■	■	■	○	■
Fundraising Events	■	■	■	■	○
Entrepreneurship (earned income)	●	●	●	●	■
Membership Dues & Fees	○	○	○	◆	○
Fees-for-Service	◆	■	○	◆	◆

◆ — Primary   ■ — Secondary   ● — Emerging   ○ — Not Applicable

Table 7.1: Common Revenue Sources By Nonprofit Subsector

Traditional Donations

Many NPOs, obviously, have to rely on the kindness of both strangers and friends for donations. Individual Americans, fraternal organizations, and corporations are very generous to NPOs. Nonprofits, with the proper tax status, are exempt from paying taxes. But, like businesses and farmers, they do not have the authority to raise revenues through coercive taxes. The amounts donated are staggering.

Charitable contributions by individuals, foundations, and corporations reached $248.52 billion in 2004, an increase of 2.3 percent from 2003 after adjusting for inflation. In 2004, religious organizations received the largest proportion of charitable contributions, with 35.5 percent of total estimated contributions going to these organizations.[1]

Furthermore, the Trust for Philanthropy of the American Association of Fund Raising Counsel (now The Giving Institute) reported that $203.45 billion was donated to nonprofits in 2000. Research, arts, and entertainment nonprofits receive about 41 percent and human service organizations receive about 20 percent of their total revenues from donations annually. Almost half of the private colleges and universities in the United States are NPOs that count on donations for 13 percent of their total yearly revenue. Nonprofit health care organizations receive almost $19 billion in donations each year.

The competition for donations among nonprofits is heavy. Some contributions are received by nonprofits indirectly from the public by the following methods:

- Through solicitation campaigns conducted by federated fundraising agencies or organizations such as the United Way

- From a parent organization or another organization with the same parent

- From subordinate organizations

At times, obtaining funds from these sources demands a competitive spirit. For example, United Ways in cities use funds that they have collected to achieve an equitable distribution to meet community needs. The amount they have to allocate is limited to the results of their fundraising campaigns. Agencies that rely on receiving funding from a local United Way have to submit proposals that are evaluated on the basis of quality outcomes and need. They have to be as responsive and professional as possible in their proposals and presentations. In making their case, agencies have to do their best to maximize the amount of money they receive. Likewise, obtaining federal, state, or foundation money usually requires that an agency adopt a competitive demeanor. Even national organizations like the American Red Cross, the

United Way, and the YMCA often present programs for which local affiliates and subordinate organizations must compete.

Grants from Government

Government sources account for one-third of total nonprofit revenues. Government grants are payments from the government to an NPO to further the organization's public programs. Some states allow tax credits so that donors can write off a portion of a donation from their tax obligation at rates higher than the typical itemized charitable deduction. The federal government is a source of funding for many, if not most, NPOs in the arts, social services, health care, or education arenas. The exception is religious organizations. Faith-based funding is a relatively new and controversial funding mechanism led by President George W. Bush's administration. People who oppose faith-based funding fear that such a mechanism is a threat to the constitutional requirement for the separation of church and state. They fear there is a violation of the U.S. Constitution's so-called Establishment Clause in the First Amendment that states: "Congress shall make no law respecting an establishment of religion . . ." Many others fear that the involvement of church-based programs will reduce the opportunities of secular NPOs to acquire their share of the federal funding pie. Still others fear that church-based programs will attempt to convert clients to their faith. Proponents of faith-based funding believe it does not violate the establishment clause found in the U.S. Constitution and that they can work without proselytizing.

Grants from Foundations

Foundation giving comes from private entities heavily invested in bond and stock markets and other types of investment. These are NPOs that are financed by corporations, individuals, or groups. These organizations operate under some restrictions: They are prohibited from making investments that jeopardize the financial well-being of their organizations and cannot spend money to influence legislation or provide support for political campaigns. There are thousands of foundations in the United States that fulfill various missions.

Fundraising Events

Many NPOs undertake campaigns or special events that raise funds for the operations of a their programs. The old Saturday-morning serial *Little Rascals*, which often played at local movie houses in the 1930s and 1940s, showed the children's favorite aunt being threatened with eviction or some little pal from their neighborhood desperately needing help. As they sat fretting over the tragedy in these episodes, one or the other of the rascals would snap his fingers or have a light bulb appear above his head and pipe up, "I got it! Let's put on a show!" They always saved the day by raising enough money to solve the episode's problem.

Fundraising events, though numerous and varied, take a lot more than the Little Rascals approach. Dances, auctions, bowling tournaments, cookie sales, and so on are just a few of hundreds of known event ideas.

Social Entrepreneurship

Related and unrelated businesses are becoming more and more popular for NPOs. Related businesses are those that are consistent with the mission of an NPO. An example is a pharmacy doing business in a nonprofit hospital. Unrelated business income is income generated by a trade or business activity that is not substantially related to the exempt purpose of the organization and not regularly carried by that organization. An unrelated business is one that has absolutely nothing in common with an NPO's primary mission, even if the all the profits made from the business are used by the NPO to carry out its mission. Unrelated business ventures are subject to income taxation. Unrelated businesses will be discussed in detail later in this chapter and in Chapter 10.

Membership Dues or Fees

Many NPOs rely on the interested public to become members of their organization. A typical example is the local YMCA, which provides numerous services and activities. Members usually pay an annual membership to belong. For some activities and services, members must pay an additional fee to participate. Other types of NPOs that sell memberships as a source of revenue include organizations involved in the following:

- Museums (fine arts, antiquities)

- Performing arts

- Sports

- Professional societies

- Religious activities

- Community service organizations

Fees for Service

Fee-for-service organizations are NPOs authorized under IRS Code 509(a)(2). This type of organization includes universities, museums, hospitals, and other organizations that receive their primary revenue from providing a service that is supported by the fees they charge their clients. These organizations are also tested in order to be eligible for the IRS designation. The first test is the one-third public financial support test.[2] This test may include related businesses for fee-for-service organizations, not to exceed one percent of total income. A college bookstore, a hospital pharmacy, and museum souvenir shop all fall in the category of related businesses.

Hospitals come to mind as an example of NPOs that must charge for services rendered to patients. Other health care providers do the same. Many NPOs that provide social and legal services charge fees for their services. Usually, clients pay for services on a sliding scale based on a client's income and ability to pay.

Selling Assets

From time to time, NPOs decide to divest themselves of their assets in order to meet a particular need, for example, to reduce maintenance costs for a building whose use is questionable. That example is a responsible reason for divesting. It is irresponsible when an organization sells off its assets in order to raise cash to meet operating obligations. Operating expenses, by definition, are recurring obligations that need to be balanced against recurring revenues. If assets are sold to generate revenue for operating expenses, there is pretty good reason to believe that the devil will claim his due when the same level of operating expense is owed in a subsequent period but the bank account is empty.

NPOs should sell off capital assets as a component of a coherent strategy designed to return as much property as possible to private hands, remove government obstacles to economic growth, reduce expenditures, and ultimately lower the tax burden on the individual citizen or in the case of nonprofits, the loyal donor. It also makes little sense to hold on to assets that have lost their utility to the program. Keeping a yard full of unused turf equipment is a drag on staff productivity when its salvage value from its disposition might cover the purchase of an improvement to the irrigation system that would cut water use and save future operating expense.

In some cases, selling an asset is the only way for an organization to survive until the financial picture improves. The authors know of a case of a private nonprofit traditional women's college that was selling off high-maintenance assets even as it was changing its whole image. One can speculate that the college had determined that changing attitudes meant that the particular assets would no longer have an attraction to young women. On the other hand, if the college were selling just to save on maintenance costs, without consideration of the attraction of the assets to future students, they could have been undercutting future performance. The world is not an ideal place. Natural disasters, legal actions, or community needs may exceed an organization's short-term ability to respond (either with liquid assets or insurance). The sale of capital assets could be a viable strategic, if temporary, alternative.

Organizations are beginning to outsource more operations to the private sector, so assets that were formerly used to perform those duties in-house are no longer needed. When an organization begins to outsource, it does so mostly in the area of equipment. The funds generated from the sale of equipment that is no longer used can be redirected to other operational areas.

Fundraising Responsibilities

Most NPOs rely on the board to raise some of the funds that are used to maintain the organization. Fisher Howe said, "the buck stops with the board."[3] The best board members will be well-placed, if not influential, in a community and should know when and how to ask for philanthropy.

The staff has the responsibility of developing a fundraising strategy in cooperation with the board. A nonprofit's director and staff must tune in to fundraising opportunities. Most of the fundraising success an organization may have is due to the effectiveness of staff.

Key elements of an NPO's fund development program include donor acquisition and fundraising events, an annual giving program, major gifts from individuals, grants, and corporate and foundation giving. Supporting elements include cultivating relationships with donors, gift entry and acknowledgment, database management, and donor research.

Board Responsibilities

Board members of nonprofit organizations (NPOs) are community members who should believe in the vision, mission, goals, and objectives of the NPO they govern. It is critical that NPO board members understand that the NPO financial needs are ever-changing and need to be attended to. Fundraising opportunities often change as well, and it is the board's responsibility to help the NPO stay ahead of the fundraising challenge. One of the specific responsibilities of a board is to consider investment authority, including permission to invest in stock. The board should delegate investment decisions to investment managers, investment committees, and staff. Most important is the responsibility of soliciting funds from community contacts, engaging in personal fundraising, and making generous contributions to the NPOs they govern. Finally, they should support all fundraising efforts that the NPO decides to participate in.

Staff Responsibilities

An NPO's chief executive officer is critical in revenue development, especially where that responsibility rests solely on the person in that position. It is important that the CEO ensure a strategic and comprehensive fund development plan that identifies prospects and donors and that enhances the short- and long-term diversified funding base for the agency. In many instances, he or she must establish a diverse donor base that consists of individual, corporate, foundation, and public funding agencies. Thus, the CEO must personally build loyal and long-term relationships with key donors. The CEO must actively seek out funding sources and apply for grants and other support.

Agencies that are fortunate enough to hire a development director rely on that person to engage in a variety of fundraising activities that carry out the vision of the board and the CEO. The person serving as development director should serve as the lead strategist for agency fund development, helping the CEO design and carry out multiyear revenue plans to ensure the NPO will maintain or grow its programs that are consistent with its mission. Often, the development director functions as the agency's principal major-gift fundraiser.

The development director should be responsible for identifying, qualifying, cultivating, soliciting, and stewarding prospects from all sources capable of giving larger amounts of money. This person should be responsible for helping shape agency strategy and for playing a leadership role in implementing the agency's operating plan. He or she should also be responsible for working closely and collaboratively with the administrative staff.

Fundraising Consultants

Today, many NPOs outsource revenue-raising responsibilities to professional fundraisers who contract with the NPOs. The consultant, presumably, will be able to accomplish what an NPO's board and staff have decided they cannot. This form of outsourcing works well in any subsegment of the nonprofit sector, including researching and writing grant proposals, designing and carrying out annual fundraising campaigns and special events, conducting and applying funding feasibility studies, training NPO boards and staff in fundraising techniques and responsibilities, and developing fundraising materials.

LEGAL LIMITATIONS ON FUNDRAISING

Legal limitations on fundraising include the following:

- **Limitations established by the local United Way:** The period of time in which a member NPO can seek donations is limited by the period the local United Way conducts its own fundraising efforts. Thus, member NPOs must shut down their own efforts in the short period of fundraising that United Way conducts its own fundraising campaign.

- **Limitations established by the Internal Revenue Service:** Certain proofs must be demonstrated. First, NPOs must make evident that over the preceding four years prior to the review by the IRS, at least one-third of its financial support (gifts, contributions, membership fees, income from unrelated businesses, gross investment income, revenues) came from the government, the general public, foundations, corporations, or a combination of these sources (IRS Code 509(a)(1)). NPOs must demonstrate this "one-third" test annually. NPOs must do this on a continuing basis.

Social entrepreneurship is a popular activity among nonprofits today. There is a risk to nonprofits for engaging in these "for-profit" activities. They may be judged to be *unrelated activities*. Unrelated business activity might be taxable, and if it makes up the bulk of the nonprofit's activities, then the IRS can take away the nonprofit status. There are some activities that the IRS has ruled will not be subject to the unrelated business income tax. They are the following:

- Activities in which almost all the work is handled by volunteers

- Activities engaged in primarily for the benefit of members, students, patients, officers, or employees

- The sale of merchandise that has been donated to the nonprofit (thrift store)

- The rental or exchange of mailing lists of donors or members

- The distribution of items worth less than $5 as incentives for donating funds (stamps, pre-printed mailing labels, and so on.)

Certain qualifications have to be obtained before an NPO can take advantage of tax-free revenue streams. Any organization that is classified by the IRS Code as a 501(c)(3) becomes either a private foundation or a public organization. Public organizations receive very favorable tax treatment, that is, they are not required to pay excise taxes on interest income, and they enjoy exemptions from income, sale, and property taxes.[4]

TRENDS AND NEW IDEAS IN REVENUE SOURCES

There are modern challenges in fundraising that arise from a fluctuating economy, threats of international violence, and competition for nonprofit donations. A visionary board, executive, and fundraisers will always be on the lookout for money-generating ideas. There are new resources and marketing devices like *cause-related marketing* and sponsorship or the sale and use of products and brands. There are also unrelated business income opportunities emerging as sources of revenue. This section discusses several new fundraising methods that are emerging around the country and presents examples. These new income opportunities could prove to be profitable. The first example is in the growing area of unrelated business ventures, which have the potential to provide significant and permanent income streams.

Unrelated Business Income

Unrelated business income (UBI) refers to profits or income from the operation of a business enterprise or trade. For example, many institutions (or their related entities) rent their mailing lists to companies and permit the company to use the list to solicit business.

To be designated a UBI by the IRS, the business must be regularly occurring and for the most part not related to the tax-exempt mission and operation of the NPO. The purpose of such an operation is primarily to make a profit. An exempt organization that has $1,000 or more in gross income from an unrelated business must file with the IRS. If designated an UBI, it will likely have to pay income taxes at the same rate as any other similar type of business.

There are three main sources of unrelated business income: (1) unrelated business activities, (2) debt-acquired property, and (3) controlled organizations. Some general rules apply:

- All profits from unrelated business activities are taxable to the nonprofit unless they are passive income such as rents, dividends, interest, royalties, and annuities. Profits from unrelated business sales are taxed.

- Profits from debt-financed properties are taxed as unrelated business income unless they are already being taxed under source 1 or 2 or they arise from a tax-exempt mission or fall into an exemption.

- All rent, interest, royalties, annuities, and other payments to the controlling organization from its subordinates are taxed regardless of whether the subordinate is tax-exempt.

A nonprofit may make a profit from engaging in a business that is related to the mission of the nonprofit without losing its tax-exempt status and without paying taxes on that profit. It may engage in profit-making businesses unrelated to its tax-exempt mission, but it must pay taxes on the profits earned. Neither of these situations leads to a loss or denial of tax-exempt status.

Example of a UBI: Ben & Jerry's

Ben & Jerry's goal is to increase the number of their Scoop Shops. To help them accomplish this goal, they have engaged in setting up Scoop Shop business partnerships with nonprofits in recent years. They are "good guy" types giving foundation dollars to advocacy groups interested in making positive changes in the lives of Americans. The foundation's partners traditionally do not include large national agencies like the YWCA. They like local grassroots organizations whose philosophy and experience are not unlike their own organization's philosophy and experience in selling ice cream.

Ben & Jerry's PartnerShop Program does not give money for nonprofits to set up a business. They assist their partners by waiving the initial franchise fees and not charging the annual $30,000 franchise fee for their PartnerShop Program. Like all of their franchises, they provide the partner with training so that they will succeed, but they do not provide the very expensive equipment and fixtures or provide space for the scoop shop.

Cause-Related Marketing

Cause-Related Marketing (CRM) is defined as "a commercial activity by which businesses and charities (or causes) form a partnership with each other to market an image, product or service for mutual benefit."[5] Corporations will choose the nonprofits they will form partnerships with on the strength of the NPO's brand value in the global market.[6] CRM partnerships can involve one or more partners. The website *Business in the Community* has found that forging a partnership with an NPO may be beneficial to the corporation, and research conducted by Michael E. Porter and Mark R. Kramer demonstrates that the time has come for businesses to join their communities and not remain aloof in making the community better.[7]

A corporate partnership is a collaborative effort between an NPO and a private for-profit corporation designed to meet certain objectives:

- Increase the company's sales.

- Improve the company's position in the marketplace.

- Enhance the company's community image.

- Benefit the charitable organization.

Porter and Kramer write:

The trend of consumers demanding more of corporations continues to grow. Businesses are expected to be socially responsible and use their valuable resources to address community concerns. CRM is helping corporations build valuable relationships with educated consumers. These relationships create loyal consumers who can identity with a company's philosophy, positioning and brand. So, not only do corporate partnerships affect the greater good of the community, they also affect the bottom line of the corporation.[8]

CRM is worth pursuing. Cause-related marketing is a form of advertising whose popularity is growing rapidly. Porter and Kramer survey results indicate that 66 percent of respondents to a survey would "likely switch brands or retailers to one associated with a good cause, when price and quality are equal."[9] Consumers listed "providing a better future for and protecting America's children" as their top public priority in these surveys. Some critics may feel that business partners are taking away more from the relationship than NPOs. There is no question that CRM enhances a firm's brand equity and potentially increase sales. Clearly, associating with a popular charity sets a business apart and potentially makes its product more popular in its market.

Ninety percent of employees feel a strong sense of loyalty to their company when they support a cause. Yet even though CRM helps build a beneficial relationship with consumers, NPOs get the same type of exposure and often receive monetary or volunteer help in return. The value of getting seen in a niche market is real.

Public Support

Most NPOs as discussed in this text acquire revenues that qualify them for exempt status with regard to federal and state taxes. Generally, these NPOs must be able to demonstrate that two-thirds of their revenues are generated from public sources. That is, donations by private and public foundations, businesses, or individuals, grants by government jurisdictions, and other NPOs (for example, the United Way) must be calculated as meeting the two-thirds requirement. Without such protections, regulatory agencies would find it difficult to prevent NPOs from being created as tax shelters rather than organizations existing to fulfill a mission for the public good. Government and public foundation grants count in total toward the two-thirds public support while the other types of revenues are vulnerable to being determined as not tax-exempt income.

Revenue that is generated through an NPO's activities are determined to be tax-exempt because they are directly related to the NPO's charitable mission as determined by the IRS. Revenue from some activities that fall outside an NPO's mission often do not qualify as tax-exempt. For example, many NPOs engage in unrelated activities that can never be construed as connecting to their missions. A church that operates a liquor store, while an exaggerated example, demonstrates a clear non-connection to its tax-exempt charitable mission to the point that none of the liquor store revenue would qualify for exempt status. IRS rules have identified a long list of income sources that give guidance as to what may or may not qualify as tax-exempt public support.

REVENUE ADMINISTRATION

Most revenue sources live up to expectations of their agreements to provide funding to NPOs. NPOs, however, cannot count on all sources of revenue to reliably provide their promised allotments as agreed. Making sure revenue sources provide the money to fulfill their responsibility is vital to NPOs. NPOs should manage that aspect of revenue seriously. Some critical steps may need to be taken.

Collection

Whether from grants, pledges, membership dues and fees, donations, bequeathals, sometimes promised money does not show up. Someone at an NPO needs to keep track of all owed funds. This is most likely the business officer or finance officer in an organization. Whoever it is needs to organize his or her files so that none of the organization's lifeblood will be lost. When revenues are late, it behooves an NPO to make a friendly contact with the funding source.

Pledges and Membership Dues

Fundraising activities often involve pledges by individuals or other organizations. Religious organizations like churches are examples of NPOs that rely on pledges from members. Other types of NPOs rely on special fundraising activities that involve the act of making a pledge to give a designated amount of money, usually by a prescribed date. Unfortunately, collecting the money tied to those pledges is often problematic. A pledge, for example, is not a legal document. It is a promise by a well-intentioned person or organization. An NPO must have a policy for collecting pledges and membership dues. The policy should include a termination of effort plan.

Billings

A billing is an official notification to a person or other entity making the pledge. After the promise is made, the pledging entity should be sent, by letter or e-mail, an invoice-like document that serves both to notify and remind them that they have made a promise to support the organization.

DETERMINING PRICES

It has been recognized that as the traditional sources of income are declining or at least getting harder to come by, NPOs are increasingly turning to alternative funding sources that involve the selling of goods and services. An NPO getting involved in such activities must learn how to set prices accurately. According to Sharon Oster, et al., "Setting prices for these services can involve an intricate balance of economics, ideology, and common sense."[10] The pricing of goods and services is a daunting task in the nonprofit sector. Price-setting is fraught with danger. As NPOs begin to use the emerging alternative funding strategies associated with entrepreneurial endeavors, setting prices for goods and services will become a more important skill for financial and fiscal staff to possess. Among the dangers of replacing giving and grants with marketable goods and services are the following:

- Prices will be too high and clients and customers will be priced out.

- Prices will be too low and costs will not be covered.

- Price increases will exceed the demand elasticity (elasticity is a measure of interest of a consumer of a good or service in response to a change in price for that good).

- Client base may require a sliding scale.

- Charging or increasing prices may adversely affect the NPO's ability to acquire donations and grants.

- Charging fees or increasing prices may negatively affect community goodwill.

Demand and supply are not always the only factors that determine the price of a good. At least this is so, as an economist might say, in the short run. Competition usually sets where a firm in a market will price its goods. It is often believed that firms pass on all cost increases to their customers. But, in fact, firms cannot always pass cost increases on to the public by increasing prices. Consider the case of a store in a mall. If the mall administrators increase the cost of rent to storekeepers because their costs went up, can the storekeepers automatically pass those higher costs on to customers? The answer is, of course, maybe. Competitors outside the mall may see the opportunity to increase its competitiveness with a mall shop when they recognize an opportunity to increase their volume. The mall shop owner has the advantage of high-volume traffic but may have to keep prices at least stable in order to compete. This problem is exacerbated for the NPO that has to engage in price setting for goods and services in markets that may have no elasticity.

Complicating the difficulty of price setting is the fact that the market in which an NPO operates may actually be what is called a *market failure*. The term means that the demand for a good or service that an NPO provides probably is not profitable enough for private firms to enter the market. This market failure makes pricing in the nonprofit sector even more difficult. The following questions need to be addressed in such a circumstance:

- How will the price affect the bottom line?

- How will the price affect other funding alternatives?

- What information will the price convey about the organization and its services?

- Under what conditions can an NPO price-discriminate?

- How effectively will the price discourage overuse of your scarce service?

- What services does a membership fee entitle a member to? [11]

The following are critical factors in pricing an NPO's goods and services:

- Strategic goals
- Competition
- Costs

Strategic plans should include services to be provided, appropriate pricing for client affordability, staff salary plans and objectives, growth volume, desired new programming areas, and other factors. NPOs must determine the costs of direct materials, labor and overhead facilities, utilities, taxes, insurance, security, and other general operating costs of the business attributable to the good or service being provided. Knowing these costs will give the NPO useful information to determine a break-even cost. These costs have to be, at least, understood even if they are partially funded by grants or donations. It is also important to consider what similar agencies, if not direct competitors, are charging for similar goods and services. It is not unreasonable to examine comparable agencies that lie outside an NPO's market area. Such agencies must have similar circumstances and characteristics so that the influence on prices will be comparing *apples to apples.*

According to Edward Gurowitz, a suggested "Easy Formula: Cost Plus Time Plus Margin" does not fully capture all the factors that NPOs have to consider, but it does provide a basis for creating a cost formula that could serve NPOs.[12] So first the NPO must account for its costs to produce a good or service. If materials are involved, it should be fairly simple to determine the cost. If an NPO, for example, is producing a cookbook to sell throughout the community, the material costs will be paper, ink, photography, graphics, and whatever other costs there are in producing a book. This is determined by estimating the number of books to be produced, the total costs of printing, and other material costs. To that, the costs of time, that is, labor per book, is added into the price. Finally, the margin represents the markup on each book. Margin in the private sector represents profit. It is expressed as a percentage. The margin is an arbitrary factor that reflects the values of the NPO. Adding all this together yields the price for one book. Using the cookbook example, consider the following:

Material Cost per book = $ 7.35

Labor costs per book = $ 5.45

Margin = 25%

Price = Costs + Margin

Price = (7.35+5.45) = $ 12.80+ ($12.80 * .25)

Price = $12.80+ $3.20

Price = $16.00

If the price had been determined to be, for example, $16.13, an NPO would probably round this price up to $16.25 following the rule of thumb that pricing which includes un-rounded cents confuse customers and probably checkout clerks. If an NPO obtains a grant that subsidizes this cost, it would probably reduce the price by a calculated amount. The margin should reflect consideration of the client. Perhaps in the pricing discussion between the staff and board members, some may consider a 25-percent margin to be outrageous, while others may consider it reasonable and justifiable. There are no stock-holders to worry about, and the use of revenues from the markup will be sub-jective. In the end, the NPO may overestimate the demand for the book, and most of the books printed will be marked down, probably down to cost.

There are other types of pricing that can be used and could be investigat-ed by the finance experts at NPOs.

FORECASTING REVENUE

Nobody can accurately predict the future. A line in William Shakespeare's *Macbeth* reads, "If you can look into the seeds of time, and say which grain will grow and which will not, speak then to me."[13] This is especially true when try-ing to get a handle on future revenues. Forecasts, unfortunately, are not prophecies. All revenue forecasting, no matter how sophisticated, is based on assumptions, political views, trends, and judgments. Theoretically, forecasting provides aid to decision makers in implementing control over revenues and spending. In reality, especially since the 9/11 violence and Hurricane Katrina, forecasting is more confusing than ever.

Some Administrative and Political Issues

The chief administrator of an NPO needs to support forecasting and ensure it is done properly and on a timely basis. All involved in using forecast-ing must realize that it is a tool, not a panacea. An organization has to decide if forecasting should be for the short term, medium term, or long term. Forecasting can compel those in charge to be forward-thinking by requiring a systematic review of what is likely to occur. Forecasts must be presented in an understandable format. All assumptions need to be known and apparent. Forecasts should be tied to a plan of action.

Short-, Medium-, and Long-Term Forecasting

Three types of forecasting as they are related to time are discussed in this section. *Short-term forecasts* are associated with putting a budget together. Metaphorically, forecasting is akin to being on a level plane and looking out on the horizon, which offers limited elevation. You just cannot see very far. You need to get to a higher place to see the way you want to go. In other words, you want more or better information. Predicting cash flow is a fiscally prudent activity, especially in times of highly volatile interest rates or inflation. Such times can erode the value of money long before a fiscal period ends. Budgeters are usually looking one year on the revenue horizon. But, as many nonprofits are experiencing these days, monitoring revenues is vital and a plan for adjusting the budget has to be part and parcel of the budget process.

When one climbs up a hill to take in the view, the horizon expands. It requires, however, more of an effort, more expense. *Medium-term forecasts* are used to avoid *management by crisis.* For example, by anticipating budgetary shortfalls two years in advance, crises can be averted. Medium-term forecasts identify fiscal gaps that can be dealt with in advance of their actually occurring. Early decisions can be based on early estimates of problems. NPOs that are subject to balanced budget requirements can be served well by medium-term forecasts.

Small NPOs rarely use *long-term forecasting.* The primary reason for this is the level of sophistication involved requires specialized expertise. Long-term forecasting is akin to climbing a mountain in order to see how you arrived at the peak and how you are going to get where you want to go. It is associated with moving an NPO in a certain policy direction. Long-term forecasting uses numerous variables in various combinations, like the size and composition of a population, income, level of investment, and the like.

Types of Revenue Forecasting

No matter what method is used for forecasting, the forecaster must attempt to see into the future using the limitations that are inherent in predicting. There are many factors that can affect a prediction, so no matter what technique is used, it is extremely important to consider all relevant components of possibilities for revenue or expenditures.

Expert

Prediction of revenue or expenditures made by a person who is familiar with the particular source of revenue or element of expenditure is an example of expert forecasting. No single method can describe this type of forecasting. There is little accountability associated with this method. Also called "judgmental" techniques, the type includes the Delphi technique, brainstorming, and other techniques common to many governments and nonprofit agencies. The Delphi technique is discussed next.

Delphi Technique

An interesting and sometimes effective expert method of forecasting is the Delphi technique. It is named after the Greek Oracle at Delphi who offered prophecies to Greeks in the thirteenth century B.C. Delphi is a forecasting procedure that originated in the nonprofit industry (the Rand Corporation) before expanding to other sectors of the economy. It is useful for accomplishing the following tasks:[14]

- Predicting revenue scenarios
- Examining the significance of historical events
- Evaluating possible budget allocations
- Putting together the structure of a model
- Developing causal relationships in complex economic or social phenomena
- Distinguishing and clarifying real and perceived human motivations
- Exposing priorities of personal values

Using this technique in revenue forecasting, a selected panel of *experts* are asked to give their opinions on what revenues will be over a period or designated periods of time. The experts are asked questions that lead to their predictions and are also asked to explain how they arrived at their predictions. The predictions of the panelists are assembled by a designated panel director and tabulated. Forecasts are decided after several iterative rounds. A designated director of the panel collects the initial conclusions from the experts. The information is processed, analyzed, and filtered for relevance. Experts are given the opportunity to review the results and may give additional input. This process is repeated several times until a consensus emerges. Experts remain anonymous during the process to avoid undue influence on each other. After four rounds, the NPO will have valuable input for making revenue predictions. This method brings in a broad array of perspectives and avoids *groupthink*. It is economical in that it can occur by snail mail or e-mail and is simple to implement. On the other hand, it is not by any means a quantitative unbiased method. It does, however, complement other more rational methods.

Trending

Trending allows an NPO to make predictions of revenues based on changes in the revenue in prior years. This method can be enhanced by studying monthly cash flow charts over several prior years. Consistent observations of revenue peaks and valleys during these prior years yield knowledge of seasonal fluctuations in income and expenses. This gives the NPO an opportunity to base forecasting on an accurate history and allows it to work external factors into the forecast. Essentially, you arrive at a more solid *guesstimate* than you would without this analysis. Of course, many unforeseen issues may change the forecast as the year goes on. Trends are used to project the future based on previous levels of the variable. Regression analysis is a common technique, with the predominant variable being time as the independent, or causal, variable.

Trend regression is a rather simple calculation of a causal relationship between time (in this case, a year) and revenues. It is a calculation of distances from the mean over time. The closer revenue measurements are to the mean over several years, the more reliable the prediction. Time is called an independent variable (x), while revenues are called the dependent variable (y). The regression equation is:

$$y = a + bx$$

This calculation results in an estimate of a future year based on changes in time. This formula is depicted graphically in the trend line shown in Figure 7.2. Table 7.2 shows the historical annual revenues going back six years. This

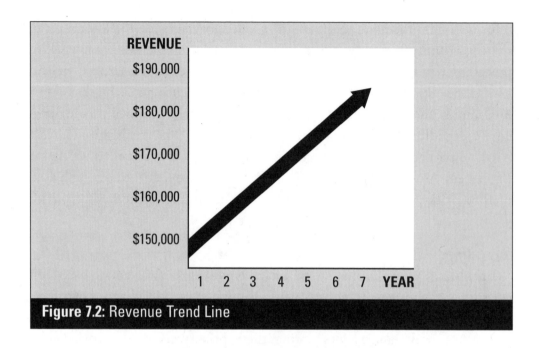

Figure 7.2: Revenue Trend Line

YEAR	REVENUE
1	$150,000
2	$159,000
3	$160,000
4	$169,000
5	$175,000
6	$180,000
7	To be predicted

Table 7.2: ABCNPO Historical Revenue

data will be plugged into the trend regression formula to predict revenue for *ABCNPO* for year 7.

In Figure 7.2, the x axis is the horizontal axis labeled *Year.* The y axis is the vertical axis labeled *Revenue.* In the formula, the a is a measure of the intercept. In Figure 7.2, the intercept is the point where the slope crosses the vertical revenue axis. Again, in the formula, the *b* is a measure of the changes in slope. For every change in *x,* there is a corresponding change in y. That is shown in Figure 7.2 by the steepness of the slope. The more responsive the change, the steeper the slope.

In order to avoid manual calculations, the calculation of ABC NPO's year-seven revenue is accomplished using Microsoft Excel. Take the following steps on your own using Excel and calculate year-seven revenue:

1. Starting in Column A, Cell 1, duplicate the years in Table 7.2. Input the revenue for each year starting in Column B, Cell 1.

2. Open the **TOOLS** menu.

3. Click on **DATA ANALYSIS** (Note: If that option is not showing, you must install it as follows: Open **TOOLS**, then click **ADD INS**. You will see a series of choices. Put a check mark in the box next to **ANALYSIS TOOLPAK**. Then follow the instructions to install).

4. Click on **REGRESSION** and then OK.

5. In the **REGRESSION** menu, you must select the values in Column B to Input Y Range.

6. Select Column A as you Input X Range.

7. Select Column A, Cell 1 as your Output Range.

8. Click on OK. Ignore the **REGRESSION STATISTICS** and **ANOVA** box.

9. In the bottom box, take the Intercept value in Column B. Copy it and paste it in Column B, Cell 31. Then copy the **X VARIABLE** value and past it in Column B, Cell 32.

10. Place your cursor in Column B, Cell 33. Type in and enter the following formula "= B31 + (B32 * 7)." B31 is the intercept (a), B32 is the change in the slope (b), and 7 is year seven (x). These are the variables in the regression equation. B31 should equal 144,800. B32 should be 5914.286.

11. If you got the result 186,200. Congratulations! ABCNPO is expecting its revenue to reach $186,200 in year seven.

This calculation of ABCNPO's year-seven revenue is a mere illustration of a simple regression attempting to use time as the only independent variable. Using more variables increases the potential in making fairly accurate predictions. Deterministic forecasting tends to use a number of variables in predicting revenue. The formula for a multiple regression containing more than one variable will look like this:

$$Y = a + bx + b_2x_2 + b_3x_3 \ldots b_nx_n$$

Any good business, public administration, or nonprofit statistics book will explain this concept in more detail.

Deterministic

This prediction type is based on a percentage of change in social, economic, or other variables that directly affect a revenue outcome. In other words, deterministic models take trends a step further by looking at variables other than time. This type of prediction does not necessarily mean the use of regression analysis. It assumes the reliability of pre-established standards. In other words, changes are compared to a base period of time and to certain expectations. Deterministic methods range from gathering information from various relevant publications to sophisticated econometric modeling. The example that follows for the fictitious Beechtree Beach, Missouri, Nutt House Theatre Company, illustrates the deterministic prediction type.

The Nutt House: A Case Analysis

The Nutt House theatre is a private not-for-profit company whose ticket sales generates its revenue during the tourist season, May through September. The theatre is equidistant from the state's two largest metropolitan areas and is located on a large lake. Each January, the theatre finance director meets with the city finance director to assess tourism for the next summer season. The theatre's annual revenue from summer productions is historically 30 to 40 percent as large as the city's tourism tax revenue. The city finance director reports the following data:

- There are 7,986 housing units in the city, 504 of which are seasonal.

- The average per unit property tax collected on behalf of the city is $224.

- On average, these households are 75 percent full during the 12-week tourist season.

- A seasonal household spends $203 per week on retail purchases.

- 65 percent of the city's 4,000 jobs are seasonal.

- The average retail spending per worker per week in the city is estimated to be $93.

- The average family trip is 2.5 days long.

- The average family spends $168 per trip for lodging, sustenance, and other purchases.

- The city projects 1.9 million family tourist days.

- The city sales tax rate is 2 percent.

The two finance directors schedule a follow-up meeting for the next week. Over the weekend, news breaks that the city's finance director is arrested for embezzlement. The company's board meeting was planned for the night of the scheduled meeting between the two finance directors. The theatre company's finance director had never actually calculated the tax revenues, and it turned out the now-jailed city finance director had never shared his methodology with anyone, even the city council. He always managed to be fairly accurate. So, armed with this data, the company's finance director conducted an analysis of information in Exhibit 7.1.

With the information from the city now calculated and resulting in an estimated $2,742,944, the company's finance director created three scenarios for the board for the evening's meeting. The economy looked good and would likely not affect tourism. Weather, he knows from experience, would then be the critical factor affecting tourism. It was likely that tourism revenues would be reduced by ten percent of the city's anticipated revenues if the summer brings cooler than normal temperatures, because fewer people would be interested in spending time at the lake. On the other hand, if temperatures would go higher than normal because of a warming trend, then the estimate is ten percent over the crooked city finance director's estimate. Ultimately, the finance director made a call to the local television meteorologist and as a result of that conversation felt safe to be in the middle of the range, predicting revenues would be 35 percent of the predicted $2,724,944, or $954,080. It looked like it would be a very good summer indeed.

7,986 housing units		
504 seasonal housing units		
$224 average property tax	$112,896	Seasonal houses times average property tax*
$203 seasonal household weekly spending	$18,416	Seasonal houses times seasonal household spending times 12 weeks times 75 percent (units full) times sales tax
4,000 jobs		
2,600 jobs, 65% seasonal		
$93 weekly spending by workers	$58,032	Seasonal jobs times weekly spending by workers times city sales tax times 12 weeks
2.5 days average family trip		760,000 trips—family tourist days divided by average family trip
$168 avg. spending per family trip		
1,900,000 projected family tourist days		
2% city sales tax	$2,553,600	760,000 trips times average spending per trip times city sales tax
	$2,742,944	TOTAL

*Owners have to pay property their tax whether their unit is being used or not. This is an annual payment, not a weekly payment. I attributed the property tax on seasonal housing units to tourism.

Exhibit 7.1: Nutt House Theatre Company Forecast of City Revenues

Why Forecasts Sometimes Fail

Revenue forecasting is an intelligent process, because it gives educated "what ifs." Ultimately, the final decision is an art (intuition), not science (forecasting techniques). The science of forecasting informs the art. Forecasting revenues is a risky duty in all organizations, and especially in nonprofits, and external events only make it more difficult. Let it be known that forecasts are impossible to get right. The real standard of accuracy is to be "close enough," but being under the actual amount is better than being over. Forecasting poorly over more than one budgetary period may result in a loss of credibility as well as the inability to provide funding for mission-based programs.

No one would have forecast the effects on the nonprofit sector as a result of the 9/11 terrorist attacks that resulted in the deaths of nearly 3,000 people. Immediately after the attacks, volunteers flocked to nonprofits in a moving expression of the nation's spirit of resilience and hope. Along with the giving of personal time and energy through volunteerism, donations poured into nonprofits. Although much of this outpouring was given to charities in New York City, local nonprofits across the country benefited as well, to the surprise of many.

This period was followed by an era of low interest rates. Foundations, as a result, made less on their investments and had less money to give. Government budgets were similarly affected. Individuals lost jobs. United Ways across the country suddenly had trouble meeting their goals. In fact, in some communities that experienced major layoffs, gifts pledged to United Ways went unfulfilled. Virtually all nonprofits experienced funding cuts during the middle of the year 2002. Then over the course of several years, as federal money was redirected toward the military engagements in Afghanistan and Iraq, fewer federal dollars seemed to be available for human services. Nonprofits, like for-profit businesses, cut staff, merged programs, and postponed capital plans. As this was happening, people in need seemed to come out of the woodwork. More services were needed. People were out of work and in need of basics such as food. All of these uncontrollable events made forecasting extremely difficult for governments and nonprofits.

During this period, there was one interesting phenomenon. Nonprofits began to partner together to deliver services. They looked to others in the nonprofit community for partnerships, and to the business community for both volunteers and cash. Programs merged for survival. Waste was cut. Agencies bonded in coalitions to apply for grants. Although, in the long run, these steps will increase the capabilities of nonprofits, none of these events was predicted. None was forecast. This is not to say that one should not forecast. No one plans to fail, but often people fail to plan. Forecasting helps NPOs plan for success.

TAX CREDIT POLICY

Charitable donations constitute the majority of revenues for nonprofit organizations. If certain legal and tax conditions are met, charitable donations give donors the right to deduct their donations from their tax liabilities. This is an long-standing practice that has been enhanced in recent years as some states across the nation have sought tax policies that benefit specific classes of NPOs. The discussion in this section covers tax policies that affect NPOs.

Public policy often promotes principles that encourage charitable giving, that safeguard voluntary donor choice, and that strengthen public trust in charitable organizations. These principles include the following:

- Encourage giving to ensure that all charitable contributions are deductible from taxable income.

- Encourage individuals to exercise a special leadership responsibility in charitable giving.

- Support private donor choice by making sure that specific charitable activities or organizations qualify for deductions.

- "Do no harm" to giving by avoiding tax law changes that have adverse effects on giving.

Special tax credits offered by states and the federal government include the following:

- Tax incentives for charitable giving that benefit all nonprofits that are qualified under section 501(c)(3)

- State sales tax exemptions for nonprofit 501(c)(3) organizations

The Youth Opportunities Program (YOP), which is offered through the Missouri Department of Economic Development, provides a typical example. After a nonprofit agency is declared eligible, donors to the agency may receive tax credits that allow them to deduct the amount they donate, up to $250,000, from their tax liability. The credit can be carried forward up to five years. It gives nonprofits the opportunity to increase donations to their programs by providing potential donors with the opportunity to reduce the taxes they owe. The YOP has $6 million in tax credits to award annually. Each project may request a maximum tax credit of $250,000 tax.

The purpose of the YOP is to broaden and strengthen opportunities for positive development and participation in community life for youth and to discourage young people from engaging in criminal and violent behavior. (Authorization: Sections 135.460 and 620.1100 to 620.1103 RSMo, 1995.)

Tax credits are awarded to donors to approved organizations that administer positive youth development or crime prevention projects. Approved organizations secure contributions from their community, and contributors receive tax credits for those contributions. There are 50 percent tax credits for monetary contributions and wages paid to youth in an approved internship, apprenticeship, or employment project, and 30 percent tax credits for property or equipment contributions used specifically for the project. Eligible projects include:

- Degree Completion
- Internship/Apprenticeship
- Youth Clubs/Associations
- Adopt-a-School
- Mentor/Role Model
- Substance Abuse
- Violence Prevention
- Youth Activity Centers
- Conflict Resolution
- Employment
- Counseling

The potential benefits of YOP are demonstrated in the fictitious case analysis presented next.

A Tax Credit Case Analysis:
The Swobodaville Community Action Resource Institute (SCARI)

SCARI has obtained YOP tax credit authority. Tax credits are now available to state taxpayers so that they can make an eligible contribution to SCARI during the taxable year. If Joe Taxpayer donates $1,000 to SCARI, the agency will mail a form to Joe to complete and return to SCARI, who forwards it on to the Department of Economic Development (DED). Based on the information provided, Joe is eligible for a 50 percent tax credit, or $500 off the income tax liability that he owes the state. DES sends an eligibility certificate to Joe, who places it with his other tax records. Next April, Joe figures his state income tax liability on the tax long form and finds that he owes the state an additional $700 in taxes over the amount withheld from his paychecks.

Joe attaches his $500 eligibility certificate to the appropriate tax form and writes a check to the state for just $200 ($700-$500), the difference between his tax due and the tax credit. The credit in the donation may be carried forward over the next five consecutive income tax years. Joe can also file for a federal tax deduction for making a gift to an NPO. If Joe is in the 36 percent tax bracket, he may be eligible for an additional credit of up to $350 on his federal return. If that turns out to be the case, Joe will have donated $1,000, and written off $850 from his total tax liability. The actual liability Joe experienced, as it turned out, was $150 to give $1,000 to SCARI.

SUMMARY

Philanthropy seems to be an instinctive and innate portion of many people's being. People want to help others. NPOs are positioned to accept much of this philanthropy to fund their operations and missions. Government and corporations also are inclined to redistribute or contribute money to NPOs. Sometimes philanthropy and government support do not meet the perceived needs of many NPOs. For years now, NPOs have been seeking other and new sources of funds to help them reach their goals. There are a lot of direct and creative fundraising practices that can be adopted and adapted across the nonprofit sector. Fundraising as a practice is not only art and science, it has become a profession. NPOs of all types are hiring personnel or contracting with consultants to raise desirable funds. The mix of funding sources tends to be different for different types of NPOs. Even so, large and small NPOs alike must compete for dollars either within or across subsectors. Financial skills required these days include the need to determine service prices, forecast revenue, and closely and professionally administer revenue programs. Revenue forecasting is becoming a most useful skill in the nonprofit sector. There are many ways to approach predicting revenue. The more diverse revenue sources become, the more revenue administration becomes another vital financial skill. Among other skills also needed is the ability to manage tax credit policies, as shown in the fictitious example from Missouri.

DISCUSSION QUESTIONS

1. **Government Subsidies and Private Donations:** A debate of increasing intensity in the public economics literature surrounds the relationship between government subsidies and private donations to the nonprofit sector. One hypothesis is that public spending displaces or "crowds out" private giving; competing hypotheses, however, say that subsidies leverage ("crowd in") philanthropy, or alternatively, that the two sources of funds are independent. This question has practical implications for both nonprofit executives and public administrators. Discuss the impact of government subsidizing nonprofits through grant programs. How does an NPO benefit? What are the disadvantages of government subsidies? How are various stakeholders affected? If you were a donor to an NPO and it obtained a large government grant to run a new program, what would you want to know about the NPO and the grant?

2. **Special Sources of Revenue:** There are many opportunities that nonprofits can consider to raise funds. Fundraising ranges from formal grant applications to soliciting donations to selling products to holding special events. Discuss in class or write a paper on the unique or innovative NPO sources of revenue that you have either observed or been a part of. Describe the source. Which type of NPO was the beneficiary of this source? What was the context of the source— mission-related fundraising? Capital project? Other special circumstance?

EXERCISE

Consider the following revenue history of the Enpio Agency.

YEAR	REVENUE
1	$28,500
2	$29,590
3	$32,380
4	$31,400
5	$33,350
6	$34,700
7	To be predicted

Table 7.3: Enpio Historical Revenue

Using Microsoft Excel (be sure to download the Analysis Toolpak):

1. Starting in Column A, Cell 1, duplicate the years in Table 7.1. Input the revenue for each year starting in Column B, Cell 1.

2. Open the **TOOLS** menu.

3. Click on **REGRESSION** and then OK.

4. In the **REGRESSION** menu, you must select the values in Column B to Input Y Range.

5. Select Column A as you Input X Range.

6. Select Column A, Cell 1 as your Output Range.

7. Click on OK. Ignore the **REGRESSION STATISTICS** and **ANOVA** box.

8. In the bottom box, take the Intercept value in Column B. Copy it and past it in Column B, Cell 31. Then copy the **X VARIABLE** value and paste it in Column B, Cell 32.

9. Place your cursor in Column B, Cell 33. Type in and enter the following formula "= B31 + (B32 * 7)." B31 is the intercept (a), B32 is the change in the slope (b), and 7 is year seven (x).

Interpret the results for the Enpio Agency.

INNOVATION: BRANDING

Branding is the marketing process of drawing people's senses to an entity based on its renown. The brand manifests itself in the form of people's recognition of a logo or the sound of the entity's name. Many companies are known by their signage: McDonald's golden arches and their many advertising jingles over the year bring to mind food that many people crave. The Red Cross has such brand strength. Experts at Philanthropic Research, Inc., believe that "an organization's greatest asset is its brand."[15] A few NPOs have made brands of their initials, which are recognized by nearly everyone, for example, YMCA and AARP. These initials make the organizations more recognizable than their actual names—the Young Men's Christian Association and the American Association of Retired Persons.[16]

How to Get Branded

Branding is supposed to take an organization from obscurity to being *well-known*. But getting there through branding is not a simple process. If an NPO wants to develop a recognizable brand locally, regionally, nationally, or internationally, it will have to develop a process. A theoretical model of branding provides a foundation for such a process. The NPO must take stock of how it is perceived. The NPO must determine how its clients, companies, and the public in general know about the NPO. This sort of baseline data is compared to the NPO's goals with regard to being recognized by a logo, initials, or some other feature. This information leads the NPO to a planning process to become branded. Finally, successful branding requires buy-in, not only by the NPO board and staff, but by all stakeholders and various media.[17]

NOTES

1   *Annual Report: Giving USA 2005* (Indianapolis, IN: AAFRC Trust for Philanthropy, 2005).

2   Herrington J. Bryce, *Financial and Strategic Management for Nonprofit Organizations* (San Francisco: Jossey-Bass, 2000).

3   Fisher Howe, *The Board Member's Guide to Fund Raising* (San Francisco: National Center for Nonprofit Boards and Jossey-Bass, 1991).

4   Herrington J. Bryce, *Financial and Strategic Management for Nonprofit Organizations* (San Francisco: Jossey-Bass, 2000).

5   Business in the Community, "Brand Benefits of Cause-Related Marketing," April 2004. Online at http://www.bitc.org.uk/resources/publications/brand_benefits.html (accessed April 25, 2008).

6   Michael E. Porter and Mark R. Kramer, "The Competitive Advantage of Corporate Philanthropy," *Harvard Business Review* Dec. (2002): 56.

7   Ibid.

8   Ibid.

9   Ibid.

10 Sharon Oster, C. Massersky, and S. Beinhacker, *Generating and Sustaining Earned Income* (San Francisco: Jossey-Bass, 2004).

11 Charles M. Gray, "Pricing Issues for the Nonprofit Manager," *Nonprofit Times* (Apr. 2001).

12 Edward M. Gurowitz, Ph.D., "Positioning Products and Services Accurately," *The CEO Refresher,* 2001. Online at http://www.gurowitz.com/articles/TheCEORe.pdf (accessed August 14, 2008).

13 William Shakespeare, *Macbeth,* Act 1, Scene 3.

14 Harold A. Linstone and M. Turoff, *The Delphi Method: Techniques and Applications* (Newark: New Jersey Institute of Technology Publishing, 2002).

15 Philanthropic Research, Inc., "Nonprofit Branding: Unveiling the Essentials," April 2007. Online at http://guidestar.org (accessed April 25, 2008).

16 Philanthropic Research, Inc., "Initial Success: Expressing Your Nonprofit Brand through Initials," 2007. Online at GuideStar.org (accessed April 25, 2008).

17 Bill Nissim, "Nonprofit Branding: Unveiling the Essentials," *Nonprofit Marketing and Branding* (December 2003). Online at http://guidestar.org/news/features (accessed May 19, 2008).

CHAPTER 8
Expenditure Management: Spending, Purchasing, and the Time Value of Money

This chapter's discussion of expenditures balances that of the previous chapter, which covered revenues. Expenditure administration in the nonprofit sector is designed to ensure that agency officials properly use the money intended to fund their mission. They are expected to do so in the most efficient way and within the framework of the stakeholders' trust. Because this is so important, expenditure administration—like most areas of nonprofit financial administration—is a dynamic process affected by technology and, it is hoped, the development of better processes. This chapter discusses the impact of time on spending and purchasing practices, and presents criteria that can be used in making spending decisions. The time value of money, that is, inflation, is an important concept for those who make NPO purchasing decisions. After a discussion of that topic, the chapter considers cost and value analysis. The chapter ends with an examination of purchasing management.

TOPICS
- Value, Time, and Money
- Criteria-Based Spending Decision Making
- Procurement: Theory and Practice
- Summary
- Discussion Questions
- Exercise: Cost-benefit and Cost-effectiveness Analysis
- Innovation: Supply Chain Management

The gratification of wealth is not found in mere possession or in lavish expenditure, but in its wise application.

-Miguel de Cervantes

VALUE, TIME, AND MONEY

One of the truths of expenditure administration for NPOs is the constant dilemma of providing the same or increased services every year with limited dollars. Some years are better than others. Complicating the already difficult job of making financial choices are the limits on nonprofits that come from economic conditions such as recession and inflation, as well as other external factors. At the same time, the demand for improvements in quality of life— and therefore, increasing services—continues. The demand for cost containment, that is, getting the most *bang for the buck* is the rule rather than the exception.

A necessary foundation for studying the performance management subsystem is an understanding of the time value of money. This understanding provides a basis for using some of the other concepts addressed in Chapters 7, 9, and 11, including forecasting revenue and expenditures, capital budgeting, debt management, and so on. Money is the important medium for value in nonprofit financial administration. Without money, nonprofit programs do not exist. It therefore becomes vital to understand money from a theoretical and practical perspective. Central to this understanding is the time value of money. Time, obviously, can have a great effect on the financial position of NPOs.

The most intrinsic value of money is that of an exchange medium. The dollar, or any currency, is easy to understand with respect to how it translates into prices and affordability. Anyone who wants something, assuming they are morally opposed to stealing it and assuming no one is willing to give it away, must trade for it, or more likely, buy it with money. So the United States and virtually every other society in the world allow money to be the marker of all things.

Time Is Money

While we may let money be the marker, it is vulnerable, like our own bodies, to the effects of time. Thus, the value of a dollar spent today is higher than a dollar spent one or two years from now. The phenomenon of the declining value of money (that is, rising prices) is called inflation. Inflation is an important issue in forecasting revenue, estimating expenditures, analyzing costs, retaining and hiring quality personnel, and many other aspects of financial administration.

Inflation is the key culprit in the declining value of money. The inflation rate is most commonly measured by the Bureau of Labor Statistics (BLS) Consumer Price Index (CPI). There are several inflation calculators that yield inflation outputs when you provide some minimal information (see the websites www.westegg.com/inflation and www.bls.gov). The discussion in this section of the chapter covers the formulae that support the products of those website calculators. Just as soldiers must understand their adversaries, it is incumbent on financial administrators to be aware of how inflation is calculated.

The CPI is the measurement of the cost of a basket of consumer goods. The BLS tracks changes in the costs of the components of the CPI every month. Prices from 85 selected locations around the United States are collected, weighted, and averaged to produce this important index. The seven components of the CPI are the following:

- Food and beverage
- Housing
- Apparel
- Transportation
- Medical care
- Entertainment
- Other

Since 1917, the BLS has provided this index every month. The ultimate use of the CPI is to compare the index and prices to what they were some time in the recent past, including a base period. The CPI is an important measure of inflation, and it is a primary tool used in economic decision making. For example, econometric models that attempt to predict the near future of economies must always include a measure of inflation. The CPI is also used as a determinant in collective bargaining for labor agreements, pensions, and many other economic transactions. To determine the inflation rate (percentage change in the CPI) for the entire basket of consumer goods or in particular components of the CPI, the BLS uses the following formula:

Assumptions: Inflation rate for a given period of time, assuming a new CPI index of 110 and an old index of 103 representing the previous year's CPI.

New CPI - Old CPI x 100, thus:

$(110 - 103)/103$ x 100 = $(7/103)$ x 100 = .0068 x 100 = 6.8 percent

Inflation in this period of time, then, is 6.8 percent.

Often, finance people are concerned with the value of the dollar relative to a previous period of time. Calculating the value of the dollar at any given time is a function of selecting a base year and applying the following formula:

Assumptions: The base year at 100 (100%, or \$1 = \$1) and the new CPI is 107, the new CPI value of the dollar is:

Base year CPI x 100

New year CPI

$(100/107)$ x 100 = .93 x 100 = 93 percent

Thus, the value of the dollar in the new year is 93 percent of what is was in the old.

NPO financial planners have to take into account the changing value of money, that is, inflation, in order to do proper budgeting and to adequately fulfill an NPO's fiduciary role. Managers should make an assessment about what will likely happen to inflation by studying economic sources and seeking how external events will affect the prices of goods and services, payroll, and other factors that affect strategic uses of money.

Effects of Local, Regional, National, and World Changes

Over and above inflation, there are uncontrollable and often unpredictable factors that can have negative and positive impacts on spending by NPOs. These can affect NPOs in both the long and short term. Hospitals have to be concerned about federal regulations affecting the medical industry. Rural health centers that have difficulties attracting physicians must be aware of regional medical school graduation rates. Social service agencies that provide safe housing to protect children from domestic abuse should be aware of birth rates. Hurricanes in the Caribbean and Gulf of Mexico have substantial impacts on nonprofits at the local and regional levels and even at the national and sometimes international levels. Compliance with the provisions of SOX have cost companies and nonprofits more for auditing services. We can continue to add to this list forever and never identify all external factors that impact NPOs. They fall under various categories, including the following:

- Natural (heat, cold, storms, epidemics, and so on)

- Demographics (birth and death rates, aging, population change, and so on)

- Social (crime, neighborhood deterioration, and so on)

- Economic (business growth, wage and salary levels, layoffs, and so on)

- International (political upheaval, natural disasters, economic shifts and so on)

Some of these occurrences take the form of trends and can be planned for strategically (demographics, wages and salaries), while others are not trends and cannot be planned for (natural disasters, political upheaval). Not all have a direct impact on every NPO. But all NPOs will be affected by some changes in the situation at the local, regional, national, and international levels. These changes should be evaluated for their effect on NPOs.

Prices, Opportunity Costs, and Discounts

Buy now and save! How many times has the reader heard or read this warning that prices are on their way up? Most likely, it is hyperbole. Prices reflect opportunity costs. Opportunity cost is defined as the value of foregone opportunities, that is, the other best possible use of the money one spends on a good or a service. This implies the need for decision making, because using money in one way means you cannot use it another way, that is, to buy something else. Inflation and opportunity costs are two of the considerations of the concept of discounting, which is vital in NPO finance and decision making. Discounting is the procedure for estimating the present value of costs and future benefits that will be realized in the future. Net present value is the means of calculating the economic viability of a project that discounts the future by taking into account the erosion in the value of money. Thus, if discounted properly, the cost and benefit streams of different projects can be compared and policy decisions can be simplified.

A problem arises for NPO financial leaders when they have to select the proper discount rate. If everyone agreed on what factors go into selecting a discount rate, then decision making would be easy. But people do not always agree. In fact, there are and should be many points of view expressed in the making of critical decisions. NPO financial planners have to be careful in choosing an appropriate discount rate because the higher the discount rate placed on benefits involved in a decision, the less the present value (the value of dollar today) of a benefit stream will be. Conversely, the lower the discount rate, the higher the present value of a benefit stream. Discounting benefits and costs transforms gains and losses occurring in different time periods to a common unit of measurement. Programs with positive net present value increase social resources and are generally preferred. Programs with negative net present value should generally be avoided. Thus, when associated with a selected interest rate, the effect on the value of money is quite evident.

The following simple present value formula shows the effect of discounting on the cost of a program. In the formula, the discount rate will be set at

$(1 + r)^{time}$ where:

1 = a constant

r = a selected interest rate

$time$ = a period of time, usually measured in years

The formula is

Cost or Benefit Stream

$(1+r)^{time}$

To calculate the effect of a discount rate over time, it is divided into the benefit of an NPO policy or a program in order to determine the present value of the benefit. Three alternative discount rates and their effects are shown here related to the cost of implementing a new nonprofit program. Remember, this is a simple example.

Let's say the agency wants to open a free day care program for a targeted group of people. The total benefits of the program are valued at $100,000. Shown here are three different interest rate estimates. The time period for receiving the benefits of the program is two years.

$$\frac{100,000}{(1 + .05)^2} = 90,703 \qquad \frac{100,000}{(1 + .06)^2} = 89,000 \qquad \frac{100,000}{(1 + .07)^2} = 87,344$$

We will deal with the use of discounting more in Chapter 11 when discussing capital budgeting and decision making. For now, note the differences in the outcomes for the three different discount rates. There is an inverse relationship between the size of the discount rate and the outcome of the calculation. The lower a discount rate, the higher the outcome of the calculation (cost or benefit stream) will be. Like passengers in a boat displacing a lot of water, the greater the number of passengers, the lower the boat rides in the water. Each time a passenger disembarks, the boat rises higher. This formula shows two things: The discount rate has an effect on the estimate of what costs and benefits will come from the investment of money in an NPO policy or social service program, and the selection of a discount rate requires careful consideration.

There are two problems involving the selection of an appropriate discount rate that nonprofit financial managers and planners may encounter. The first problem comes in selecting an appropriate rate from the many possibilities in private markets. The argument involves the familiar issue of the opportunity foregone by investing in the private financial markets, which are best reflected by tangible rates like the prime rate, the T-bill rate, and so on. There are so many different kinds of instruments in private markets that settling on one interest rate is a difficult and subjective choice.

The second problem the nonprofit sector might encounter is based on the fact that the private discount rate ignores the consideration of social costs such as externalities like pollution, birthrates, public health, poverty, and so on. While more of a concept that is important to governments, to take into account the problem of these non-market considerations, an NPO may consider using what has been termed the social discount rate (SDR). The SDR is an attempt to use a rate that will take into account not only the market discount rate but also other factors that do not have an inherent monetary value, including health and social factors, way of life, life expectancy, intergenerational equity, and other relevant factors. These factors, of course, will be unique to each decision being made. The value of these factors is mostly judgmental and subject to scrutiny.[1] Organizations vary in the impact resulting from these factors. The market discount rate will rise or fall depending on the weight of each factor included in the estimation of the SDR. Looking to the federal government, since 1969 the Office of Management and Budget (OMB) has required federal agencies to use a real discount rate of 10 percent unless a special rate is set by law or as a result of a formula or guidelines required by law. Perhaps the most unique difficulty in arriving at an appropriate and acceptable SDR is the fact that most people simply do not appreciate being quantified.

CRITERIA-BASED SPENDING DECISION MAKING

The art of spending requires forethought. If done correctly, the benefits to an NPO will be the ability to get the most bang for their buck. Competent expenditure administration relies on three criteria for judging expenditures that have to be made in the mission of nonprofit agencies: economy, efficiency, and effectiveness. These three Es can be measured through relevant and legitimate output and outcome standards that can be developed by NPOs. These standards generally should be developed on a per-agency basis.

Another way of measuring *proper* spending is to compare rates of expenditure and prices with expenditures and prices paid by other agencies. This gives NPOs the ability to find reasonable industry standards for certain criteria for making spending decisions.

There are also specific cost analysis techniques available to aid in decision making. Cost-effectiveness analysis and cost-benefit analysis are two techniques that, if used correctly, enhance administrators' ability to assist decision makers. If financial managers make good use of these tools, they can greatly assist board members in making tough policy decisions captured in the annual budgets and deciding where and when to spend money.

Cost-Benefit Analysis

Cost-benefit (CB) analysis is a method of evaluating a major spending decision that attempts to discover if the major economic benefits of the project outweigh the economic costs. The hope and the challenge of cost-benefit analysis arises from the need to reduce all costs and benefits to a single measure—the dollar—and to calculate the ratio between costs and benefits. Before calculating the CB ratio, an agency has to determine how it is going to measure costs and benefits and how it will collect the data on each identified cost and benefit. While this requirement is often misunderstood, the essential idea is quite logical, and part of human nature. Children, for example, can be observed scrunching up their faces as they weigh the pros and cons of breaking into a cookie jar. When this basic concept is applied to major spending decisions, cost-benefit analysis helps NPOs to identify and understand both the expenses and the payoffs as well. The decision rule is that if the benefits of a project outweigh its costs, then it is advisable to go ahead with spending money on an object or objective. Conversely, it is not advisable to go ahead and spend the money if costs exceed benefits.

The word *weigh* is useful in explaining this concept. Consider the illustration in Figure 8.1. Picture a brass scale with bowls suspended on either side of a balancing lever and a pile of green rocks and red rocks in front of the scale. A homebuilder is deciding whether to purchase a piece of property where both green rocks and red rocks are found. Green rocks are better on a property than red ones. The pile of rocks is

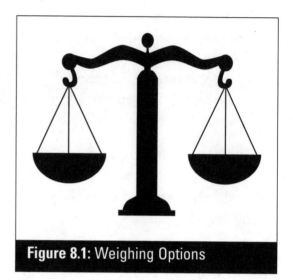

Figure 8.1: Weighing Options

a sample that the builder will use to make a decision about purchasing the property. If the green rocks outnumber the red rocks, the builder will go ahead with the purchase. He places all the green rocks in one bowl and all the red rocks in the other bowl. In the end, the green rocks outweigh the red rocks in the sample, which convinces the builder to go ahead with the purchase.

Applied to real-world decision making, the cost-benefit decision-making process would involve the following:

- Listing all costs and benefits of a program

- Putting dollar values on all costs and benefits

- Comparing costs to benefits and developing a ratio of costs to benefits (total benefits divided by total costs)

A positive ratio (more benefits than costs) indicates that a decision to spend money makes sense. The simplest use of cost-benefit analysis is to calculate a ratio that only measures easily estimated dollar costs.

A Case Analysis: Applying Cost-Benefit Analysis

The following example applies the cost-benefit concept to the purchase of two instruction process alternatives for the fictitious Heads Up agency. The first alternative is a teacher-applied kit for improving language skills. The other is a self-directed software program for accomplishing language skill improvement. The agency wants to determine a cost-benefit ratio for both products before making a decision. Both products have successful track records in other local Heads Up agencies. Table 8.1 lists the costs and benefits of alternative *A*, a teacher-applied kit.

COSTS	AMOUNT	BENEFITS	AMOUNT
Five year student fee	$24,000	Improved test scores	$14,000
Teacher training time	14,000	Child self-esteem	14,000
Cost of replacements during training	2,400	Parent satisfaction	8,000
Administrative costs	10,000	Increased financial support from state for improved performance	14,000
Total	**$50,000**	**Total**	**$52,000**

Table 8.1: Heads Up Agency Language Program – Alternative A

The cost-benefit ratio would be calculated as *TB/TC* (total benefits divided by total costs)

C/B Ratio = $52,000/$50,000 = 1.04

This result is positive. The decision rule for cost-benefit analysis is that if a positive ratio is achieved, then spending money on a project is advisable. But the Heads Up agency is comparing two alternatives. Cost-benefit analysis of the other alternative would allow the agency to compare the alternatives for a higher cost-benefit ratio. Table 8.2 shows the result for alternative *B*.

The agency went through the same type of analysis as for the first prod-

COSTS	AMOUNT	BENEFITS	AMOUNT
Five year student fee	$26,000	Improved test scores	$16,000
Teacher training	4,500	Child self-esteem	14,000
Annual license	4,000	Parent satisfaction	8,000
IT staff training	6,000	Increased financial support from state for improved performance	14,000
Administrative costs	10,000	—	
Total	$50,500	Total	$52,000

Table 8.2: Heads Up Agency Language Program – Alternative B

uct and determined the cost-benefit ratio for the second product to be 1.03. Based on the decision rule, both alternatives are candidates for purchase. Assuming that all bias for one alternative or the other has been controlled for and all other things being equal, the agency would make a better decision to select alternative *A* instead of alternative *B*.

Cost-Effectiveness Analysis

Decision making can be based on the old maxim of getting the best bang for the buck. Cost-effectiveness analysis attempts to accomplish this by calculating a ratio of cost to outcome and comparing that one to one or more alternatives. The alternative with the highest cost-effectiveness ratio would have an edge over the other. It is generally believed that the military services were the inventors and strongest users of cost-effectiveness analysis—measuring the ratio of costs for a weapons system against either kills, lives saved, or other relevant measure. Other sectors also use it to help make purchasing decisions as well, especially health care providers when considering medical treatments. When two or more treatments are being considered, applying cost-effectiveness analysis makes comparisons on the basis of determining how effectively an alternative produces an outcome. Unlike cost-benefit analysis, cost-effectiveness analysis is a straightforward quantitative calculation. It reduces the comparison of alternatives to a comparison of costs per unit.

Using the Heads Up agency example, look at the tables just presented. Note that the benefits column looks at improvements in reading skills as a factor in arriving at a decision. We can use that here to demonstrate cost-effectiveness analysis. Assume that the alternatives A and B have track records for an average increase in language skills for students using them in other local Heads Up agencies. The average increase in language skills per student using alternative A is 4 percentage points above the expected increase over a six-month period and using alternative B is five percentage points above the expected increase over the same time period. The cost-effectiveness formula follows:

Cost-effectiveness ratio = Cost per student/average improvement in language skills

The cost per student is determined by calculating the total cost by the number of students served. The estimate for the number of students served over a six-month period is 100. The cost per student is calculated by dividing the total program costs by the number of students served and inserted in the equations here.

Alternative A =

Per student cost = Total cost divided by students served

= 50,000/500 = $100

Cost-effectiveness ratio = $100/4 = $25.00

Alternative B =

$50,500/500 = $101

$101/5 = $20.20

So even though the total cost of implementing alternative B is somewhat greater than alternative A, the incremental increase in reading skills is larger for B than for A. This results in a lower incremental cost for alternative B. The cost-effectiveness analysis decision rule is that the lower the incremental cost or cost per unit, the better the cost-effectiveness. Thus, alternative B would be selected instead alternative A.

Exhibit 8.1 summarizes an adaptation of Gurowitz' four buying criteria.[2] NPOs should consider functionality of an object of purchase before finally deciding to purchase it. NPOs should also consider reliability, convenience, and cost as discussed here.

Functionality refers to the all-important concern about the usefulness of the purchased object. Does the product under consideration assist the agency in carrying out its mission? Do affected staff persons find it useful? Does it

One view of buying decisions is that they are based on four elements.

Functionality

Relevance – to program mission

Applicability – to the NPO's organizational needs

Features – of the object of purchase that differentiate it

Fit – with programs and personnel preferences

Reliability

Integrity – of the product

Trust – in the seller

Sustainability – through the life of its need

Convenience

Proximity – location to the NPO

Ease of use – compared to rival products

Accessibility – at the appropriate time

Cost

Economies of scale – cost does not increase with increase in use

Cost of use and maintenance

Exhibit 8.1: Elements of Buying Decisions

have all the features desired by its primary users? Does it have too many features that will never be used? Reliability is an important quality. This is an important research issue that requires a mini-audit process. Obviously, the first thing to investigate is whether the object will fail in its purpose. Does it do what it is supposed to do consistently and on demand? Does it break down too often? Who owns the product, and do they endorse it? Also important is the seller of the product or service. What is the seller's reputation, especially with regard to the product or service under consideration? Convenience is a relevant factor. If the amount of work involved in using a product or service is burdensome in the minds of the users, then it would be wrong to purchase it. Finally, of course, is the issue of cost, which has been discussed in great detail in the previous subsections.

Controlling Expenditures

Revenues and expenditures are very different concepts. Metaphorically, fundraisers are hunter-gatherers, and program people are traders in goods and services. At their base, they have different purposes: The fundraisers acquire money, and the program people spend it in legitimate ways. Sound cash flow management, which will be discussed later, demands that the rate of expenditures is kept consistent with the flow of revenue. While some grants are given in a lump sum, others are apportioned or allotted in monthly, quarterly, or other intervals by the funding agency or by the financial officer of the NPO itself. Such a process prevents the spending of money too quickly and provides control over those staff whose primary job is to spend money. It keeps spending in conformance with the budget and prevents the exhaustion of budgeted funds. Such a process also keeps money in reserve to cover urgent and unforeseen needs and the effects of inflation. Not having this type of control puts the most efficient and effective use of precious resources at risk.

Many NPOs charge for services rendered or goods sold at prices that have to be determined by someone or some group like an NPO board. Contracts with other entities to provide costly services are usually obtained through bidding and negotiation. The margin for reducing organizational costs can result in big cost savings. Preparing a request for bids (discussed in the next section of this chapter) or indeed responding to one forces NPOs to engage in an effective cost analysis that sometimes requires development of complex financial proposals. An NPO's chief financial officer should be responsible for the preparation of cost proposal packages as well as for conducting proposal negotiations with outside firms, consultants, and employees. Negotiating costs with clients, partners, vendors, and subcontractors helps to ensure the quality of operations and effective cooperation with the board, staff, and managers.

Someone in every NPO needs to have responsibility for overseeing the procurement process, including responses to solicitations, providing technical assistance on developing cost proposals, and working with executives to incorporate strategic planning and budgetary principles into the development of proposals. The designated procurement officer needs to review the proposals and contracts to make sure the NPO remains compliant with important regulatory requirements. Costing should occur in an appropriate context. Thus, an NPO should match the approach to costing with program needs. Such a strategic approach will ensure that the effects of costs on budgets and strategic plans will be controlled. Of course, unit costs, not just total costs, must be examined to determine cost-effectiveness. This will require due diligence in research and analysis and thorough monitoring of quality and uniformity. Carefully maintained records and files will ensure terms of the relationship with respondents or contractors and will give the NPO a basis of knowledge for future procurements. Of course, a solid review and analysis of how the program or project will be financed is vital. Negotiations with the proposer or contractor can help lower costs. Finally, someone in the NPO should be responsible for monitoring agreements for accuracy and compliance, and for negotiating changes in the contract if necessary.

PROCUREMENT: THEORY AND PRACTICE

Predictable spending is its own reward. Investors in debt (buyers of bonds and lenders) want reassurance that money lent or invested will result in a profit. Grantors want to know that the trust they put in an NPO is well placed. The way nonprofit money is spent tells the entire financial agenda of a nonprofit agency. Donors to NPOs might be well advised to examine the spending patterns of NPOs, especially the amount of money actually spent on programs. Expenditures can encourage particular types of investment and discourage others.

Competitive bidding and subsequent contracting is a widespread tool NPOs use for spending money to acquire necessary goods and services. Competitive bidding provides NPOs control over their costs.

Competitive bidding is a very common technique for spending money in NPOs. It is a form of expenditure that is designed to maintain control over legal and binding contract terms. The agency that contracts out maintains responsibility for the service being provided and ownership of any capital involved. Therefore, the agency usually oversees work conducted under the contract. Generally, contracts for goods and services are solicited through a Request for Bids or Request for Proposals, and the contractor is selected on the basis of price, responsiveness to the solicitation, and responsibility, that is, ability to do the job in an effective manner.[3]

Procurement is a catchall word designating the purchasing process. All individuals acquire goods and services. When we spend personal funds, most of us usually look for the best deal among alternatives. At other times, we are forced to shorten the length of time we engage in comparing possibilities so that we can deal with more pressing concerns, or even emergencies. We all also acquire the products and services we need based on our own experience with a product and our loyalty to a store or brand. Sellers of products assist us through advertising and marketing that creates interest and informs us of the features and benefits of their products. This all comes together, in theory, at the time of purchase. Embedded within this simplified statement of the theory are a few complexities that make procurement policies and procedures necessary.

Procurement in General

Procurement is a word that should be understood to mean *doing what it takes to acquire, implement, and manage goods and services.* Theoretically, the objectives of procurement activities in any organization are to do the following:

- Acquire goods and services and obtain the best pricing and greatest benefit for the NPO.

- Increase the value obtained for organization dollars.

- Guarantee that procurements meet professional and legal requirements.

The objectives of an NPO's procurement and contracting policies are to acquire goods and services and to carry out the use of those services in a manner that enhances the achievement of the NPO's mission.

Procurement Model

The following are the tasks of a workable procurement model:

- Plan procurements.

- Follow regulatory or policy requirements by using appropriate requests for proposal (RFP), invitations for bid, and requests for price quotation (RFQ) in order to obtain contracts with qualified vendors.

- Develop specific selection criteria to evaluate bidders.

- Apply evaluation criteria to arrive at a quality decision.

- Oversee contract to make sure the contract provisions are met.

- Monitor the process and report needed revisions in procurement procedures.

- Conduct a backward review after conclusion of a contract that includes contracts that have been terminated early for any reason.

- Maintain good vendor relationships and complete vendor lists.

The following guidelines from the National Association of Educational Buyers explain a lot about the philosophy of procuring goods and services in the private and nonprofit sectors.[4] The guidelines constitute a theory of purchasing that can be applied to all public and private organizations and are as follows:

- Give first consideration to the objectives and policies of my institution.

- Strive to obtain the maximum value for each dollar of expenditure.

- Decline personal gifts or gratuities.

- Grant all competitive suppliers equal consideration insofar as state or federal statute and institutional policy permit.

- Conduct business with potential and current suppliers in an atmosphere of good faith, devoid of intentional misrepresentation.

- Demand honesty in sales representation, whether offered through the medium of a verbal or written statement, an advertisement, or a sample of the product.

- Receive consent for original or proprietary ideas and designs before using them for competitive purchasing purposes.

- Make every reasonable effort to negotiate an equitable and mutually agreeable settlement of any controversy with a supplier; and/or be willing to submit any major controversies to arbitration or other third-party review, insofar as the established policies of my institution permit.

- Cooperate with trade, industrial and professional associations, and with governmental and private agencies for the purposes of promoting and developing sound business methods.

- Foster fair, ethical and legal trade practices.[5]

Improved understanding of purchasing rules and responsibilities will help avoid the following:

- Economic and programmatic failure, and other consequences of bad or inappropriate purchasing decisions

- Loss of institutional authority, loss of funds, poor relations with the business community

- Loss of public trust and confidence in our purchasing decisions

- Individuals being held liable for improper or incorrect actions.[6]

Competitive Bidding

An NPO's procurement policies should include various procedures for acquiring goods and services, including those procedures using both competitive and noncompetitive arrangements, and group procurement. A highly honored method of purchasing goods and services in most NPOs is competitive bidding. Basically, this means that an entity will obtain more than one price or proposal for providing a good or service and then choose the one that best meets the entity's needs. In reality, it is a lot more complex and involved. It is generally believed that competitive bidding is the best way of obtaining the lowest price for needed goods and services. Competitive bidding is believed to be open and fair and to eliminate the perception of inappropriate deals or favoritism in purchasing. The economy has a great stake in this system's being fair, because competitive bidding theoretically gives each bidder an equal chance of being selected to provide a good or service.

Competitive bidding can be good for one-time, short-term purchases. However, complex contracts can affect the bid selection process.[7] If a contract bid is chosen solely for the lowest price, selection is simple. When multiple factors such as price, quality, and possible subsequent contracts for related products or services are considered, contracts become more complex.

When bidders decide not to participate in the competition, problems can arise from one bidder dominating the market and stifling entrepreneurship.[8]

Noncompetitive Procurements

Competitive bidding should almost be the default procedure for an NPO. When it is not appropriate as part of their procurement policies, some NPOs acquire goods and services through noncompetitive procurement, that is, private and individual negotiation. Economists have studied the reasons some organizations choose to use private negotiation instead of competitive bidding. Reasons include the costs associated with setting up a bidding contest, dealing with multiple bidders, and not wanting to—as K. M. Johnstone et al. explain—"disclose potentially negative private information to outside parties."[9] Negotiating relies on interpersonal factors and relationships that allow parties to reach an agreement together. The majority of negotiation efforts should occur in prenegotiation planning. This will increase the opportunities for a successful and fair outcome.[10] In general, the negotiation process should be approached as a joint and collaborative problem-solving endeavor. It is inappropriate to ask, "Who is winning?" Long-term success is based on achieving outcomes mutually beneficial to both parties. But the process is subject to bias and favoritism.

Group Purchasing

Group purchasing arrangements can save money for nonprofit organizations. What is group purchasing? It's simply strength in numbers. Organizations can join together with other organizations and get a better price from a vendor and negotiate discounts on goods and services. Group purchasing is not a new concept. Hospitals have benefited from group purchasing arrangements for many years. It is almost always necessary to belong to an association or group in order to take advantage of these kinds of discounts. Cities often enter into group purchasing arrangements for the purpose of saving money. Most states offer subdivisions (counties, states, special districts) the opportunity to purchase goods from the state vendor list. These lists are populated by vendors approved by the state purchasing office because they have met the states' terms for price, suitability, and availability of products and services. Likewise, states often associate with nonprofits for the purpose of purchasing arrangements. An example can be found at www.ga.wa.gov/pca/forms/nonprofit.doc.

SUMMARY

Spending money is the easiest activity in the world. Spending wisely is a great challenge. This chapter demonstrated this challenge through its emphasis on expenditure management. The chapter began with a discussion of the effect of time on money available for spending. This is an important factor for NPOs that engage in strategic planning. Erosion of the value of money must be a part of the strategic planning process. The chapter put great emphasis on the mechanics of making wise spending decisions and the criteria for doing so. Specific techniques like cost-benefit and cost-effectiveness analysis were demonstrated in some detail. The chapter closed with a discussion about the procurement process. It discussed the advantages of competitive and noncompetitive bidding and when each is appropriate for NPOs. Clearly, spending is one of the critical parts of performance management conducted by NPOs.

DISCUSSION QUESTIONS

1. Pick one of the external factors discussed in the section "Effects of Local, Regional, National, and World Changes." Select one of the listed changes that could have an impact on spending decisions. Develop a strategy that an NPO you are familiar with can implement to mitigate the impact. Compare and contrast the strategy you use with those of other students in the class. What are the lessons learned from external events?

2. Some experts argue that an agency would be better served if it were allowed to engage in purchasing processes that bypass competitive bidding. The argument is that negotiations with a firm supplying a good or service can result in a better price than can be obtained through competitive bidding. So what? Why should or why should an agency not engage in competitive bidding? Explain your position.

EXERCISE: COST-BENEFIT AND COST-EFFECTIVENESS ANALYSIS

In doing the following exercise, please refer to the discussion in this chapter on cost-benefit and cost-effectiveness analysis. Cost-benefit analysis is the means of evaluating all costs on a dollar basis, even those costs that do not have a dollar value attached to them. After all other calculations have been made, the analysis needs to conclude with calculating the ratio between costs and benefits. The result will result in an aid to decision makers. Consider the following example from the fictitious Community Medical Center.

The price of a new machine is $795,000.

Staff training costs over three years, when considering direct costs and loss of productive hours while in training, will be $70,000.

The actual operating costs of the machine in the three-year period will be $35,000.

On the benefit side, there will be an increase in staff productivity. It was calculated on the average hourly rate of the ten affected staff ($55) and the number of hours freed over the three year period (1,150).

Patient wait time will be reduced by 1,000 normal workday hours. The average hourly rate of patients is estimated at $25 per hour.

As a community hospital with an investment in every aspect of the community's well-being, life expectancy is considered in the cost calculation. The medical center's board has dictated that the value of increased life expectancy should be included as a benefit to the medical center. The lives of 50 patients are expected to be extended by an average of three years. The average annual wage of a patient (including all men, women, and children) is estimated to be $17,157. This factor assumes those working during the treatment will continue to work until their death.

Calculate the cost-benefit ratio. Is it positive or negative? If positive, would you go ahead and replace the old machine? Or would you do a cost-effectiveness analysis? Referring again to the earlier section dealing with cost-effectiveness, take the following data and calculate a cost-effectiveness outcome:

Old Machine: Annual operations and maintenance costs = $33,500; annual training costs = $2,500; number of patients treatable per year = 490.

New Machine: Annual operations and maintenance costs = $35,003; annual training costs = $2,500; number of patients treated per year = 500.

Based on this information, what would you advise decision makers regarding the old and the new machines? Justify your recommendation.

INNOVATION: SUPPLY CHAIN MANAGEMENT

Two natural disasters, Hurricane Katrina in 2005 and the tsunami in Thailand in 2006, were so huge they required effective methods of getting the right supplies to the people who needed them.[11] The answer was the use of *supply chains*. A supply chain is a network of vendors and "users"—those involved in the relief efforts—needed to provide the resources and materials that go into creating a product or service in a timely way. Supply chain management is vitally important to many organizations. Managing a supply chain means to plan, implement, and supervise the processes and people in the chain from its origin to the user. The chain metaphor is obvious.

Supply chains are popular in the business sector but not so much in the nonprofit sector except for hospitals, medical centers, and the large charities that deal with disasters. The goal of supply chains is reliability of availability.[12] The greatest advantage is that supplies are available when needed. The major disadvantage is that it takes a considerable effort to establish and maintain the supply chain. When managed correctly, a supply chain will create a well-stocked inventory. In the case of disasters, emergency relief agencies will be able track supplies. Relief workers will know what is available at supply centers in order to keep an adequate amount on hand, what has been dispatched, and when it will arrive where it is needed. The key word is control. There will be no scrambling around looking for potential suppliers.

There are four major decision areas in supply chain management:

- Location: Acquiring suppliers in strategic places for responding to a supply need

- Production: Closeness of the supplier

- Inventory

- Transportation[13]

NOTES

1   R. Brent, "Country Estimates of Social Discount Rates Based on Changes in Life Expectancies," *Kyklos* 46 (1993): 399.

2   Edward M. Gurowitz, Ph.D., "Positioning Products and Services Accurately," *The CEO Refresher,* 2001. Online at http://www.gurowitzcom/articles/TheCEORe.pdf (accessed August 14, 2008).

3   Charles M. Gray, "Pricing Issues for the Nonprofit Manager," *Nonprofit Times* (April 2001).

4   Mike Chielewski, "Ethical Procurement," *Educational Procurement Journal,* National Association of Educational Procurement. Online at http://www.naepnet.org (accessed May 20, 2008).

5   Ibid.

6   Ibid.

7   V. P. Goldberg, "Competitive Bidding and the Production of Pre-Contract Information," *Bell Journal of Economics* 8 (1977): 250–62.

8   D. A. Hensher and M. E. Beesley, "Contracts, Competitive Bidding and Market Forces: Recent Experience in the Supply of Local Bus Services," *Australian Economic Papers* 28 (1989): 244.

9   K. M. Johnstone, J. C. Bedard, and M. L. Ettredge, "The Effect of Competitive Bidding on Engagement Planning and Pricing," *Contemporary Accounting Research* 21 (2004): 47.

10   H. Farrell and A. Héritier, "Formal and Informal Institutions under Codecision: Continuous Constitution Building in Europe," Governance (2003): 601–623.

11   Tash Shifrin, "Charity Uses Supply Chain Management Tool to Help Deliver Aid to Katrina Victims," *Computer Weekly* (Sep. 2005) and "Katrina and the Tsunami in Thailand, New Humanitarian Logistics Qualification," *Logistics & Transport Focus* 8 (2006): 62–66.

12   Ganeshan Ram and T. P. Harrison, in Carter McNamara, *Procurement (Purchasing) Practices in Small Organizations (For-Profit and Nonprofit),* 2007. Online at http://www.managementhelp.org (accessed April 25, 2008).

13   Ibid.

CHAPTER 9
Cash and Investment Management

This chapter talks about the topics of cash and investment management. Topics under cash management include cash flow budgets, cash management through a budget year, cash reserve management, petty cash, and cash strategies. On the investment side, a comparison and discussion of short- and long-term investments provides the reader with an understanding of the usefulness of these financial instruments in managing an organization's cash. The discussion includes the limits of investing strategies set by law and by agency policies for the protection of donors and stakeholders.

TOPICS
- Cash Is King
- Cash Payment Strategies
- Technology Strategies: Wire Transfers and Online Banking
- Managing Cash Needs
- Investment Management
- Summary
- Discussion Questions
- Exercise

CASH IS KING

We do not yet live in a cashless economy. This chapter discusses what NPOs should be doing with their cash to maximize their financial power for the good of agency missions. NPOs generally do not invest in the stock market or other types of risky financial markets. They do, however, put money into bond markets and more secure investments. They also invest in bank certificates of deposit and savings accounts. All these strategies have the goal of stretching the value of each dollar by making interest earned on investments an additional funding source.

CASH PAYMENT STRATEGIES

The infamous political machine, Tammany Hall of New York City, was one of the best-known and most corrupt nineteenth-century political machines in the United States. One of its cash management practices was to simply not pay selected vendors who did work for the city. Another was to force vendors to accept much less repayment than they were owed. The vendors would eventually write off the money the machine owed them, or they would accept a reduced amount of money, such as ten cents on the dollar. They were powerless to do anything else because of the power the machine possessed. This gave Tammany Hall the ability to provide political favors to their supporters.[1] While the history presented here demonstrates unethical and illegal behavior, it also leads to a discussion of legitimate and widely used practices by organizations to meet their budgets. Of course, the practices are not done to the degree of the Tammany Hall political machine, but they do provide ways to get by in hard times. Among the strategies used are the following:

- Delaying payments on bills
- Making partial payments
- Centralizing payments
- Creating zero balance accounts

Clearly, some of these cash management strategies in tough financial times can affect vendors and clients. For example, delaying payment on bills that have come due and making partial payments can be practiced by organizations, but such practices may border on the unethical and can certainly endanger relationships and reputations. There is little to nothing that a vendor or contractor can do about it. It is certainly inconvenient—at best—when the vendors have to pay their own bills with their own resources, usually having to pass the ill treatment on down the line to their own creditors.

Delaying payments might occur through the use of organization credit cards. If this is the practice, NPOs should maintain zero balances on credit cards and make all payments within 30 days, the amount of time that most payables come due. The strategy of delaying a payment is not necessarily to miss a payment deadline but to hold on to the money until the last possible moment. On the other hand, if the vendor offers a cash discount of ten percent, that offer forces the NPO to determine if the savings from the discount are greater than the money earned by holding it to the last moment. If the discount and the interest earned are equal, the NPO should favor making the payment early.

Taking advantage of cash discounts is a crucial step that all prudent organizations should undertake. By determining the most cost-effective time to pay a vendor when they offer time-related discounts and charge additional fees for late payments, organizations can increase earned interest and maintain good relationships with their vendors.

If an NPO has relationships with subcontractors on a project involving a government or foundation grant, it should tie payments to two factors: services rendered and grant reimbursement. Thus, the NPO with fiscal responsibilities should not pre-pay its subcontractors. It should include in all agreements a clause that describes the payment method.

A line of credit is one way to ease cash flow problems. This may mean that the NPO will have to make interest payments, and it may be charged to the line of credit as needed to meet monthly budgets. Banks often compete on the basis of the interest they charge for line-of-credit borrowing.

A non-centralized payment system can often take months to turn around payments. Centralizing payments reduces confusion and problems with vendor payments. Centralizing the accounts payable function is an effective way of managing cash flow. If staff and vendors take excessive time to turn in their timesheets, expense reimbursement requests, and invoices, payables grow. It can take months to turn around the payments. Centralizing accounts receivable and having staff people actively seeking out payment documents of staff members and the vendors to ensure proper routing of and payment is definitely hard work, but the results of improved cash management are well worth the effort.

A practice that is used in some organizations is the zero balance accounts or ZBAs. The organization sets up one account, a "home" account with its bank. The bank maintains the cash balances; other accounts are utilized for payroll and general disbursements. When checks are cleared from the various accounts, money is credited from the main account to "zero out" the various accounts.

A few other ideas include the following:

- Pay as many creditors and service providers as possible, like insurance companies, monthly instead of an advance lump-sum payment for the full year.

- Shift payroll from hard-copy paper checks to direct deposit into the bank accounts. Not having hard copies reduces the costs of payroll.

Applying the strategies discussed in this section for delaying payments is not necessarily a good idea. Most vendors and contractors do not like delaying tactics. Some may decide not to do business with an NPO that regularly delays payments. In that scenario, a local retail establishment may refuse to accept an NPO's purchase orders and demand cash upon delivery of a good or service. Likewise, delaying payments to employees is one form of cash flow management that should be avoided at all costs. Delayed payroll is known to result in reduced morale, reduced productivity, and increased expenses for specific projects. It might also result in the loss of key workers.

TECHNOLOGY STRATEGIES: WIRE TRANSFERS AND ONLINE BANKING

People and organizations often pay their bills by knowing when the bill will arrive and holding on to their money as long as possible in order to capitalize on the interest that accrues in their bank or credit union. Another delaying tactic that was used by many organizations in the past was to conveniently forget to sign the check for payment to a vendor. The payee would then write a polite letter to the payer and return the check looking for a signature. Today, however, banks and other payees have become wise to these tactics. The use of electronic wire transfers (EWTs) of funds can help an organization receive funds quicker. Internet banking has taken payment processing toward the threshold of the immediate. Electronic wire transfers and Internet banking have reduced the turnaround for reimbursements to 2 to 10 days or less for electronic and Internet claims from the 20 to 45 days required for paper claims. With the introduction of electronic banking, banks began living in the age of technology. If an organization sets up accounts to pay as well as receive funds, it will save on paper and postage and reduce the chance of mistakes in payments. In addition, regularly scheduled payments can be automatically processed using EWT that offer instant confirmations.

With the passage by Congress and implementation of the Check Clearing for the 21st Century Act (Check 21) in 2004, banks are beginning to better leverage technology in order to reduce the delay between debt incurred and cash outlay. Essentially, the Check 21 Act makes possible a reduction in the time between issuing a check and cashing it by creating a new document called a substitute check. This substitute check is an electronic check and carries the same legal weight of a paper check. Check 21 makes check *kiting* (passing bad checks) far less risky for the payee.[2] The law does not require the use of electronic checks, however, and allows people and businesses to continue to use paper checks.[3]

Use of the Internet allows consumers and organizations to more efficiently manage when they receive money and pay bills. Thus, it is a potential new delaying tactic for NPOs that allows them to reduce operations costs. It lets them go down to the wire without paying late fees.

MANAGING CASH NEEDS

If an NPO is to do well, cash should flow into and out of an organization consistently and reliably. Or at least it must seem to do so because of the actions taken by NPO financial leaders. That is what this chapter is about—

making sure that there is enough money to consistently and reliably meet the budget each month. For many NPOs, the cash flow experience seems like flood water events followed by periods of severe drought. Cash in an NPO is usually scarce. Therefore, the processes used to manage these funds needs to be comprehensive, efficient, and effective, and it is extremely important to identify and plan for how the money will be spent. Without cash on hand, NPOs must beg, steal, or borrow just like any other entity.

The best way to avoid begging, stealing, and borrowing is to engage in what is called cash flow management. Cash flow management, according to the Alliance for Nonprofit Management, "refers to the need to have cash come in—flow in—at the right times so that it is available to flow out as needed."[4] In the worst case scenario of the practice of poor or no cash management, an NPO will have more expenses than revenues. Having good cash management prevents the trouble this scenario causes. Cash management is knowing when and how much money is coming in and going out and, therefore, knowing that there will always be cash available. It includes the need to know when cash is coming in, and therefore when and how fast goods and services can be purchased to meet operational needs. Someone in every NPO needs to smooth the inflows and outflows of the organization's cash. Common sense and knowledge of cash flow management techniques—planning, monitoring, and controlling—will help avoid disaster.

Cash Flow Budgets

A cash flow budget can help managers stay on top of money needed to meet an NPO's needs within a given period. The first aim of cash management is to reduce costs at the front end through the purchasing function. The second aim is to stretch the use of available dollars by what is done with the cash on hand. The working hypothesis is that close attention to the use of cash will increase purchasing power. In other words, NPOs should get as much money as they can, spend it as slowly as possible, and accomplish as much as possible while it is still around.

The purpose of a cash flow budget is to achieve effective cash management. Effective cash management means determining the timing and magnitude of projected cash needs as well as any projected cash surpluses. In other words, knowing the flow of cash during a budget period is vital information.

The form shown in Exhibit 9.1 is a tool for maintaining a cash flow budget. In the revenue portion, the form begins at the beginning—cash on hand at the beginning of the first month of the budget year (in the cell in the upper left-hand corner of the form). To this beginning balance is added grant and other anticipated revenues: receivables, donations, fundraising, and so on. In the expenditure portion of the form, all monthly expenditures are projected. The difference between one month's revenue and expenditures is the basis for smoothing out expenditures and revenues. Thus, projections should be made for the entire month. Each month, the cash flow budget for the entire budget

REVENUE	Jan	Feb	Mar	Apr	May	Jun	July	Aug	Sep	Oct	Nov	Dec
Beginning Cash Balance												
Grant Payments												
Receivables												
Donations												
Fundraising												
TOTAL (estimated)												
EXPENDITURES												
Payroll												
Operating Expenses												
Insurance												
Other												
TOTAL (estimated)												
Estimated Cash												
Cash Required												
Surplus/shortage												

Exhibit 9.1: Monthly Cash Flow Budget Format

year should be revised to reflect changes and improved knowledge of cash flow in the coming months. If it does nothing else, a cash flow budget treated in the way just described should at least motivate an NPO to do two things. First, it should stimulate an effort to find ways to increase efficiency and effectiveness of money usage. Second, it should feed back into the NPO's strategic planning process by giving it a view of the desired cash position.

Case Analysis: A Lesson on the Need for a Monthly Cash Flow Budget

After returning from vacation, the executive director of a fictitious NPO found the agency's budget in disarray. The monthly financial report showed a $60,000 shortfall. The director realized that the agency's cash management policies were deficient. The agency's fiscal year was concurrent with the calendar year. Each December, the director would make an educated estimate of monthly revenues and expenses for the next fiscal year. Starting in January, he would rely on monthly reports from his outsourced accountant on the agency's monthly cash position. That monthly report was submitted to the director 15 days after each month ended. The director always examined this report as well as the monthly bank statement, which was received on the 10th of each month. Each month, the director's assistant assembled all the invoices and bills the agency received along with copies of checks and financial transfers from granting agencies and sent them to the accountant so a monthly report could be prepared. The director did not examine the transmittal slips that summarized the bills and invoices.

When the director discovered the shortage of funds, he immediately began looking for a reason. In the previous month, there had been a $20,000 shortage, and the director felt compelled to use reserves to cover the deficit. He then reconciled the bank statement and found it showing a $26,000 deficit in its end-of-the-month report. He immediately started checking all the numbers he could. He examined the originals of bills, previous months' reports, his monthly revenues and expenditures estimates, and the annual budget. He fearfully asked how this could this have happened. Was the assistant embezzling? Was the accountant incompetent? Was the situation as bad as it looked? No, no, and no. Several events and a misunderstanding had created the situation. All of the following events had been proper and were reported to the accountant in a timely fashion:

- The director had made large lump-sum payments to subcontractors in advance of their contracts.

- A subsidiary agency in the next county postponed its fundraising activity, pushing back revenue from the event by four months.

- A break-in and theft of computers, routers, and printers required the agency to pay a large deductible, and the replacement costs were high for the new machines and software.

- The accountant's report allocated equal portions of the revenues received over 12 months rather than when revenue was received and in what amounts.

- It did the same with lump-sum payments like the annual professional liabilities insurance.

The result of these events was that although there was an actual deficit, it was not as bad as it appeared. The problems were created by not fully understanding the relationship between the monthly accountant's report and the bank statement, and by not recognizing when payments and revenues were actually received. A monthly cash flow budget would have reflected the irregularity of income and expenditures and would have made true adjustments to spending. Instead, the director relied on the accountant's report, which amortized income and payments over a 12-month period and came in fifteen days after the end of the month. The director never got a true reading of his agency's cash position because he relied on the accountant's report over the cash flow budget. He did not understand that by failing to anticipate actual revenue streams in a cash flow budget, he failed to recognize the need for adjustments.

Planning Cash Flow

It is not unusual for an organization to have experienced poor financial and fiscal performance due to inadequate cash management that led to cash flow problems. Bad control, management, and planning can put an organization at the point of laying off workers, losing funding, and experiencing difficulties in meeting mission goals. Uncontrolled spending, other bad decision making, and not balancing expenditures properly can result in negative effects on any organization. Budgets and cash flow projections should be the basis of cash flow management. The agency budget and cash projections can help decision makers determine what strategies to implement to control cash flow. Financial manager should create and maintain a cash flow budget in order to know what cash is coming in and going out, because mapping out budgets and costly projects helps alleviate cash flow problems.

As a tool for organizations, the modern importance of cash management goes back to the runaway inflation rates of the 1970s. However, even low inflation does not argue against an effective cash management policy. Planning cash flow and cash flow budgets means projecting and scheduling revenues and expenditures in a systematic way. A cash flow budget or plan should also include the anticipation of contingencies to the extent possible. Projections of these elements translate into revenues, expenditures, and investments for a particular budget period. Both historical and new knowledge about when an NPO's funds are received into an NPO and subsequently disbursed is the place to begin the planning process. The budgeted funds then can be broken down into heavy and light periods, with the ultimate goal being to even out available cash over the course of the budget period. For each portion of the budget period, the NPO is interested in (month, quarter), available cash and cash needs can be planned. This concept is called a cash flow budget, which theoretically can smooth out cash throughout the year. The Alliance for Nonprofit Management explains that "a cash flow budget or projection should not be confused with a financial statement called *Statement of Cash Flows* which describes changes in cash from year-to-year."[5]

Revenues and expenditures move cash in opposite directions. Put another way, staff members who raise funds have very different goals and motives than program staff members who spend the funds, and the NPO must resolve these competing functions. The key to a successful relationship between revenues and expenditures is careful planning and realistic projections. This is where a good financial analyst is worth his or her weight in gold. Cash management is the key.

An NPO must look at historical revenue and expenditure patterns as one of the bases for cash flow projections for future budget periods. Next, anticipated new program funding, new spending, or loss of revenues must be added to the mix. These changes might include when your programs are offered, what programs are offered, new funding sources or expiration of previous funding, increases or reductions in interest rates, and so on. While this new cash flow projection will largely correspond to your budget, some cash flow may come in from receivables from the prior year, cash may go out for payments made for last year's bills, and some income and expenses for the current year will be delayed until next year and would therefore not be included in the current year's cash flow budget.[6]

Cash Shortages

Sometimes incoming cash does not even out over the course of the entire budget period. When bills need to be paid and there is not enough cash on hand, NPOs can consider some creative means of making payments, although those creative methods may not be the most comfortable to those in an organization. The first creative method is to borrow or create a line of credit from a bank or other source. Obviously, this is a decision of last resort because it costs money. Borrowing should be something the NPO can do comfortably. Another possible tactic to turn to is to speed up collection of receivables. Like borrowing money, collection activities are potentially uncomfortable, but if payments to the NPO are past due and affecting the cash flow, collection activities must be considered. Another option is changing a scheduled fundraiser or adding a fundraising event. This is dictated by the old nuance *if possible*. There could be a number of obstacles to doing this, not the least of which may be a staff revolt against additional work. Lowering payments through financing or leasing of equipment is also a reasonable means of meeting a shortage.

The next two tactics—selling off assets and cashing out investments—are probably the most difficult of all. The former is most dangerous because it may result in weakening the NPO's capacity to operate efficiently. Disposing of assets should be done without crippling the ability of an NPO to meet mission obligations and goals. The latter—the liquidation of investments—may be built in to the cash flow budget as will be discussed later.

Finally, delaying payments to vendors may make a finance officer squeamish, but it also might get an NPO through slack times. NPOs are sometimes reluctant to delay payments because they are usually part of a community where public trust and reputation have great meaning. However, vendors may sometimes be understanding and cooperative and may be willing to negotiate an agreeable payment plan, especially if the alternative is no payment at all or a loss of business with the NPO.

Cash Surplus

At first glance, a cash surplus seems like a gift to be celebrated. On the other hand, it might be pointing to the fact that poor planning has occurred. Donors might react to a cash surplus by withholding their contributions on the basis that the NPO has more money than it needs. That is the dark side. The bright side is that the lucky NPO may be in a position to use the surplus to the benefit of the NPO itself or of its clients. The reader can probably imagine several legitimate uses of a cash surplus. A cash surplus can be used to purchase useful supplies that will be used up in the budget year and to make short-term gains from legitimate investments.

There are two primary reasons to invest the revenue of NPOs in financial markets. One is for the long term, that is, to make money with one's assets and increase the wealth in a fund. Pension plans do that in order to make money to meet retirees' needs. The other is operational and has to do with the fiduciary responsibility of organizations to use cash efficiently and effectively. In other words, it is the task of engaging in cash management.

Having just the appropriate amount of cash on hand to ensure liquidity without incurring late charges and earning returns on idle cash is the essence of cash management. Many nonprofits carry cash balances in excess of those necessary for immediate transactions. There is a cost involved in doing this. Exhibit 9.2 gives an example of a cash flow budget.

FISCAL ITEM	JAN	FEB	MAR	APR	MAY	JUN
Budgeted revenues (all sources)	35,000	30,000	33,000	26,000	32,000	30,000
Budgeted disbursements	30,000	31,000	36,000	28,000	35,000	29,000
Receipts less disbursements	5,000	(1,000)	(3,000)	(2,000)	(3,000)	1,000
Cash at beginning of month	1,000	6,000	5,000	2,000	0	(3,000)
Cumulative cash position (end of month)	6,000	5,000	2,000	0	(3,000)	(1,000)

Exhibit 9.2: Cash Flow Budget Example

As Exhibit 9.2 shows, the organization runs deficits in the first three months of the year. It did not plan for this shortage of revenue and will have to do something to meet payroll.

Projecting cash flow gives NPOs the obligation and opportunity to invest wisely. An organization that does not plan for using cash management is courting disaster. It will be hard to recover from not meeting payroll because someone forgot to plan for those periods of least revenue. To summarize the earlier discussion, one way to make up for periods when no money is coming in is to put money aside prior to the anticipated no revenue period. Borrowing from the bank is another option. Another is to sell short-term investments. A fourth is to delay payments to vendors and creditors. Unfortunately, these methods all come with costs. Preparing and implementing a cash flow budget helps avoid such costs. An organization in the nonprofit sector using donated funds to pay those costs is at risk of not meeting its fiduciary responsibility. A more sensible strategy is to invest surplus cash and make money doing so. Proper planning and good management can, and usually do, create a positive cash position.

The Inventory Cash Management Model

Cash management often reflects the challenge of maintaining a balance between the opportunity cost of having cash on hand (inventory of cash) and the real cost of buying and selling securities such as stocks, notes, and bonds. To explain how this works, assume that an organization's holdings comprise cash and liquid securities that can be sold in a secondary securities market, that is, cash and stocks and bonds. One theory of cash management is the *inventory model*, which can determine the amount of ready cash needed within a certain time in order to keep that amount on hand while leaving surplus cash in short-term securities. The strategy for an NPO under this model is to put all cash, *C*, in marketable securities *(M)* except for *X* dollars with which to begin the year. *X* is spent as needed. So when *X* reaches zero, sell *X* dollars of securities *(M-X)*. The model is shown in Figure 9.1.

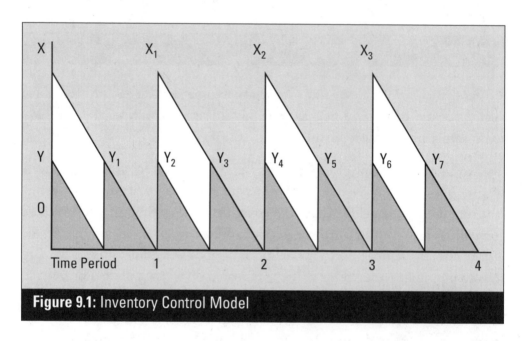

Figure 9.1: Inventory Control Model

For example, in Figure 9.1, *X* is the beginning of the year, and the finance officer determines that expenditures in a given period will average $200,000. That much cash will be on hand for spending at the beginning of the period giving the NPO the basis for managing its cost to the end of the period. All reserve funds that the organization possesses will be invested in short-term securities. The NPO keeps the reserves invested until the end of the first period and then will sell $200,000 of the invested money. Look at point *X* on the vertical axis in the graph in Figure 9.1. That point represents $200,000 that is not invested at the beginning of the year. Follow the red line from the vertical axis to the horizontal axis at point *1*, the end of the first period. At that point, all of the allocated money will have been spent. Then, enough liquid securities will be sold to replenish the $200,000 for the second time period. There are three such transactions per year at points X_1, X_2, and X_3.

Calculating the Effective Use of Cash Under the Inventory Model

The inventory model is complicated by the fact that cashing in short-term securities has an associated transaction cost *(TC)*. A certificate of deposit generally results in a penalty for early withdrawal. That cost should be included in the effectiveness calculation of the inventory model. The way to do this requires a formula that begins by calculating the average cash balance during each time period. So the average cash balance during period one is calculated as follows:

X/2

Thus,

$200,000/2 = $100,000.

The opportunity cost is calculated as X/2 times *i* (the average cash holdings times the rate earned on marketable securities). Perfect effectiveness is reached when the earnings on short-term investments minus the cost of transactions are equal to zero at the end of the period. If equal to zero, then the cost of the transactions has efficiently and completely offset the amount that could have been made if the money had been left in the NPO's investments. This measurement of the effectiveness of the cash management is then determined by the following formula:

X/2(i) – TC

Thus, assuming an opportunity cost of five percent:

(200,000/2) (.05) = $5,000

Transaction costs should be no more than this amount.

If six percent:

(200,000/2) (.06) = $6,000

If TC minus interest earned is greater than zero, then not enough has been invested in liquid securities. If the amount is less than zero, then too much has been invested.

Note that points Y1 through Y7 represent a different strategy. In that case, the organization would cash in short-term investments at intervals that are closer together.

Control Theory and Cash Management

If an NPO's need for cash is volatile, it helps to have control limits that trigger cashing in or investing money. The Control Theory is shown in Figure 9.2. If an NPO's cash situation reaches its upper limit, that is, if it has a surplus of cash, the organization may need to buy securities in order to reduce its opportunity costs. If the NPO is approaching its lower limit of cash needed, that is, if cash on hand is too low, it triggers the need to sell liquid securities. In Figure 9.2, the vertical axis measures the amount of cash on hand. The horizontal axis is a timeline representing a budget year. The jagged line is a curve that represents the relationship between time and cash on hand, that is, the amount of cash on hand at any given time. The curve shows how volatile that available cash is during the year. The red and blue lines are control mechanisms imposed by the NPO that trigger the sale or purchase of market securities. The blue line A measures the minimum that the cash balance should be allowed to reach, while the red line B measures the maximum that a cash balance should be allowed to reach. If cash starts toward zero, (A) dollars, marketable securities are sold and the new balance again becomes higher than A. Thus, at points 1 and 3 on the horizontal axis, the red curve breaches the control line, A, which triggers the sale of securities to increase the amount of cash available. When the curve goes above the line B, the control mechanism signals the need to buy securities to unload unneeded cash. Note that for most of the time the curve is safely distant from the lines A and B.

INVESTMENT MANAGEMENT

In discussing cash management, we brought up the need to invest surplus cash to make the best possible use of organization revenue. There are several

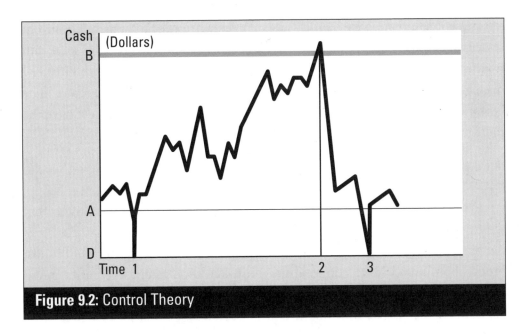

Figure 9.2: Control Theory

factors that affect investment decisions, not the least of which is politics. Some NPOs get involved in social investing. Such investing restricts investing in certain movements or causes that hurt people, the environment, or nations. The expertise for investing money or finding outside investment managers rests with the NPO's financial manager.

An important approach of investment management is to invest with capital preservation in mind. This is a concept that guides an organization to invest at a conservative pace in solid performing and reliable investments. This is an excellent strategy for an NPO. Another way to describe this strategy is that it is a way of avoiding unreasonable risks in order to prevent loss. Investing in safe municipal and blue-chip bonds, or in market instruments that offer acceptable returns, is assured with this strategy. This is a good way to serve the natural tendency of many NPO boards and executives to be risk averse. By investing in a diverse basket of low-risk financial instruments, an NPO can be reasonably assured of healthy returns. The result is that cash will be readily available when it is needed to carry out an NPO's mission. Having written policies is the best strategy for using cash to make money, because such policies are driven by the board of directors. Of course, the board needs to be advised by professional investment managers.

Consistent return is a term to describe the avoidance of unpredictable returns as a good strategy to keep cash flowing. In order to achieve consistent returns, one must look at funds that are of low volatility, which means funds with returns that have remained more or less the same over the recent past. Financial managers have to sift through the many factors that affect risk and return. The bottom line, however, is the portfolio that managers put together must have the right mix of securities to make the investment strategy successful.

Financial Markets

Primary financial markets include stock, bond, and commodity markets that sell initial public offerings (IPOs) of stock ownership certificates (stocks), initial bond sales, and other financial instruments to raise large amounts of funds. Stocks, bonds, and other commodities continue to be traded even after initial offerings of stocks and bonds in secondary markets. Investors trade in secondary markets that, led by the New York Stock Exchange (NYSE), deal in re-sales of stocks and bonds. The major purpose of primary and secondary financial markets is to facilitate the flow of funds from savings to the production sector for investment in business projects. Markets in the United States are regulated by the Securities and Exchange Commission (SEC). The SEC regulates the stock market and prevents dishonest practices by people and organizations that are tempted to manipulate markets or to take advantage of inside information.

A financial market is made up of all traders, exchanges, and transactions that occur within a particular financial market. A secondary financial market provides a network for buying and selling securities. These markets reflect the combined actions of investors in stocks. The link between a firm, investors, and the financial market is the price of securities. Most secondary market transactions do not involve the issuing company. Stocks are exchanged by outside investors with portfolios of all sizes. Secondary markets concern financial managers because most funds in the United States are invested in secondary markets.

Stock exchanges are found across the world. They organize securities issuers and traders, and set the rules for trading. Shareholders place orders for buying and selling. Floor brokers do the actual trading. Trading in a secondary market is like an auction in which the securities go to the highest bidder. Floor brokers are supervised by specialists and are assigned specific stocks to ensure the orderly exchange of ownership. Floor brokers are the people among a throng of shouting people that you see in television reports and movies. The New York Stock Exchange is the largest and most famous of the stock markets. There are 1,200 companies listed on the NYSE and 85 percent of American stocks are traded on the NYSE. The American Stock Exchange (AMEX) is the second largest. Ironically, the NYSE is legally a nonprofit organization under the New York law that regulates nonprofits.[7]

There are other types of financial markets that trade in bonds and commodities. Capital bond markets trade financial securities called bonds that are a form of debt acquired by investors for long periods. Corporations, governments, and many NPOs issue bonds in the capital market. The purpose of selling these instruments is to acquire capital for capital expansion. There is a secondary market for capital bonds. Money markets trade short-term debt instruments such as notes, bills, and commercial paper. Secondary commodities markets trade ownership certificates in agricultural and industrial products. Each of the financial instruments identified earlier involve different types of risk to the investors. These risks are discussed now.

Investment Risk

Risk means the potential for losing the money that is put into a financial investment. In general, investment opportunities offer higher returns than savings accounts but also involve higher risks. While investors do generally expect a return on investments, they should always realize that every stock and every bond has a risk. As a general rule, stocks and bonds that offer higher potential returns also come up with higher probabilities of total loss.

The risk for the lender (bond holder) of a bond is that he or she will receive less than the full value of the principal or less than the amount of return anticipated. Some debt has zero risk. The difference between interest on zero risk and other loans is called the risk premium. With bonds, the risk to investors comes from several sources: default by the issuer or early buyback by the issuer if interest in the marketplace is less than expected. This information is used to calculate the nominal interest rate on bonds.

Default risk (DR) includes both principal and periodic interest payments. It occurs when economic conditions for the issuer deteriorate. Risky bonds include a default risk premium in the interest rate paid on the bond. If investors perceive that risk is too great, the bonds will not be sold. Short-term borrowing is generally less risky than longer-term securities because risk is reduced in the short term.

Liquidity risk (LR) comes up when buyers are afraid that they will not be able to convert bonds to cash, or that the conversion will be slow. Bonds issued by small firms are generally difficult to market because they are not very well known. This situation will lead issuers to lower the cost on their bonds. This is liquidity risk. The liquidity risk premium is paid to compensate for the difficulty selling bonds.

Maturity risk (MR) results from the length of time required to pay back a security's principal. The longer the time to maturity for a security, the more risk there is. Because interest rates fluctuate, there is more risk for longer-term securities. This causes investors to want a discount. The formula for determining the interest rate paid on bonds is:

$$k = \text{Inflation} + \text{DR} + \text{LR} + \text{MR}$$

k is the nominal interest rate.

Figure 9.3 depicts the investment risk associated with instruments from

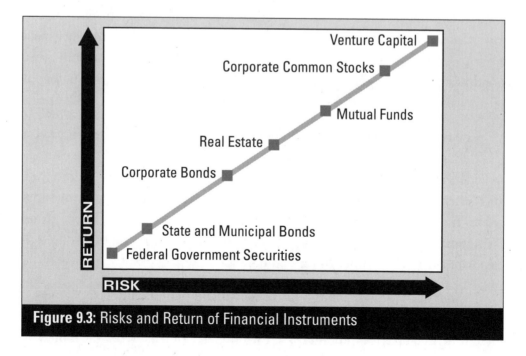

Figure 9.3: Risks and Return of Financial Instruments

various financial markets—from least risky to most risky. It shows how risk and return associated with these securities vary. Both risk and potential return have a positive correlation. The lower left-hand corner of the graph begins with government securities. As it moves up and to the right, the risk becomes greater and private-sector bonds become prevalent. Among the highest-risk instruments are corporate stocks. NPOs are usually guided away from high-risk categories. Short-term investments of concern to financial managers include Treasury bills, certificates of deposit, and the like. Longer-term securities include Treasury notes and bonds, corporate bonds, stocks, and so on. Risk and return associated with these securities vary, but generally these are fairly low-risk investments.

An Investment Strategy

Every organization should have guidelines for investing nonprofit funds. Doing it wisely and within legal limitations is a necessity. Many NPOs have limitations on how and what to invest. If they do not have such limitations, the idea of a strategy should be to maximize return on investment. Highly risky ventures, for example, should not be considered by NPOs.

Some organizations are restricted by preset priorities such as investing locally first, or not investing in certain securities that support oppressive nations or businesses. Other restrictions may be based on concerns about safety in the investment of public and nonprofit funds. These priorities have been deemed important policies by boards and need to be followed. The philosophy of the organization, then, is the strongest influence on an investment strategy. Still, within the organization's priorities, other rational criteria for creating and investing in a portfolio need to be accepted and followed.

Of course, studying the various financial markets is a top priority for investing. Knowing where the markets have been, where they are now, and where they are going reduces the risk of investing. The second priority should be to maximize the rate of return on investments. Investing in higher-risk securities like common and international stocks can be a bit riskier than other types of investments. But they might be the ones that have the greatest payoff. Less risky securities compensate for the risk of stocks. So a portfolio strategy should be based on an acceptable mix of securities using risk as the major criterion. In other words, the key to success is allocating funds among targeted financial markets. By examining the risk/return payoff, an organization can discern which securities fit which risk category and consider how each one fits into an NPO's risk averseness. There are two purposes of an investment strategy, and they counterbalance each other. They are, first, maximizing return, and second, minimizing risk. The following are some portfolio strategies that reflect target allocation policies. The first is conservative, the second involves modest risk, and the final one is clearly on the risky side.

Portfolio Allocation Strategies

INVESTMENT TYPE	ALLOCATION TARGET PERCENTAGE
Cash Equivalents	25–40
Fixed Income	40–50
Real Estate	5–10
Common Stocks (U.S.)	5–10

CONSERVATIVE

INVESTMENT TYPE	ALLOCATION TARGET PERCENTAGE
Cash Equivalents (e.g., CD's, money markets)	5–15
T-Bills, Government Bonds	20–40
Real Estate	5–10
Mutual Funds	10–15
Common Stocks (U.S.)	25–40

MODEST

INVESTMENT TYPE	ALLOCATION TARGET PERCENTAGE
Cash Equivalents	5–10
Fixed Income	20–30
Real Estate	10–20
Common Stocks (U.S.)	25–40
Common Stocks (International)	10–20

AGGRESSIVE

SUMMARY

Managing cash boils down to logical thinking. When cash does not come in, money has to be found to carry the organization until revenues arrive. If done well, investing available funds in short-term investments can help NPOs smooth out irregular cash flows. Normally, the longer the investment term, the greater the return on that investment. This affects the timing and availability of funds and investment strategies. Even if cash flow is not a problem, short-term investments of surplus funds is a great income enhancer. Most NPOs will not have appropriate investment expertise on staff, so NPOs with relatively large cash reserves should consider the services of an investment banker, advisor, or portfolio manager. The authors have used and seen other circumstances where the expertise of board members can provide sound advice to NPOs on investing short-term surpluses and cash reserves. Finally, the use of bill and invoice payment strategies can increase an NPO's effective use of its precious cash.

DISCUSSION QUESTIONS

1. Cash flow budgets vary by subsector and from NPO to NPO within subsectors. Some agencies have smoother cash flows than others. Some receive funding at the beginning of a fiscal year while others must wait until the middle or toward the end of the fiscal year. Some revenue streams are consistent from year to year while others are more sporadic. Identify some factors that could affect the nature of a cash flow budget. Clarify the reasons for these differences.

2. To what extent should projections about revenues and expenditures be informed by actual revenues and expenditures in the past? Note: This question can also vary from NPO to NPO.

EXERCISE

The fictitious Knotfer Prophet Agency is attempting to create a cash flow budget in the face of volatile revenue and expenditure profiles in the first six months of its coming fiscal year. Both revenues and spending commitments are front-loaded. The last six months of the year are quite predictable. It finds the following conditions (in dollars).

FISCAL ITEM	JAN	FEB	MAR	APR	MAY	JUN
Budgeted revenues (all sources)	68,020	60,000	69,000	62,000	68,000	59,000
Budgeted disbursements	60,000	71,000	59,000	68,200	67,000	60,000
Receipts less disbursements	8,020	(11,000)	8,020	(6,800)	(1,000)	(1,000)
Cash at beginning of month	1,000	9,020	(1,980)	6,040	(760)	(1,760)
Cumulative cash position (end of month)	9,020	(1,980)	6,040	(760)	(1,760)	(2,760)

Knowing that there was not enough cash in operations and that the reserves would have to be drawn down, the finance director decides to apply cash management using an inventory model. She divided the year into 12 monthly periods. When she came on board in July of the previous year, she noted that in earlier years, reserves, which were sitting in a savings account earning 1 percent interest, had to be used to make budget in the first six months of each year. To defend against the budget shortfall, she had invested the reserves in short-term investments that earned more than five percent interest. Converting these investments to cash, however, came with a cost. The transaction cost, a combination of charges and interest, amounted to five percent of the amount cashed in. Refer to the discussion of the inventory model earlier in this chapter and do the following:

- Estimate the average expenditures for each period.

- Calculate the measure of effectiveness, that is, the amount that transaction costs should not exceed in a period.

- Interpret the results.

NOTES

1   Alexander B. Callow, Jr., *The Tweed Ring* (New York: Oxford University Press, 1966).

2   American Bar Association, "Check 21—New Federal Law to Speed the Check-Clearing Process,"
     2005. Online at http://www.abanet.org/rppt/publications/edirt/2005/1/Zawodniak.pdf (accessed May
     20, 2008).

3   The Federal Reserve Board, *Check Clearing for the 21st Century Act,* 2005. Online at
     http://www.federalreserve.gov (accessed April 25, 2008).

4   Alliance for Nonprofit Management, "Frequently Asked Questions—Financial Management." Online
     at http://www.allianceonline.org/FAQ/financial_management (accessed May 20, 2008).

5   Ibid.

6   Ibid.

7   J. Hempel and A. Borrus, "Now the Nonprofits Need Cleaning Up," *Business Week* (June 21, 2004).

CHAPTER 10
Risk and Reward: Financial Risk and Risk Management

This chapter focuses on risks that affect NPO finances and on what it takes to manage those risks. Risk management is vital to any organization, including NPOs. The chapter also discusses internal controls, personnel, and risk management issues. The discussion includes consideration of compensation, benefits, and personnel costs; pensions; 403 (b) accounts; insurance, liability, and risk management; contracting and outsourcing; and business risk. Unrelated business ventures are becoming a very popular and often useful means of acquiring restriction-free income. But they are not risk-free. Starting a venture requires knowledge of the laws and regulations covering earned income and the tax treatment of revenue from these ventures. These topics are covered from both a legal and business perspective and are discussed in the context of costs and cost-savings strategies.

TOPICS
- Risks and Rewards
- Nonprofit Financial Risks
- Liability
- Financial Risk Management
- Related and Unrelated Business Risk
- Partnerships with Corporations
- Summary
- Discussion Questions
- Exercise
- Innovation

RISKS AND REWARDS

"I have always depended on the kindness of strangers."

- Blanche DuBois, a character in Tennessee Williams' play
A Streetcar Named Desire.

NPOs depend on the kindness of donors and grantors. They face financial risk because by their nature they are dependent for their existence on others. On a continuum displaying intensity of risk, private business ventures are the most susceptible and government programs are the least susceptible to risk. Businesses do not have either the reliability of a tax base or the authority to pass coercive tax laws. They face bad economies, bad markets, and lawsuits. Governments do possess taxing and legislative authority, but they must often face the wrath of voters. NPOs fall in the middle of the risk continuum. As will be shown, this condition can be overcome. Using boldness and creativity, an NPO can realize unique rewards.

NONPROFIT FINANCIAL RISKS

Some areas of risk typically faced by NPOs that need to be managed include:[1]

- Health
- Workers' compensation
- Risk to clients
- Staff and director risks
- Contracts
- Harassment laws
- Employment discrimination
- Errors and omissions
- Risk to volunteers
- Board risks
- Fundraising
- Property and equipment
- Wrongful termination
- Employee dishonesty

Risk is any uncertainty about a future event that threatens an NPO's ability to accomplish its mission.[2] For an NPO, everything is at risk. There are costs associated with every risk. All employees, volunteers, assets, revenue sources, clients, equipment, bank accounts, reputation, parking lots—everything—carries risk. Any loss resulting from the actualization of that risk can threaten an NPO's ability to carry out its mission.

Chapter 2 stated, "Taking nothing away from the importance of the concept of *mission,* which is the heart of any NPO, how money is raised and spent by NPOs is arguably more important than any other activity of NPO administration. Blood must get pumped through the heart." The body metaphor illustrates the role of financial and fiscal administration in an organization. Recall that money was compared to that of blood that streams through various-sized vessels leading ultimately to and through the heart. Blood keeps the body alive. The metaphor is expanded here to add the concept of risk to the body. Each time a body steps outside, it risks the dangers of the real world, such as traffic, crime, heat and cold, the environment, and so on. Risk to the body increases when it is underdressed in cold weather, a time when the body is vulnerable to bacteria and viruses. It is also a risk to life and limb to drive a car. These risks threaten one's ability to earn a living. They are, however, unavoidable. Such risks are a part of just being alive. There is a profit for taking such risks. A body can be covered warmly in cold weather, and its owner can use a hand sanitizer, take vitamin C, and purchase adequate health insurance. Motorists can slow down, wear a seatbelt, purchase plenty of insurance, drive defensively, or take other preventative steps on the freeway. Similarly, an NPO can identify financial risks, develop and implement a risk management plan, and, of course, obtain adequate insurance against damages.

Like their business and government sector partners, NPOs large and small must find ways to maintain and enhance their financial condition in order to survive and thrive. Finances, physical assets, vendors, the talent of employees, and the board all contribute to both the mission and the financial health of an NPO. Financial resources need to be protected. Without adequate financial resources, an organization will ultimately fail to accomplish its mission. It is logical that the better the financial health of an NPO, the more likely it will enjoy mission success.

Protecting financial health means tending to cash, bank accounts, and investments as well as property, supplies, equipment and inventory, employees, clients, and volunteers. There are risks to these NPO financial resources that range from disrupting the NPO's mission activities all the way to shutting the NPO down. Threats are internal and external. Damage can be caused by employee theft, workplace accidents, illegal personnel behavior, bad financial investments, violation of grant requirements, burglary, the actions of volunteers and board members, and much more. Even the possibility of terrorism needs to be considered.

NPOs must be aware of the possibility of a financial loss and take the appropriate protective actions. The impact of financial loss can create a cash flow problem forcing reductions in spending, staffing levels, or services. Most NPOs are contributing members to a community. Financial problems may reduce donor contributions, or if the problems become public knowledge, can lead to the destruction of an NPO's reputation and goodwill. Such a result would likely lead donors, volunteers, and grantors to question an NPO's viability in all areas. Controlling these risks is clearly essential. Some of the specific areas of risk are discussed now.

Budgets

Budget risk is real. A budget is a numerical expression of an organization's values. The clearest reflection of what an organization values is found in the budget document. Sometimes there are competing values. The central issue in many budget struggles is tied to what the organization values. An explanation of budget and fiscal responsibility will be lost on an audience that puts program way out in front of available funding. The authors know of an NPO director who, right after the 9/11 attacks, could not convince the board of the negative effects of 9/11 on giving. The board then set a very high budget. Consequently, the NPO had to dip deeply into the reserves and lay off two people during the budget period. The next year, as a reaction, the board passed a very conservative budget in spite of the director's advice that revenues would increase. That decision severely limited the NPO's mission fulfillment. The board finally got it right the next year. Those who are promoting fiscal responsibility need to communicate responsibility by setting realistic budget numbers and by being fiscally responsible. When realistic budget numbers are used, the organization can expand its programmatic efforts and elevate the image of the NPO to even greater heights.

Investments

Investment management was discussed in the previous chapter. Here, the concentration is on investment risk. NPOs vary in the size and mix of their portfolios. Size and types of investments generally are unique to each NPO and are based on legal and policy restrictions, available funds for investing, and the level of the board's risk averseness. This last component, risk averseness, is a major driver of investment decisions. The investments of small NPOs might be limited to the purchase of CDs, while large NPOs, that is, medical centers, universities, theatres, and museums, may work with extremely large endowment funds. Every board should establish an investment policy that will guide the nonprofit in its investment and financial decisions. The reader can imagine the fate of an executive director who ends up with deep losses after investing surplus funds in stocks with a high potential payoff but with a high risk. Even an NPO operating out of its checkbook should have a strong and sensible policy about what to do with available surplus cash.

Fundraising

Critical questions to ask about fundraising events for NPOs include, "Is there energy for a project?" and "Is it the best way to raise funds?" Sometimes in board meetings people throw out many ideas, but they have no idea how much work it is to implement them. The authors have seen boards like that with ideas for a multitude of events. They think that having another event will solve a financial problem, but there is no guarantee. Often, fundraisers are associated with a recreational activity in the community that can put the NPO in the public eye in a carefully planned way that tells the NPO's story. While fundraising events are a lot of work, they can also be great for building team spirit. There is nothing better than the euphoria of a group of people reaching a goal together. There should be, however, a concern that someone will get hurt at a recreational fundraising event. Obviously, insurance against this can mitigate costs, but it cannot insure against bad publicity. In the field of NPO finances, fundraising events produce the least amount of money.

Partnerships are discussed in detail later in this chapter, but a corporate partner seeks a payoff from its relationship with an NPO in the form of good publicity, and ideally, profits. NPOs want to establish goodwill and garner publicity that leads to more money or more volunteers. There is a risk in this relationship. There is potential for negative publicity if that corporation behaves in a way that causes donors to form a negative opinion. The effect on the NPO's reputation and goodwill could be disastrous. Any potential partnership needs to be evaluated carefully in order to avoid these types of losses.

Sometime a fundraising event involves selling a product to the public. Many NPOs hire or purchase products that they in turn sell. Like any other business, NPOs can lose money on such ventures. NPOs must ask themselves if the payoff is worth the effort.

Turning Down Revenue Sources

NPOs should not dance for dollars. Revenue opportunities will arise from time to time that should be passed up. The key criterion for rejecting a revenue source is, of course, the fit with an NPO's mission. While no NPO can succeed without money, mission ranks way ahead of money as an NPO value. If a revenue source is far removed from the mission, it should be turned down. There are other reasons for turning down a revenue source that have to do with financial and insurance risk. The authors know of an example with a social service agency that was asked to create a mentoring program in cooperation with a golf program. Mentors would have been recruited using golf as a basis for relating to children. It was suspected that the leaders of the golf program had motives for private gain that were not compatible with the NPO's mission. The NPO turned down the potential partnership.

Buildings, Grounds, and Equipment

To own property of any kind is to be subject to risk. And all physical property is vulnerable to events such as theft, fire, flood, storms, and other acts of mankind and natural disasters. Property includes equipment and assets that have a replacement value and are vital to the operation of an NPO. Risks to physical property can occur from human acts such as vandalism or theft and from unforeseen events such as electrical malfunctions or fire, tornadoes, hurricanes, floods, wind, and explosions. The authors know of a social service agency that was burgled three times in one week by the same person until locks could be changed and a more effective alarm system installed that alerted police. The perpetrator was arrested, tried, and convicted. The agency's insurance costs rose as the result of this crime. Regardless of the cause, property loss has both operational and financial consequences that include the loss of use and/or the necessity of replacing the property.

Employment Practices

The costs resulting from employment policies and practices include the need for directors' and officers' liability policies. Risky practices include wrongful termination; sexual harassment; gender, age, national origin, and religious discrimination; workplace conditions; and general harassment. These situations are covered by federal, local, and state laws.

Fraud

Fraud is deliberate deceit. Fraud risks, including the threat due to theft or the misuse of funds, can have severe consequences. Cases of embezzlement are frequent. The American Red Cross, Rainbow Coalition, United Way, and others have experienced instances of fraud or the appearance of fraud at the highest levels of their leadership. Each year, losses that are due to fraud are commonly estimated to be in the billions of dollars. NPO policies should include internal controls along with checks and balances to alleviate the risk due to fraud.

LIABILITY

An NPO is liable for damages if it is found to have failed to take an appropriate level of care; if it was negligent in its responsibility to protect individuals, groups, or the general public; or if it was negligent in its obligation to carry out its duties in a reasonable manner. The required standard of care, however, varies with the situation, the people involved, and the community in which the incident takes place. Nonprofits serving children and other vulnerable populations must exercise a higher level of care than agencies that serve adults.[3] Part of a good risk management strategy is to have policies in place to deal with liability and potential loss. These policies need to be monitored to ensure ongoing compliance with ordinances, laws, and regulations.

FINANCIAL RISK MANAGEMENT

A risk evaluation and prioritization strategy must be led by two criteria: potential cost (financial and others) and probability of a risk becoming an actual event. The worst-case scenario is that someone—a client, an employee, or a passerby—could somehow be injured as the result of an NPO's actions, either because of negligence or by accident. The mere act of holding an event carries with it exposure to risk. As an example, a fundraising event—a bowling party, picnic, carwash, and so on—creates the probability of a risk becoming an actual event. Likewise, workplaces, vehicles, and surroundings are also vulnerable to risk.[4]

One of the purposes of managing risk is to reduce financial losses, which in turn will reduce insurance costs or the number of program-related injuries to staff members, volunteers, clients, or others.[5] A risk management program can also have other purposes, including screening volunteers for qualifications and criminal backgrounds; finding appropriate property and liability insurance to protect against principal exposures; mitigating dangers associated with fundraising events; or developing policies and procedures covering liability stemming from relationships with partners of organizations.

Corporations tend to view risk management as a financial function. Even though risk seems to mean much more to an NPO because of its reputation and goodwill as a member of a community, an NPO is right to view risk management as a financial function. The easiest measure of loss is ultimately financial in nature, because a disaster has the potential to put an NPO out of business. It can easily lose its financial security. Thus, risk management necessarily means preventing the loss of operating revenue. Risk management means ensuring that exposure to the events discussed in the previous section are covered and that risk is minimal. Primarily, managing risk involves calculating the probable costs of errors and omissions that come just from operating. The costs of risk management—insurance premiums, salary for oversight, upgrading property and equipment—result in real dollar costs and must be factored into products and services.

Organizations often ignore the early signs of risk. For example, financial wrongdoing by employees such as embezzlement and theft can often be prevented. If the proper accounting controls are in place, the systems should alert someone to possible fraud. Established checks and balances should be procedural. Accounting controls should clearly identify authority and approval, documentation, and physical security and should be signed for early detection of problems.[6]

Legal Requirements

NPOs tend to be extensively regulated by various levels of government because of their special status and the fact that many receive government grants that constitute large portions of their budgets. In addition, most NPOs establish internal operational policies to deal with legal issues. Examples of regulated NPOs include health clinics, because they handle hazardous waste, and NPOs that serve children, because of the potential for child abuse. Some churches have been rocked by scandals involving targeted legal liabilities such as child sexual abuse and sexual harassment.

Responsibility Distribution

Given its oversight responsibilities, the NPO board is ultimately responsible for the entire organization. A board's responsibility includes making sure the executive and managers are implementing risk management and monitoring risks as well as keeping policies up to date in order to protect people and the NPO's reputation and goodwill. The board members are liable for their failure to act and their mistakes. The board should be proactive and measure risk management performance against goals and objectives; it should also delegate day-to-day management to the executive director but monitor activities with timely discussions and checks.

The executive director should have authority for making sure that the policies dealing with the various areas of risk—finances, property and asset protection, employment practices, errors and omissions, negligence, and fraud and abuse—are up-to-date and are followed, and that insurance policies are both adequate and maintained. The executive director should appoint a risk management committee to identify risks and recommend risk coverage.

Strategies to Reduce Risk

An NPO can take important steps regarding risky activities that threaten mission fulfillment. The first is to continually assess the probability and damage potential of each risk. Secondly, an NPO should avoid highly risky operations and activities. Avoidance means either not offering a service, ceasing to provide a service, or not conducting a service or activity considered too risky. Third, the NPO can modify its activity and redesign it to reduce the exposure resulting from that activity. Risk-sharing with another organization can mitigate but not eliminate risk. Insurance pooling is one example. Negotiating a contract that sets out responsibility with a partnering organization is another risk-reducing step.

Insurance is a risk financing tool. It is not the same as risk management, and it does not change the need to manage risk. Not every risk can be covered under an insurance policy. For example, an errors and omissions policy does not cover loss of supporter base because of illicit public behavior by an employee. Insurance does, however, provide coverage for tangible items like negligence on the part of employees.

Most NPOs cannot afford to self-insure. An NPO should buy insurance that covers the likely specific risks that threaten its ability to carry out its mission. A combination of insurance coverages will likely be necessary, because a single insurance policy will not address the specific exposures facing individual NPOs. Claims made against NPOs fall into three general categories: claims and lawsuits filed against the nonprofit and its staff, claims by staff, and claims to repair or replace property a nonprofit owns or controls. The various types of insurance instruments that are available to cover these claims include the following:

- **General liability policies** cover directors, board members, and employees against claims alleging property damage or bodily injury caused by the nonprofit's operations or activities. This type of liability insurance includes broad coverage for damage to the property of others, bodily injury to outsiders, and personal injury (false arrest, malicious prosecution, and defamation).

- **Directors' and board members' liability insurance** is intended to protect against claims related to potential wrongful acts by an NPO.

- **Professional liability insurance** covers claims related to the delivery of professional services. This is found predominantly in medical and legal practices to protect against malpractice lawsuits, although some policies cover other professionals found in the nonprofit sector.

- **Property insurance** safeguards against damage to buildings, grounds, and equipment that a nonprofit owns or for which it is responsible.

- **Fidelity bonds** protect against employee theft and embezzlement.

- **Workers' compensation** covers an NPO's liability for employees' injuries that occur in the execution of their duties on behalf of the NPO. In some cases, NPOs can secure coverage for their volunteers.[7]

There are a few other insurance-like instruments that an NPO may purchase depending on the nature of its mission and operations. These instruments are designed to cover financial risk by reducing harm. These include liability waivers, hold harmless agreements, indemnification clauses in contracts, and disclaimers. The person or organization that is covered voluntarily (theoretically) releases the NPO from responsibility for certain activities. These instruments include the following:

- Waivers, which are agreements with participants in an NPO-sponsored activity that hold it harmless from the potential claims by participants in an activity.

- Hold harmless agreements, which are specialized contracts between NPOs and other parties. The other parties assume all legal liability and indemnify the NPO. The party agreeing to hold the NPO harmless also agrees to pay the cost of any injury or lawsuit. It works in reverse when an NPO holds a funding source harmless against claims against the NPO.

- Disclaimers are a denials by NPOs made in writing for any responsibility for any type of injury, transaction, or performance failure that may occur.

- Indemnifications are intended to hold another party harmless. Many times, NPOs indemnify important contributors such as volunteers, board members, and others from any liability in the performance of their contribution to the organization.[8]

RELATED AND UNRELATED BUSINESS RISK

A related business reflects an NPO's mission. An unrelated business does not. The purpose of both related and unrelated businesses is to increase NPO's cash flow.

Related Businesses

A related business operated by an NPO is roughly the opposite of an unrelated business. Both are legal statuses that require an attorney's involvement to avoid problems with the IRS. A related business is integrated into the NPO's normal operation and mission. Profits from officially designated related businesses are not taxed. A fundraising event—such as a bingo night, or an annual dinner-dance, or walk for whatever—is a related business that does not disqualify an NPO for tax-exempt status. An onsite pharmacy operated by a nonprofit hospital can be construed as related to the hospital's mission of delivering health care. Likewise, a church that operates a bookstore may continue to be tax exempt.

Unrelated Businesses

New devices in fundraising and marketing have created possibilities for the nonprofit sector to tap into resources offering potential solutions for shortfalls in revenue. While NPOs are not expected to act in the same way as their private-sector counterparts, Kevin Corder notes that "there are compelling reasons to believe that NPOs will behave in ways similar to other private firms.[9] One of the interesting manifestations of this conjecture is the movement toward unrelated business ventures. NPOs are starting private-sector businesses that are beginning to compete for shares of private-sector markets. All NPOs that are normally tax-exempt under the terms of the IRS 501(c)(3) designation are subject to a tax on unrelated business income. As discussed in earlier chapters, unrelated business income is income generated by a trade or business activity not substantially related to the exempt purpose of the organization and regularly carried out by that organization. An unrelated business is one that has absolutely nothing in common with an NPO's primary mission, even if the all the profits made from the business are used by the NPO to carry out its mission. An unrelated business venture is one that is subject to income taxation because it is in actuality removed either physically or by the nature of its financial transactions from the NPO's normal not-for-profit operations. It does not directly affect how an NPO operates, nor does it further its mission as established under the terms of 501(c)(3). The word *substantial* is important. If an NPO's business venture is substantially related to the NPO's mission, the IRS may determine the NPO will not lose its tax-exempt status.

A business activity that is not related to the main reason for the NPO's existence and that is intended to make a profit constitutes and unrelated business venture. For example, a space museum running a screen printing business that is a full-service print shop has no connection to the museum's purpose. Likewise, a human services agency operating an offsite restaurant, a nonprofit hospital purchasing and operating an auto body shop, and a theatre selling cruises on a regular basis are all examples of unrelated businesses.

The Logic and Risks of Nonprofit Business Ventures

The primary reason for an NPO to venture into the world of business is often uncertainty about its usual revenue sources for furthering its missions and goals. Consequently, many NPOs are finding themselves willing to take on the headaches and risks of running a business other than their primary operation. The potential upside for these risks is a new regular source of income that for the most part can be spent without the restrictions that generally come attached to government and other large foundation grants. The downside risks are, first, that an NPO will lose the money ventured into a business and second, that even though the business may prove to be successful, private donations will shrink substantially as donors come to the conclusion that their generosity may not be needed.

The Upside

Perhaps the greatest potential benefit of operating an unrelated or related business is simply an expanded budget. More money applied to fulfilling an NPO's mission is an executive director's dream. Another potential benefit is the ability to use profits from the business without restriction. A New Jersey NPO executive once explained why the $5,000 annual profit from an unrelated business in an annual budget of more than $1 million was important.[10] He said it was the only unrestricted source of funds in the NPO's budget and that he could use it for staff training. A business that earns in the neighborhood of hundreds of thousand dollars, or more, of unrestricted funds after taxes is even more significant; it allowed the organization to have cash not only for valuable employee training, which was not allowed by this NPO's funding sources, but also for supplementing grants that may restrict spending to personnel costs and not allow spending on equipment. This benefit opens up all manner of opportunities for budget planning.

The Downside

Obviously, the most critical concern about NPOs venturing into the world of related or unrelated business is the risk of failure, that is, the risk of losing money. It has become accepted that 80 percent of new businesses fail after a short period of time. NPOs, therefore, have to ensure that the decision to start an unrelated business will either succeed or will not result in major losses if business failure occurs. There is another unique kind of risk that NPOs may encounter. Some scholars are concerned about the potential negative effect on private giving of government or major foundation grantors allocating money to nonprofits.[11] The same risk is likely to be involved in a decision to start an unrelated business. Traditional donors may conclude that their donations are not needed as much as they once were and may reduce or eliminate their support for the NPO. Whatever turns out to be true, it is clear that NPOs have entered into a new era where they operate leaner and more efficiently by choosing to emulate business models.

PARTNERSHIPS WITH CORPORATIONS

Many corporations are turning to cause-related marketing by partnering with nonprofits that share an affinity for the NPO's mission. Most NPOs are perpetually on the lookout for money-generating ideas. This is also true of the YWCA in Fort Worth, TX. There are new combined resource/marketing devices like cause-related marketing and sponsorship or the sale and use of brands. There are also emerging unrelated business income opportunities as a source of revenue that could prove to be profitable even though there could be organizational restrictions as well as tax implications. Nevertheless, there is a growing potential that these unrelated business opportunities have the potential to provide significant and permanent income streams. The YWCA in Ft. Worth raised several million dollars to restore a historic facility, raised money from government and private donors to support programs, and partnered with community organizations to support its programs. This assertive agency also looked into a corporate partnership opportunity to make money for the organization several years ago. Its examination resulted in an agreement to open an ice cream shop, an unrelated activity. This partnership with Ben & Jerry's turned out not only to be a steady revenue source but an enhancement to the YWCA's mission to help young women on career testing and women who have aged-out of foster care, housing child care, or transitional housing.

The following appears on Ben & Jerry's website. It discusses some of their ongoing partners in various parts of the country and the world:

Ben & Jerry's PartnerShop Program is a form of social enterprise, a growing movement in which nonprofit organizations leverage the power of business for community benefit. In establishing PartnerShops across the country, Ben & Jerry's partners with nonprofit organizations that offer supportive employment and job training to people who may face barriers to employment. Our PartnerShops are built around great ice cream and goodwill just like our other Ben & Jerry's scoop shops across the country. The difference is that Ben & Jerry's donates PartnerShops to nonprofit organizations by waiving the standard franchise fees and provides additional support to help nonprofits operate strong businesses. As PartnerShop operators, nonprofits retain their business proceeds to support their programs. PartnerShops help people build better lives. We plan to expand the PartnerShop Program and are looking for new partners in major metropolitan markets. Criteria for new partners: nonprofit status, experience in youth development, vocational training and/or social purpose enterprise development, an interest in providing job training to youth in a retail foodservice setting, the desire and capacity to operate a social enterprise business, a staff and board with small-business expertise, an excellent credit history, financial acumen and stability, a record of fundraising success, the willingness and the capacity to manage the complexities of developing a new business.[12]

The PartnerShop does not give money for nonprofits to set up a business.

The way they assist their partners is that they waive the initial franchise fees and do not charge a franchise fee of $30,000 yearly. Like all of their franchises, they provide the partners with training so that they will succeed. They do not provide the very expensive equipment and fixtures nor the space for the scoop shop.

The YWCA ultimately entered into an agreement with Ben & Jerry's. It turned out to be a very good decision. Choosing to accept the risks involved, Ft. Worth's Scoop Shop, located on the west side of the city, has met the goals both for itself and for the partner, Ben & Jerry's. It is turning a profit while it is meeting its mission goal of preparing young women for the world of work. Ben & Jerry's is selling a lot of ice cream.

What message does such a partnership send to donors and other backers of a nonprofit agency? For many of these people, it would mean very little. It might lead to a small drop-off in donations, but nothing significant. Organizations that start ventures like scoop shops may find that the business end would generate enough income to more than compensate for any financial drop-off in contributions, and the backers would in fact be donating by frequenting the shop instead of making a straight cash donation. If an NPO is considering a partnership, it needs to evaluate the compatibility of its mission and goals with the company's statements of social consciousness. The company will certainly evaluate the NPO's compatibility before becoming involved with it, so the NPO should do the same.

For the NPO, there is an important question to answer: "Is there the energy to do such a project?" It ultimately will be the board that makes the decision to go forward, but it has to know if the staff member who is in charge of the project can be stretched enough to develop the project. If there is enough money to hire someone who is knowledgeable about running a profit-making business to take the lead, having someone available to do the job might not be a problem.

Deciding to Venture into Business

One of the major responsibilities of NPO board members is raising funds, so taking on an unrelated venture is a major board decision, not one of the staff. Board members must either give or raise funds, preferably both. NPOs can make a profit through a business venture, but to be non-taxed, that profit must be spent on their missions. Making a profit to increase savings is equally acceptable. Just like any other business venture, there will always be bad years, and it is essential to have cash in the bank to cover lean times. A related or unrelated business venture should not be begun to save a financially desperate agency. Correcting that kind of problem requires other kinds of assistance. Instead, any NPO that has achieved a reasonably successful financial status and has a source of finance and the staff and energy to venture into a new area of operation is a reasonable candidate to start up a business.[13]

Steps to Success

Develop a business plan. If a business is to succeed, there must be a plan. Business plans will be expected by potential financial backers. Furthermore, a business plan is very much like a strategic plan for the NPO starting the business. It lays out goals, objectives, alternatives, funding possibilities, expected outcomes, and so on.

Line up financing. Possible funding for this type of venture might be venture capitalists who need tax write-offs and understand the big picture of an entrepreneurial venture. The NPO should talk to people running businesses who have been at it for a long time as well as to several new entrepreneurs running the same type of business. They can provide information about the good, bad, and worst aspects of entrepreneurship.

Start and stay within your means. This advice goes beyond your ability to provide money; it includes having the right staff and a sufficient number of staff to equip and run the venture. Make sure current staff are available and have cleared their schedules to make their individual contributions. The best decision, if possible, is to hire managers who have experience in operating a business, if not running one that is in the same area of business, or at least from the same geographic location or catering to the same clientele.

Effects on NPO Tax-Exempt Legal Status

According to the Free Management Library, "The IRS limits the amount the revenue a nonprofit can make that is not directly associated with the mission of the nonprofit. This is in order to prevent nonprofits from unfairly competing with for-profit organizations."[14]

An NPO's tax-exempt mission is the key measure of whether or not income earned by a business is taxed or not. Simply put, a related business remains tax-exempt along with all other mission-related activities. It loses that exemption if the IRS determines the business is unrelated to the NPO's mission. An NPO's business income that is determined to be nonexempt is taxed at a common business or corporate rate. The reasoning is that the tax exemption would give the NPO an economic advantage in the private market in which the unrelated business operates. This gives private competing companies protection from a *clear* and *substantial* advantage in the marketplace. In other words, a bookstore operated by a nonprofit home health care agency does not have an economic advantage over a mom-and-pop bookstore because of its tax-exempt status. Likewise, a print shop operated by a museum would benefit in not having to pay taxes and perhaps charge lower prices than competitors.[15]

Unrelated Ventures Exempt from Taxation

The U.S. Supreme Court has found that NPOs operating a trade or business or other commercial activity are allowed to do so.[16] If the following are present in the running of a venture, NPOs operating unrelated business activities are exempt from income taxation:

- Activities of the unrelated business do not occur on a regular basis.

- Work is performed by volunteers.

- Substantially all merchandise being sold has been acquired as a gift.

- Work is being conducted for the convenience of the organization's members, students, patients, visitors, officers, or employees.

- Profits flow directly from the business into the NPO.

If an operating business substantially meets these conditions, it is likely exempt from income tax liability.

SUMMARY

Every organization faces financial risks and needs to insure or self-insure against those risks. Unfortunately, not all risks are insurable. The only way to insure against many risks is to be very careful and create risk policies that are intended to reduce risk. Risk management by NPOs is important to the organization, to staff and the board, to clients and stakeholders, and to the public, because somewhere along the line all are susceptible to risks but deserve to be protected. One area of risk to NPOs comes from business ventures, especially unrelated ventures. Because of their ineligibility for tax exemptions, these business ventures must face the same operational risks that regular businesses face. There is also a great potential for reward, however, and all NPOs should not simply ignore the potential financial reward of operating a business-like activity.

DISCUSSION QUESTIONS

1. Consider a well-endowed private women's university in a Midwestern town of about 100,000 residents. Founded in the 1800s, the university has been experiencing enrollment decline from its glory days (which started in the second decade of the last century and ran through the 1960s). The university owns many assets that are well recognized by residents, like its golf course, stables, lakes, beautiful old buildings, and attractive homes. These and other assets have been opened up to community use. Its graduates include one U.S. Secretary of State, corporate presidents, actors, newswomen, and other famous people. As enrollment declined, the university experienced a decline in revenue and has begun to seek assistance from the board of directors to tap into the university's endowment fund for operating revenue. The board lost confidence in the previous president's ability to solve the financial and enrollment crisis. A new president is hired to try to turn the situation around. Her vision is to recruit more men, sell off assets, and raise prices to the community to use the university's assets. In a close vote, the board has bought into the president's strategy. Identify some of the risks to the university's goodwill from the new president's strategy. Describe some of the associated financial risks.

2. Interview a nonprofit executive or finance director and ask that person to identify some of the financial risks of doing business. Also, find out what that NPO's risk management plan is to avoid financial loss. Discuss with your class what you have discovered.

EXERCISE

From the following list of NPOs, select a type of NPO for analysis. If your instructor allows it, you can select any other type of appropriate NPO:

- Youth mentoring agency
- Church, synagogue, or mosque
- Preschool
- Legal services agency
- Children's museum
- Cancer research institute
- Community radio station

Assignment

Investigate the type of agency you have selected to determine as much of the following information as possible about that type of NPO:

- Identify the financial risks to the organization you have selected.
- Prioritize each of those risks in terms of intensity of financial loss.
- Identify the relative costs of taking mitigating steps.
- For each risk, list some steps the NPO can take to mitigate the risks.

INNOVATION

Specialized risk management software exists to assist NPOs in developing personalized risk management plans. The authors have had personal experience with the software package offered by the Nonprofit Risk Center found at www.MyRiskManagementPlan.org. Other private companies have developed their own proprietary risk management software or training programs. Using this kind of software is a good step for the serious NPO to take to protect itself from the types of risk found in Table 10.1 and discussed in this chapter.

NOTES

1   Alliance for Nonprofit Management, "Frequently Asked Questions—Risk Management." Online at http://www.allianceonline.org/FAQ/risk_management (accessed April 28, 2008).

2   Alliance for Nonprofit Management, "Frequently Asked Questions—Financial Management." Online at http://www.allianceonline.org/FAQ/financial_management (accessed May 20, 2008).

3   Charles Tremper and G. Kostin, *No Surprises: Controlling Risks in Volunteer Programs* (Washington, DC: Nonprofit Risk Management Center, 1993).

4   Peggy M. Jackson, L.White, and M. Herman, *Mission Accomplished: A Practical Guide to Risk Management for Nonprofit Organizations* (Washington, DC: Nonprofit Risk Management Center, 1997).

5   E. S. Gere, P. C. Vitrano, and S. T. Schmelz, *Be Prepared: Nonprofit Organizations Legal Risks and Protection* (Washington, D.C.: ALTRU, LLC and Ross, Dixon, Bell LLP, 2005).

6   Bruner-Cox LLP, "Accounting and Budgeting: New Risk-Based Assessment Standards," May 2007. Online at http://www.brunercox.com (accessed April 28, 2008).

7   M. Lai, T. Chapman, and E. Steinbeck, *Am I Covered For . . . ? A Guide to Insurance for Non-Profits* (San Jose, CA: Nonprofit Risk Management Center and Consortium for Human Services, Inc., 1992).

8   American Bar Association, *Guidebook for Directors of Nonprofit Corporations* (Washington, DC: Nonprofit Risk Management Center, 1993).

9   Kevin Corder, "Acquiring New Technology: Comparing Nonprofit and Public Sector Agencies," *Administration & Society* 33 (2001): 194.

10   Special Report: "Making Money with a Mission." *Chronicle of Philanthropy* (January 11, 2007): 6.

11   A. C. Brooks, "Do government subsidies to nonprofits crowd out donations or donors?" [Abstract] *Public Finance Review* 31 (2003): 166–179 and E. T. Boris and C. E. Steuerle, eds., *Nonprofits and Government: Collaboration and Conflict* (Washington, D.C.: Urban Institute Press, 1999).

12   Ben & Jerry's, "Ben & Jerry's PartnerShops." Online at http://www.benjerry.com (accessed April 28, 2008).

13   Richard Larson, *Venture Forth!* (Minneapolis, MN: Fieldstone Alliance, 2007).

14   Free Management Library, "Tax Information for Nonprofits," 2008. Online at http://www.managementhelp.org/tax (accessed April 28, 2008).

15   M. A. Hoffman, "Tax-Motivated Expense Shifting by Tax-Exempt Associations," *Journal of the American Taxation Association* (Spring 2007): 1.

16   Herrington J. Bryce, *Financial and Strategic Management for Nonprofit Organizations* (San Francisco: Jossey-Bass, 2000).

CHAPTER 11
Capital Budgeting, Evaluating Capital Investment Decisions, and Debt Management

The focus of this chapter is on capital budgeting, evaluating capital investment decision making, and capital debt. The central theme is decision making and using techniques that provide information to NPO leaders whose responsibilities include making critical capital investment decisions. One of the critical decisions many NPOs are faced with, for example, is deciding whether to rent facilities and equipment, to purchase them, or to find some other creative alternative that meets the needs of their organization. These types of decisions must be made whether the question at hand is the possible construction of a huge new wing of a nonprofit hospital or the potential purchase of a modest home by a small community-based NPO to house abused women and children. Thus, decision-making techniques are helpful and important. The chapter includes a discussion of the relationship of capital budgeting and decision making to the strategic plan, and closes with discussion of the critical topic of debt and debt management.

TOPICS
- Capital Budgeting and Cost of Capital
- Capital Budgeting and the Strategic Plan
- Capital Decision Making
- Financing Capital Projects
- Capital Debt Policy
- Summary
- Discussion Questions
- Exercise
- Innovation: Leasing Technology to Free Up Capital

CAPITAL BUDGETING AND COST OF CAPITAL

Generally speaking, capital expenditures are made to support the acquisition of property, buildings, additions to buildings, equipment, software, and technology that have a life of more than one year. Capital expenditures nearly always involve large cash commitments with major implications for the achievement of an NPO's mission and goals. Such expenditures require careful and analytical decision making for two reasons: First, after the items are acquired, they become a major part of an agency's operations, and second, because after operations using the acquisitions are started, they are almost impossible to terminate. When capital acquisitions are thought of as investments, the preparation of a strategic plan provides an opportunity to consider these long-term and costly items as things that can be deleted, reduced, or increased in scope prior to committing funds.[1]

Regardless of the legitimacy of the need, NPOs often overlook the fact that bringing these kinds of facilities into existence requires more than the one-time cost of construction. There are ongoing operation and maintenance activities associated with them that require ongoing operating funds. These continuing costs must be accounted for in the annual budget process for the life of the facility. The three most important considerations in capital budgeting are planning, evaluation of alternatives, and financing. These considerations should be a visible part of a strategic plan that deals with investing in capital. Evaluation of alternative projects or programs comes about through applying appropriate decision-making techniques. Because of the long-term life and high expense of capital projects, the consideration of financing usually necessitates proper debt management.

NPOs can eliminate some types of indebtedness by implementing strategic planning practices into their financial analysis. Using such practices will allow them to plan investment strategies that are designed to enhance their surplus funds. Surplus funds can be applied to an NPO's shortfall in its cash flow and/or working capital, and it can be used as an emergency fund for unexpected acquisitions and/or spending.[2]

Although this chapter emphasizes the investment of surplus cash and borrowing to finance capital projects, many NPO's have no cash reserves, and many are not in a position to borrow. Many exist in a day-by-day, flying-by-the-seat-of-the-pants, putting-out-fires manner and do not have the time, energy, and the knowledge by and large to implement the type of strategic/financial planning and investment strategies described here. Such agencies are confined to purchasing capital items when a specific donation is given or by using pay-as-you-go financing.

CAPITAL BUDGETING AND THE STRATEGIC PLAN

Extensive planning and ongoing research is crucial in all areas of NPO management. As stated before, for many NPOs the strategic planning process will include a long-term capital budget. In view of unlimited projects competing for limited resources, the requirement to have a strategic plan in place is nonnegotiable. The capital budgeting process is a comprehensive effort that includes an inventory and assessment of existing capital assets, estimations of the need for new capital items, and a determination of the capital assets that will need to be added or replaced. The capital budget, as defined in and flexibly controlled by the strategic plan, will include a time line for expenditures that specifies financial goals and plans for capital acquisitions and the purchase or replacement of equipment and other fixed assets.

In addition to determining needs, the strategic plan should include estimates of costs and financing possibilities. Strategic planning and capital budgeting provide an opportunity for ongoing examination of the assumptions that go into investing in capital projects and programs that help fulfill NPO missions. Like any business entity, NPOs should have an ongoing practice of reexamining of capital needs, because these high-price items will use up a significant amount of resources. Furthermore, the processes of making decisions, estimating costs, and financing need to be carefully done, because mistakes in these areas are magnified due to the high costs of the big-ticket capital items. Finally, as observed, organizations must not be myopic in understanding the capital budgeting process. Clearly, an NPO must consider the influences of board members and strongly interested and influential stakeholders in the overall process, but the big picture provided by the strategic plan must not be ignored.[3]

Planning capital budgets is commonly identified as a continuous process involving several steps. The first of these is to define a project under consideration. Defining a project means to clearly understand the nature, costs, and function of each alternative project within the NPO's understanding of the strategic plan. Next, the process requires identifying and ranking alternatives and selecting the best among them. This requires an understanding of each project and the sort of payoff or return on investment it will contribute to meeting the NPO's mission. The selection should balance project quality with affordability. Next, a cash flow analysis must be conducted. This means determining life-cycle costs, including financing, as well as operating and maintenance costs and salvage value, if any. Implementation needs to be planned just as well as anything else. Project management (part art, part science) is a vital part of planning. Finally, a project review program should include interim, final, and ongoing sub-steps.[4]

CAPITAL DECISION MAKING

"If all needed capital improvements had been made before Hurricane Katrina, the levees would not have broken and the effects on New Orleans would have been just that of a normal hurricane. When I hear about what could have been prevented, my internal reaction is: yeah, and if we had made the decision to remove the icebergs, the Titanic would not have sunk."

– Anonymous

Good decision-making skills are imperative, because consideration of opportunity cost means that money spent on the decision made cannot be spent on the alternatives. There are two types of decisions confronting organizations with regard to capital budgeting. The first is the classic go/no-go decision involving one project. The question is, "Do we go ahead with this project or not?" The second type of decision is when a decision must be made from among two or more alternatives. The operating question is, "Which project do we choose?" NPOs need to carefully analyze and evaluate all proposed capital expenditures and all the alternatives.

Capital budgeting analysis and decision making is a process of evaluating and selecting investments in capital projects. The purpose is to determine if the benefits of a project, however measured, best fit an organization's mission and are efficient and effective. We include the opinions and ideas of others into the decision. Group or team decision making is usually much better than one person analyzing the decision. So, critical stakeholders, including the executive director, the board, and consultants, should not be afraid to put their heads together.

All capital project decisions affect the future of an NPO and its stakeholders and clients. A hospital adding a wing, a social service provider deciding on whether to join other NPOs to create a *one-stop shop* location in a community, a museum considering making a major exhibit purchase, and a religious institution finding itself ready to build a children's center are all examples of NPOs contemplating capital projects, which demand good decisions. The business sector is highly oriented toward making decisions about production capability and other profit-inducing projects based on quantitative information. The nonprofit sector should be no less attentive to the extent that capital *needs* can be measured in dollar terms. Businesses focus on present values to understand the dollar outcomes of investments today and their effect on dollars returned in the future.[5] This section will discuss and demonstrate the use of net discounted cash flows and associated quantitative techniques that can be helpful to decision makers. These associated techniques include *net present value* (NPV), *internal rate of return* (IRR), and *payback period* (PP). In discussing these issues, readers need to keep in mind that NPOs must consider both financial and nonfinancial criteria in making their decisions. Quantitative analysis should not be the lone determining factor. NPOs may be influenced to make capital needs decisions based on community or other needs assessments. Businesses do not tend to be so motivated. For NPOs, all reasonable assumptions about the project and the community must be considered. It is also important that wisdom and judgment be applied to capital project decision making. Quantitative analysis will inform that wisdom and judgment.

Cost and Benefit Streams

A word about returns on investment is appropriate here. It may be necessary for an NPO to measure returns (benefit streams). While capital projects are often easy to measure in dollar terms, many projects will not result in clear monetary benefits. Recall from Chapter 8 the case analysis of the Heads Up Agency, which was trying to decide between two programs using cost-benefit analysis. There was a need to compare the costs and benefits of one project to the costs and benefits of another. To do that, it was necessary to reduce the comparison of projects and programs to a single unit of measurement, that is, to measure apples against apples. Dollars are the best measure because they are quantitative in nature, and because dollar values are easily understood. Nevertheless, some costs and benefits were not easily given dollar values, and it was recommended that key players be involved in developing monetary values for costs and benefits. That process may be necessary for measuring the cost and benefit streams of capital projects in some NPOs.

Discounting

Chapter 8 also introduced the concept of the time value of money. This concept is an important aspect of talking about discounting and what is called an annuity. An annuity is a financial instrument where the buyer of the annuity will receive money at regular intervals in the future. A discount is nothing more than the rate at which the value of an annuity erodes. The problem for the buyer is that inflation, uncertainty, and opportunity costs affect the *real dollar* value of those future payments. For a buyer, in calculating the value of future payments, there is a need to discount the value of the future payments in order to predict their *buying power*. The buyer's key players must agree on the effects of inflation to be included in calculating the value of an annuity's payment stream. Another factor affecting future payments is uncertainty about the future. For an NPO, this may not be measurable in dollar terms as easily as it would be for a person trying to build a retirement portfolio or for a business. But in pure annuity terms, many external and internal events could affect an investment in an annuity: war, changes in demographics, economic upheaval, loss of a key staff person, and so on. Finally, Chapter 3 introduced the concept of *opportunity* cost as it affects the strategic plan. A discount rate should reflect the value of what a buyer gives up in order to purchase an annuity. It is up to the NPO and its stakeholders and board members to select a discount rate that makes the most sense for its programs.

The following discussion refreshes the concept of the time value of money here, because NPV, IRR, and PP use this concept in discounting future earnings streams. These simple calculations are provided to demonstrate how the estimates work. All three concepts deal basically with the concept of present value. Present value brings all future earnings back to their value in the present for the purpose of comparing alternatives. Recall the basic formula for the present value of an annuity that divides a stream of benefits by a formula as follows:

Stream of Costs or Benefits

$$PV_A = (1 + r)^{time}$$

Where: PV_A = (present value of an annuity) = stream of costs or benefits.

r = the discount rate.

(1+r) = an expression that will form the basis of the annual discount rate. For year 1, the expression is $(1 + r)$, year 2 is $(1 + r)^2$, year 3 is $(1 + r)^3$, year 4 is $(1 + r)^4$, and year 5 is $(1 + r)^5$ and so on.

time = period of time (usually a year) labeled as 1, 2, 3, 4 and 5 but calculated as an exponent.

Example:

$1,000 per year for five years   Discount rate (r) = 10 percent.

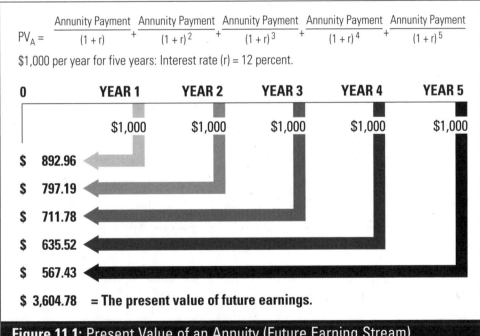

Figure 11.1: Present Value of an Annuity (Future Earning Stream)

With this example as a basis for demonstrating the concepts of present value and discounting, the discussion turns to PP, NPV, and IRR, using the following simple illustrations of selecting the better of two projects. Projects are compared using all three techniques in Figures 11.3, 11.4, and 11.5. The following income streams of Projects One and Two are noted in Figure 11.2 and apply to all three examples.

YEAR	PROJECT ONE	PROJECT TWO
0	($90)	($110)
1	15	75
2	55	50
3	85	30

Figure 11.2: Project Benefit Stream

Payback Period

Payback period is a straightforward technique that demonstrates how fast a project pays for itself, that is, how fast it pays the investor back for the original investment. It does not actually use discounting, but it is useful to many investors. That is, *PP* shows decision makers when a project's payback reaches the value of the original investment in capital. Some people and some NPOs would hold faster repayment as a value, but not everyone holds that value. The formula calculates a time period. In the example in Figure 11.3, the project with the lowest *PP* is the one that is selected.

The initial investment for Project One is $90 and Project Two is $110. To find the payback period for these projects, you must first determine the year in which the cumulative income stream equals or exceeds the original investment. See the following:

In Project One, the first year income of $15 is added to the original investment. Thus, after year 1, $75 remains to be paid. After year 2's income of $55 is subtracted from the balance to be paid back, $75, there remains $20 to be repaid. In year 3, the income of $85 is $60 more than the remaining $25, leav-

	PROJECT ONE		PROJECT TWO	
INITIAL INVESTMENT		$90		$110
YEAR	**Annual Payoff Income**	**Balance**	**Annual Payoff Income**	**Balance**
1	15	($75)	75	(35)
2	55	(20)	50	15
3	85	65	30	45

Project One payback occurs during year 3. Thus, payback occurs in 2 full years plus part of the third year.

Payback Period = 2 + (20/85)   Payback Period = 2.35 years

Project Two payback occurs during year 2. Payback occurs in 1 full year plus part of the second year.

Payback Period = 1 + (25/45)   Payback Period = 1.595 years

Best selection is Project Two if Payback Period is the preferred strategy.

Figure 11.3: Payback Period

ing a balance of $50 over the initial investment of $100. Thus, Project One is paid back before the end of the third year. In other words, the project is paid back in two years plus a portion of the third year. The portion of the year is calculated by dividing the income stream, $85, into the balance at the end of the previous year ($20), resulting in a payback period of 2.375. Thus,

Payback Period = 2 plus $30/$80 = 2.375

For Project Two:

Payback Period = 1 plus $25/$45 = 1.595

The Decision:

The project with the smaller *PP* would be selected because the sole decision-making criterion is how fast the project "pays back" its original investment. Project Two is selected. Remember that *PP* does not discount cash flows. It assumes that all cash flows are known with certainty. Finally, it does not measure the profitability of the projects. In fact, Project One has a higher return on investment, that is, profitability.

Go-No Go selection: If only looking at one project, the NPO would have to apply its own reasoning to whether the calculated PP is sufficient to do the project.

Net Present Value

NPV is calculated as the difference between the present value of future income streams and the current cash outlay to pay for an investment. Note that net present value includes a discount rate in the calculation. The formula is:

$$NPV = \sum_{t=0}^{n} \frac{CF_t}{(1+k)^t}$$

where CF = cash flow, t = a given year, k = the discount rate.

When comparing two projects, the project with the highest NPV should be selected. The reason for using a criterion of a higher NPV is that the NPV is a measure of wealth, and the higher the NPV, the more money that is returned. In the example here, assume a discount rate of ten percent (see Figure 11.4).

$$NPV_{One} = -\$90 + \frac{\$15}{(1+.1)} + \frac{\$55}{(1+.1)^2} + \frac{\$85}{(1+.1)^3}$$

$$= -\$90 + \$13.63 + \$45.45 + \$63.86$$

$$= \$32.94$$

$$NPV_{Two} = -\$110 + \frac{\$75}{(1.1)} + \frac{\$50}{(1.1)^2} + \frac{\$20}{(1.1)^3}$$

$$= -\$110 + \$68.18 + \$41.32 + \$15.03$$

$$= \$14.53$$

The rule is to select the largest NPV. Therefore, if NPV is an organization's strategy, select Project One.

Figure 11.4: Net Present Value Less Initial Investment

Again, the key to understanding the example is that net present value measures real dollar values. Therefore, its concern is the maximization of wealth. For this reason, NPV is the most popular decision-making technique used by business.

The Decision:

Selection between alternatives: select Project Two.

Go/No Go selection: If only one project is being considered, if the NPV is positive, it is a candidate to be selected.

Internal Rate of Return

IRR, like NPV, discounts cash flows using a selected discount rate. The goal of IRR is to select the project where the difference between costs and benefits equals at least zero. The project whose IRR exceeds zero is presumed to be economically viable. The goal is not to maximize wealth. The goal is to find the internal rate of return, that is, the discount rate where costs and benefits are equal. Note that the calculation of the IRR is not simple. While there are computer programs and business calculators that calculate this measure, to hand calculate means having to guess at a starting point and then arrive at the point where IRR exactly equals zero through trial and error.

$$\text{IRR} = 0 = \sum_{t=0}^{n} \frac{CF_t}{(1+k)^t}$$ where CF = cash flow, t = a given year, k = the discount rate.

The project with the highest IRR should be selected. Assume a discount rate of ten percent.

See the calculation of Project Two in Figure 11.5.

IRR_{One}: $\$0 = -\$90 + \underline{\$15} + \underline{\$55} + \underline{\$85}$

$$\qquad (1+r) \quad (1+r)^2 \quad (1+r)^3$$

r is the unknown. Use calculator or trial and error.

Project One calculation and result is

$$-\$90 + \underline{\$15} + \underline{\$55} + \underline{\$85}$$

$$(1.25) \quad (1.25)^2 \quad (1.25)^3$$

$$r = \text{IRR}_D = 12.5\%$$

Project Two calculation and result is

$$\$110 - \underline{\$10} + \underline{\$60} + \underline{\$80}$$

$$(1.26) \quad (1.26)^2 \quad (1.26)^3$$

$$r = \text{IRR}_D = 12.6\%$$

If internal rate of return is the preferred strategy, then Project Two is best option because it is greater.

Figure 11.5: Internal Rate of Return

The Decision:

Selection between alternatives: select Project Two.

Go/No-Go selection: If only one project is being considered, and if the NPV is positive, it should be selected.

Capital Decision-Making Summary

The techniques just discussed are used extensively in the business sector, and there is no reason they cannot be used by NPOs. The information they provide is not a complete view of a decision. There may be limitations or community concerns that limit the use of these techniques. And NPOs need to remember that these or any quantitative technique will simply inform the decision makers and should not be used as a substitute for responsibility and judgment.

FINANCING CAPITAL PROJECTS

Financing in the nonprofit sector is an adventure in creativity. There are two primary ways to pay for capital projects, pay-as-you-go (PAYGO) and pay-as-you-use (PAYUSE). PAYGO means that you charge the costs of capital to current donors and members only. The perceived obligation is not to impose costs on future donors and members. The philosophy of pay-as-you-go financing is to pay for a project only after enough money is saved in either a special fund or a capital campaign, or after the desired project is made part of the operational budget. Putting the project in the budget is costly in terms of time but free of financing costs. PAYUSE financing is associated with borrowing the money or selling bonds needed to construct or purchase a project and repaying the money over a period of years. Using this method means the NPO will raise funds slowly, use operational funds, or borrow the money needed to pay for the project. It implies the need to go into debt. The rest of this section explores traditional and creative financing.

Paying Out of the Budget

The pay-as-you-go approach for financing a capital project is to budget contributions to a reserve fund during each budget period. This approach avoids the cost of paying interest on a loan or on bonds. It is fiscally responsible, of course, and when the fund is large enough to pay for the project, the project will be paid for in cash. Setting aside money to a reserve fund should be based on a plan with a definite time period so that everyone understands that the money is for an identifiable purpose. The plan may be long-term or short-term depending on how much money is available in each budget period for the reserve fund. The NPO should not use the money in the fund for any other purpose than the designated project. In some cases, NPOs may be able to do a large project in phases, budgeting parts of the project each year until the project cost is available in the reserve fund.

Capital Campaigns

The traditional method of funding a nonprofit project for most NPOs is to raise money from donors, businesses, and other individuals solely for the purpose of constructing one or more specific-use facilities. Agencies of all sizes ranging from volunteer organizations to hospitals and universities use this approach to financing capital projects. Such a fundraising campaign needs to be well-planned, convincing, noncompetitive with other agencies or projects, and held infrequently enough to keep faithful donors from feeling overburdened.

Grants

Occasionally, some foundations and even governments appropriate money and distribute it to NPOs for the purpose of funding all or part of a capital improvement.

Borrowing

Paying-as-you-use means that you can start a project now and pay for it later. The point of financing a project through borrowing is to provide an immediate service or activity without having to wait until money is saved. It also spreads the costs over a long period of time to make sure all those who benefit from a project over the years of its life share in the cost. The trade off is that it usually means paying more for the project than when paying cash. Repayments, which will likely include interest at some negotiated rate, must be repaid out of the annual budget. Banks and credit unions may support all or parts of loans to NPOs. A large NPO that uses the services of smaller NPOs to deliver services might be in a position to lend money without charging interest. Likewise, national and international NPOs might have loans available for local and regional projects.

Large NPOs such as churches, museums, universities, and hospitals may be able to issue corporate bonds to finance major projects. The process of selling bonds is quite complex. Such bonds can only be structured by using a consultant and bond counsel. Buyers are usually large institutions like banks that negotiate a purchase price with the issuer and its consultant. Bonds as issued by NPOs most likely cannot interest investors without what is known as a bond safety rating. This will affect the interest that the issuing agency must pay on the bonds. But while all investors make subjective decisions to take risks, risk is captured in terms of credit ratings that are assigned by the respected Standard & Poor's and Moody's companies and shown in Figure 11.6.

Moody's Investor Service	SYMBOL	SYMBOL	Standard & Poor's
Best quality, smallest risk	Aaa	AAA	Prime, highest quality, lowest risk
High quality; higher risk	As	AA	High grade, still very secure
Upper medium grade, favorable	A	A	Upper medium grade, safe
Medium grade, not high protection	Baa	BBB	Medium grade, lowest security
Judged to have speculative elements	Ba	BB	Lower medium grade, weaknesses
Not a desirable investment	B	B	Low grade investment
Poor standing, possible default	Caa	CCC	
Speculative in high degree	Ca	CC	Defaults
Lowest rated, don't invest	C	C	

Figure 11.6: Bond Safety Ratings

Moody's, Standard & Poor's, and other ratings services assign letter ratings to bonds based on the risk of default. Certain trusts and pension funds are not allowed to invest in bonds with ratings lower than investment grade. Bond rates that contain "C" in them indicate there are serious doubts in the minds of the raters about the financial condition of a company issuing such bonds.

Endowments

Endowment funds are the least painful funds that an NPO can obtain, but they are difficult to obtain. An endowment is a large and long-term fund usually set up by a wealthy donor for a specific purpose that is provided by an NPO. It is usually a one-time gift of principal intended to earn interest proceeds. Those proceeds comprise the money that can be used for the purpose. Occasionally, endowments are given in order to fund capital projects.

CAPITAL DEBT POLICY

Organizations enter into long-term debt essentially so that they can finance long-term capital projects such as high-cost capital items that require cash payments to contractors. No one likes debt, particularly a small NPO. Without the ability to borrow, however, many capital projects would be inadequate or nonexistent. There are two reasons organizations incur debt. The first is the need to finance current expenditures, such as what the federal government does at its worst. NPOs should not operate with a deficit. The second reason is to finance a capital expenditure. Regarding the former, the debt incurred may exacerbate the financial difficulties experienced by an entity whose revenues and ability to meet its day-to-day obligations fall short of estimates. The latter form of debt is related to the large capital expenditures discussed in this chapter. The financing of these expenditures can be based on the pay-as-you-use philosophy in order not to pressure current budgetary needs. The downside to this method is that the term of the debt does not exceed the useful life of the project and the NPO has to pay for a facility that has become obsolete. Sometimes, however, borrowing is necessary for meeting mission and goals. One way to offset the problem of indebtedness is to plan ahead and use capital budgeting and investments to pay for most items. The best budget usually will not pay for all capital items. It is not a financial sin to borrow, but not having an effective debt policy is a sin.

Bond markets and interest rates are external factors that negatively or positively affect the decisions to acquire physical capital assets. Obviously, the costs of borrowing are major contributors to overall costs to an organization. Cost and time savings can result from a well-constructed and planned capital debt process that is guided by the strategic plan. The intended outcome is to acquire effective capital assets that exactly meet the mission and goals of an organization. Financial advisors can provide valuable input and greater understanding of bonded indebtedness. This is especially true when an NPO needs to understand bond safety ratings services and how a repayment schedule is restructured. The more well informed the NPO is, the easier it will be to handle bonded indebtedness. A thoughtful and effective debt policy will help ensure the financial security of an NPO. It will serve board and management objectives by providing sensible guidelines for incurring, managing, and paying off debts. The debt policy should, at a minimum, address the total indebtedness that the NPO can handle in order to avoid defaulted payments on debt. The policy should also identify acceptable purposes for various types of indebtedness. Finally, the debt policy should define the structure of the debt issuances by type.

Financial resources always are limited. An enforced debt policy will help an organization maintain manageable investments in capital. Staff and board members can more easily balance the need for capital assets with the willingness of donors to pay for the high costs associated with it. A debt policy should mandate coordination with the budget to ensure that construction, repair, and replacement of capital items are consistent with limits established in the debt policy.

SUMMARY

Capital budgets, like operational budgets, need to be guided by the strategic plan. Decisions to invest in capital projects are serious responsibilities for boards and executives. For several reasons, many NPOs have been slow to adopt the techniques used in the business sector for capital decision making: the time required to using them effectively, the difficulty in pricing costs and benefits, and the lack of financial expertise. NPOs tend to be mission-oriented first, even when it comes to capital investments. But they also need to apply neutral, rational approaches when faced with making decisions for large-dollar capital projects. Such decision making requires answering both financial and nonfinancial questions that will help decide what to invest in or even whether an investment should be made. While it is best for NPOs not to incur debt to pay for high-cost items, that is not always possible. An effective and comprehensive debt policy is the next best way to approach paying for capital projects.

DISCUSSION QUESTIONS

1. The pace of change affecting nonprofit operations today continues to accelerate and grow in complexity. To create a sense of stability and coherence in this dynamic world, nonprofits should consider developing a corporate strategic plan. Capital budgeting combines planning, evaluating, and financing capital projects. What is the relationship between the strategic plan and the capital budget? For example, what effect might there be on financial performance from development and use of a strategic plan? Consider all possible aspects of the relationship between the capital budget and strategic planning.

2. The long-term capital investments made today determine the long-term value of those investments. Capital budgeting analysis forces NPOs to critically assess alternatives for their ability to create value for the organization. The decision-making techniques discussed in this chapter help to reduce the uncertainty in those critical high-cost decisions. Therefore, one of the biggest challenges in capital budgeting is to manage uncertainty. Those techniques include the following:

    *   Payback Period

    *   Internal Rate of Return

    *   Net Present Value

3. Discuss each of the techniques. Think of projects that an NPO in your sphere of knowledge is doing, has done, or is considering doing. Match decision-making techniques to these projects. Explain why you made the choices you did.

EXERCISE

The fictitious Knotfer Prophet Agency is comparing alternative projects. It has put the decision in the hands of its finance officer, who decides to take a quantitative approach. He decides to use Payback Period and Net Present Value analyses to arrive at his recommendation to the CEO and the Board. You are the finance officer. Calculate the Payback Period and Net Present Value of both alternatives and recommend which alternative should be selected by the NPO. Then explain the reasons for your selection.

Here are the facts:

Building Project Proposal A

Principal Investment (cost): $780,000

Estimated Benefit Stream (expressed in dollars):

Year 1:	$17,000
Year 2:	$11,000
Year 3:	$ 7,500
Year 4:	$ 3,900
Total:	$39,400

Discount Rate: 9%

Building Project Proposal B

Principal Investment (cost): $707,000

Estimated Benefit Stream (expressed in dollars):

Year 1:	$ 7,200
Year 2:	$11,800
Year 3:	$13,300
Year 4:	$16,500

Discount Rate: 9%

INNOVATION:
LEASING TECHNOLOGY TO FREE UP CAPITAL

Information technology (IT) is a huge capital expense for any organization and particularly for a medium-sized or small NPO. Today, IT is nearly a necessity as well. The financial challenge for NPOs is striking a balance between expensive and necessary. One way to strike that balance might be to enter into a favorable leasing agreement with a supplier. Leasing is an option used quite often with a lot of capital items—automobiles, buildings—quite regularly.

Cisco Systems, Inc. is an example of an IT supplier with a leasing program that NPOs might want to study. A customer case study showed that one of Cisco's clients, a college, wanting to preserve its cash, determined that it wanted to have a framework that could grow with enrollment and that included high-speed Internet access and the ability to add new services for students and the rest of the college. Cisco had a lease program that let the college meet these goals while enabling the college to keep its cash for other purposes that supported its educational mission.[6]

If leasing a computer system, or any other capital item for that matter, meets an NPO's needs, the NPO should explore such options. The NPO should conduct a financial analysis by using one or more of the same capital decision-making techniques discussed in this chapter. It should compare its options in two ways. First, the NPO should compare the cost of leasing versus purchasing. Second, it should compare leasing alternatives.

NOTES

1   Matt Evans, "Matt Evans on Finance—Examples of Key Performance Indicators," February 03, 2007. Online at http://www.certifiedconsultants.org (accessed April 28, 2008).

2   J. Shim and J. Siegel, *Financial Management for Nonprofits* (New York: McGraw-Hill, 1997).

3   G. E. Pinches, "Myopia: Capital Budgeting and Decision Making," *Financial Management* 11 (1982): 16–19.

4   Matt Evans, "Matt Evans on Finance—Examples of Key Performance Indicators," February 03, 2007. Online at http://www.certifiedconsultants.org (accessed April 28, 2008).

5   Ibid.

6   Cisco Systems, Inc., *Customer Case Study. Cisco Capital Leasing Agreement,* 2007. Online at http://www.cisco.com/web/UK/pdfs/cisco_capital/ROC_van_Twente.pdf (accessed April 28, 2008).

CHAPTER 12
Personnel Compensation: Salaries, Benefits, and Retirement

This final chapter provides a look at the responsibilities that the human resource management team has toward an NPO's budget and finance operations. Human beings and their labor is the major input to an NPO, not only in terms of ideas but also in terms of costs. Recruiting quality employees and retaining them for their experience is often the biggest challenge an organization faces. The chapter defines employee compensation as a delicate process requiring strategic thinking. The process also requires providing answers to the following questions: How does an NPO compete in the employment market without busting the budget? What can an NPO do to satisfy its staff members in a fair and understandable way, so that morale does not suffer? How does an NPO place a dollar value on individuals? What is an appropriate benefits package?

TOPICS
- Planned Compensation: Salary, Benefits, and Retirement Packages
- Components of a Compensation System
- Wage and Salary Structure
- Benefits
- Retirement
- Compensation Administration
- Summary
- Discussion Questions
- Exercise
- Innovation

PLANNED COMPENSATION: SALARY, BENEFITS, AND RETIREMENT PACKAGES

There is a delightful trend of people working in the business sector who are driven to help create positive social change. To do so, they are leaving their big business-sector salary opportunities and seeking employment the nonprofit sector. Even though they are willing to leave the big bucks behind, they still need to get paid. Lloyd Harger writes that, "simply defined, worker's [employee] compensation recompenses something to a worker, one who performs labor for another, for services rendered or for injuries."[1] Not to pay compensation in exchange for labor provided by a worker is the very definition of a slavery system. In a free market system, workers get paid for doing their jobs according to what the market will bear. In modern times, thankfully, most people are paid for their labor. In the United States, compensation varies among jobs and professions. Market forces, economic sectors, tradition, culture, labor advocacy, and other economic and social concepts differentiate the wages paid for skill and knowledge. Societies tend to value some jobs over others when it comes to compensation. Human resource employees must keep up with compensation trends and the salaries that can and should be offered to job candidates.

For most NPOs and most other types of organizations, human services constitute the most expensive capital resource. Compensation is vitally important to both individuals and the organizations that hire and retain them. Thus, recruitment and retention become the prime motivations for the human resource goals among NPOs. But organizations cannot pay each employee the amount that he or she thinks they are worth. Finding and keeping qualified NPO employees often depends on the amount of work required of them, the personalities of managers and of governing board members, and a variety of other individual factors. Usually, it most heavily depends on the employees receiving their desired package of income and benefits. The fact is that everyone employed in the world of work wants a larger paycheck. Organizations, however, have to balance their own resources with the availability of qualified candidates and market forces. This leads to competition among NPOs for the best workers. Competition is an important factor in employee hiring and in the retention of desirable employees, and highlights the need for an effective compensation system.

COMPONENTS OF A COMPENSATION SYSTEM

A compensation system contains the following essential components:

- Wage and salary structure

- Benefits

- Retirement

While there are a number of approaches, compensation primarily means money paid to hired staff in the form of salary in exchange for the value staff contribute to an organization's well-being. Governing boards normally are responsible for creating compensation policies. Compensating someone with a salary in a systematic way may give a person a strong motive to join an organization and to perform well, and also serves as a means for the person to meet his or her need for job satisfaction.

Basic salaries meet basic needs. Benefits that are over and above the salary for a position are frequently included in an offer and provide the potential employee with an incentive to work for the organization. While benefits are often less important to youthful employees, they often appeal to older employees, especially those with families, who often appreciate the true value of such benefits. These benefits make an organization more competitive for some employees and may provide a potential employee with sufficient compensation to make a not-so-high salary acceptable. Benefits can be offered in numerous forms, including expensive retirement programs, health care packages, and in-facility day care centers as well as less-expensive cafeteria plans and employee assistance programs.

Wage and Salary Structure

Developing an effective wage and salary structure requires some set of the following conditions and components:[2]

- A compensation committee

- Consistent executive compensation according to the organization's bylaws

- Comparability studies

- Reasonable compensation

- Fair policies to determine employee raises

- Clear bonus policies

- Attractive nonfinancial incentives

- Sensible commission policies

- Understandable overtime policies

Many employees prefer to work in organizations that provide consistent and understandable pay structures. This often means recognizable pay grades and steps in salary opportunities. Most pay structures include several pay grades and several steps within each pay grade. Each step within a pay grade is incremental in the sense that each is a percentage of the base salary within a pay grade. An example of a pay structure is found in Exhibit 12.1 in the section "Compensation Administration."

Another type of salary includes an incentive as part of or over and above the established pay grade and step. Fundraisers and volunteer recruiters are among the types of positions within NPOs that are willing to risk salary with the added payoff in the form of incentives.

Organizations usually associate compensation and pay ranges with job descriptions in the organization. The ranges include the minimum and the maximum amount of money that can be earned per year in that role.[3]

Jobs in organizations have two classifications, exempt and nonexempt. Generally, employer treatment of the concepts of exempt and nonexempt has to do with legal protections of nonexempt workers. Exempt employees generally are paid a defined annual salary and nonexempt employees receive defined hourly wages. It is common for nonexempt employees to receive lower compensation than exempt employees within an organization. Nonexempt workers are paid for overtime work for any work over 40 hours and on holidays.

Generally, exempt employees do not receive overtime compensation, but they are expected to work until the job gets done or with a structured or creative way of finishing the job.

The Fair Labor Standards Act (FLSA) is a federal law that protects nonexempt employees by setting a minimum wage, requiring overtime pay and record keeping, and defining child labor standards requirements for both employers and employees covered by the law. It does not preempt state wage and hour standards except when FLSA is more beneficial to an organization's employees. Employees are protected by FLSA if their work is performed in the United States (or U.S. territory), a true employer-employee relationship exists, and the requirements of one of the following tests are met: a) Two or more employees are sufficiently engaged in interstate commerce or in the production, handling, or selling of goods or materials moved or produced for interstate commerce; and b) The employer has gross annual sales of not less than $500,000, unless working in an enterprise not subject to this dollar-value test (that is, hospitals and nursing homes).[4]

Benefits

An employee benefit is really a form of compensation over and above salary. Some benefits, such as unemployment and workers' compensation, are required by federal law. Workers' compensation is really a worker's right, rather than a benefit. Benefits usually include health and life insurance, retirement plans, disability insurance, sick leave, and vacation time. Benefits are expensive, even though employees may contribute a portion of the cost. Most NPOs cannot afford to provide every possible benefit. Assembling a benefits package and deciding which benefits to leave in and which to leave out is one of the great dilemmas for human resource compensation experts. Medical and hospitalization insurance (commonly called health insurance) is a special challenge for NPOs who offer that benefit, because employee premiums are continuously increasing. While the range of benefits that an NPO might offer seems limitless, it is a terrible challenge for an NPO to put together a package of benefits that maintains its competitiveness for quality employees while not busting the budget. This section describes some of the most common benefits offered by NPOs today.

Disability Insurance

According to the American Council of Life Insurers, nearly one-third of all Americans will suffer a serious disability between the ages of 35 and 65. Statistics like that should make short-term disability insurance a vital piece of an overall financial plan. Normally, disability insurance covers disabilities from illness or injuries that are not job-related. By federal regulation, workers compensation programs cover on-the-job injuries.[5]

Short-Term Disability Leave

The benefit known as short-term disability leave allows employees absences because of an illness or injury. Short-term disability leave is considered accredited time toward seniority and simultaneously as a family and medical leave under the federal Family and Medical Leave Act (FMLA). By this regulation, employers are not required to pay the employee during his or her absence but are required to allow the employee to return to work. Short-term disability includes sick leave.

Long-Term Disability Paid Leave

An employer can obtain a group long-term disability plan at a cost that is lower than the cost to an individual. Long-term disability is a benefit to employees who need to be away from their work for a long period of time because of illness or injury. The typical plan will pay a large portion of an employee's normal salary while he or she is out of work. Long-term leave typically begins after 90 to 180 continuous days of disability or when short-term disability benefits end. This type of insurance, while expensive, is an attractive benefit for those employees who have, for some reason, learned to fear the disaster that can occur from a long-term illness. It is not something that the typical employee will obtain. Because of the expense, many employees are willing to risk the consequences of a long-term disability and do not sign up for the benefit. Actuarial studies suggest that the risk of an employee seeking long-term disability payments is low. So long-term disability insurance is one of the nicer benefits an organization can offer without incurring much expense. In other words, an NPO can offer it but does not necessarily have to pay for it.

Life Insurance

An employer can often make a recruiting and retention coup by offering life insurance to its employees. As defined by the Historical Text Archive, "Life insurance reflects one of the best parts of human beings: caring for others. One buys life insurance because he or she loves their spouse and children. There are benefits while living but the real reason for life insurance is to make sure others are financially taken care of."[6] This benefit adds to employees' confidence that an NPO cares for its employees and their families, the beneficiaries of the policy.

Accidental Death or Dismemberment

This special type of insurance is sometimes provided by an employer to cover fatal accidents or accidents that result in an employee's loss of eyesight or a limb. There are usually stipulations to the coverage. For example, a death must occur within the employer-designated time frame of the date an accident occurred. The death or dismemberment must be proved as having occurred as a direct result of the accident. Accidental death and dismemberment insurance should be considered as a supplement to a life insurance policy. Risky or extreme hobbies, such as skydiving, bungee jumping, or extreme sports may not be covered by this type of insurance, because you are routinely engaging in dangerous activities. Many employees would prefer to put the cost of such a policy toward the purchase of more health or life insurance coverage.

Medical/Hospitalization

Medical and hospitalization insurance (health insurance) is a special challenge for NPOs because premiums have increased at an annual average of over seven percent. The average employee contribution to company-provided health insurance has increased more than 143 percent since 2000.[7] The cost of this type of health insurance is usually paid by employers, although responsibility is increasingly becoming a shared effort between employer and employees. Health insurance is a type of insurance whereby the insurer pays the medical costs of the insured if the insured becomes sick because of covered causes or due to accidents. The insurer may be a private organization or a government agency. Market-based health care systems such as those in the United States rely primarily on private health insurance. This benefit is the most expensive benefit an employer may provide, and costs for this insurance increase at a higher rate than do those of other benefits. Many NPOs simply cannot afford to purchase this insurance for their employees.

Cafeteria Plans

Cafeteria plans give NPOs a variety of benefit choices that can be customized for individual employees. They allow the employee to defer income for tax purposes. To do so, the employee must set aside money from their salary and apply it to selected benefits offered by the NPO. Typical benefits include health care premiums, childcare costs, and medical or dental treatment programs. For example, if an employee knows in advance of the need for, for example, expensive dental work such as orthodontia, he or she can plan to have that amount deducted over the course of a year's worth of paychecks, and federal income taxes will be deferred in the amount paid. A big drawback is that if the employee fails to spend the deferred money within a year, it is sometimes lost.

ERISA

If an NPO provides pensions and health care benefits, then the NPOs must provide reliable pension and health care plans that are consistent with federal and state laws. These protections do result in administrative costs if the NPO provides health insurance and pensions. The Employee Retirement Income Security Act of 1974 (ERISA) is a federal law that sets minimum standards for most voluntarily established pension and health plans in private industry (including nonprofits). These standards insure the individual covered in these plans. The Health Insurance Portability and Accountability Act (HIPAA) is an amendment to ERISA that protects members and beneficiaries of health benefit plans. It protects employed Americans and their families who have preexisting medical conditions or are discriminated against in health coverage based on factors that relate to an individual's health. Newer ERISA amendments cover mothers, children, mental health, and women with breast cancer and ensure that certain minimums of health care coverage are included in health plans. These amendments are:

- Newborns' and Mothers' Health Protection Act

- Mental Health Parity Act

- Women's Health and Cancer Rights Act

ERISA excludes these protections from "group health plans established or maintained by churches for their employees, or plans which are maintained solely to comply with applicable workers compensation, unemployment, or disability laws."[8]

Retirement

Pension plans are normally associated with private companies and government agencies. Some NPOs include pension plans in addition to 401(k) and 403(b) tax-deferred investment plans. This benefit is costly to maintain, but it is an important aspect of a total compensation plan. Pensions are payments that are promised to employees after they get to a certain age or after another specified time, such as a combination of age and years employed. They can take the form of lifetime annuities. Some plans continue to pay the beneficiaries of retired employees after their death. The financial instruments known as 401(k) and 403(b) are employee-sponsored retirement plans.

Some large NPOs may have pension plans that must be managed to ensure that they are fully covered in the sense that they are *actuarially* sound. That is, contributions to the plan and interest earned on investments of funds must be earning enough money for the pension to pay for current retirees' pensions, and the pension must have an investment strategy that ensures that all potential retirees will be covered. Underfunded pension plans are at risk of default. Pensions are categorized on the basis of who is making contributions to the plan. There are two types: *defined benefit* and *defined contribution*.

Defined Benefit

A defined benefit plan promises to employees who participate in the plan that they will get a stated monthly retirement benefit if they meet the requirements in terms of salary, age, and length of service. Monthly benefits are usually calculated through a specific formula involving those factors. Under the defined benefit plan employees may or may not make a contribution from their salaries depending on the rules and policies of the organization. Unlike defined contribution plans, the participant is not required to make investment decisions. Funds are managed either by the employer or by a professional fund manager. The strength of that fund, however, should not be a factor in a defined benefit plan that is designed to guarantee that the employer will make specific payments.

Defined Contribution

Defined contribution plans provide an individual account for each employee who participates in the plan. The benefits are based on the amount contributed and are also affected by income, expenses, gains, and losses. Benefits are calculated based on how much has been contributed to the participant's plan account and the account's investment earnings. Some examples of defined contribution plans include Internal Revenue Code 401(k) plans, 403(b) plans, employee stock ownership plans, and profit-sharing plans. Many employers match a percentage of the employee's contribution to the plan.

IRS-regulated 401(k) and 403(b) plans are funds that defer taxation on the money put into them. The employee manages his or her own account through a fund manager selected by the employer. In theory, when the employee retires (generally after the age of 59), his or her income will likely be smaller than when he or she was employed. The result is that the employee's tax rate will be reduced.

COMPENSATION ADMINISTRATION

Human capital, that is, the NPO's employees, usually accounts for the highest costs of fulfilling a nonprofit's mission. Human resource experts have an important role in advising executives and governing boards on the costs of hiring and retaining employees. There are several key actions and tools that contribute to an NPO's ability to control its human resource costs.

Job Descriptions

It is important for employees to have the perception that their salaries are fair. Fairness can be achieved if the compensation system is codified and understood. A set of codified job descriptions is, therefore, an important part of a compensation system. The responsibility of developing job descriptions and requirements falls on human resource experts. It is an important responsibility, because a good job description captures the appropriateness of the salary for a position. From time to time, specific responsibilities change in the job market and old job descriptions can become outdated. Writers of job descriptions should make sure job descriptions reflect current language specific to the type of job being described. Additionally, job descriptions should be balanced by budgetary limitations and should exactly reflect the responsibilities, duties, and all other functional aspects of a particular job.

Salary Studies

The development of the pay structure should focus externally and should be sensitive to market considerations. Salary surveys collect salary and market data to examine average salaries for valued positions in the organization. They may also examine inflation and cost-of-living indicators, and may be conducted within a specific geographical region or across different geographical regions. An NPO cannot rely completely on the results of a salary survey when addressing employees' salaries. Some jobs are not as important to an NPO. On the other hand, some positions that are highly valued by the NPOs may actually be overvalued when compared with data from market pay studies.[9] An NPO should carefully use salary studies as information in decision making, not as the deciding factor.

Pay Structure

Perhaps the most important policy instrument an NPO can use to achieve desired recruitment and retention goals is its pay structure. As stated earlier, most employees prefer to work in organizations with an understandable and consistent pay structure. The NPO's pay structure relates the value of each position, in dollars, to the organization's mission. The result of calculating a pay structure is a hierarchy of values. Each job in the NPO receives a value, and the value grows in steps with time and merit. An example of a pay structure is presented in Table 12.1. It shows a pay structure that contains pay grades with steps equal to one percent of the previous salary. Thus, for example, for pay

POSITION	PAY GRADE	ANNUAL SALARY	STEP 1	STEP 2	STEP 3	STEP 4	STEP 5	STEP 6	STEP 7	STEP 8
Executive Director	05	$70–85k	$70k	$700 70,700	$707 71,407	$714 72,121	$721 72,842	$728 73,570	$736 74,305	(Up to $85,000)
Program Manager	04	$47–61k	$47k	$475 47,475	$479 47,954	$484 48,438	$489 48,927	$494 49,421	$499 49,920	(Up to $61,000)
Development Director	04	$47–61k	$47k	$475 47,475	$479 47,954	$484 48,438	$489 48,927	$494 49,421	$499 49,920	(Up to $61,000)
Program Assistant	03	$35-54k	$35k	$350 35,350	$353 35,703	$357 36,060	$361 36,421	$365 36,786	$369 36,367	(Up to $54,000)
Development Assistant	03	$35-54k	$35k	$350 35,350	$353 35,703	$357 36,060	$361 36,421	$365 36,786	$369 36,367	(Up to $54,000)
Administrative Assistant	02	$30–48k	$30k	$300 30,300	$303 30,603	$306 30,909	$309 31,218	$312 31,530	$315 31,845	(Up to $48,000)
Program Aide/ Receptionist	01	$27-41k	$27k	$270 27,270	$273 27,543	$276 27,846	$279 28,125	$282 28,307	$285 28,592	(Up to $41,000)

Table 12.1: Salary Structure*

*Salary increases are given in step increments. Step increases are based on one percent of the employee's previous salary. "k" represents $1,000 dollars.

grade 03 (program assistants and development assistants), step three salary is one percent higher than step two and one percent lower than step four.

The structure in the figure should not be created in a vacuum. It is only a framework and needs substance to give it meaning. According to Susan Heathfield, an NPO's compensation philosophy and pay strategy "should consider many employee factors, including the following:[10]

- Number of years of experience
- Number of reporting staff members
- Performance evaluation results
- Hazardous working conditions
- Undesirable shifts
- Education and degrees
- Professional certifications"

Pay structure development requires the following:[11]

- Grouping jobs of similar value in the organization
- Assessing those groupings
- Determining an appropriate number of pay ranges
- Establishing salary ranges with minimum, middle, and maximum points within groupings
- Determining the amount of overlap across ranges and amounts to elevate salaries consistent with promotions

A recent innovation in pay structures is called strategic work valuation (SWV). Heathfield states that SWV "emphasizes both the market pay rate for the job and the value of the job to the organization."[12] The distinguishing feature of SWV is that the factors used in valuing a particular position are organization-specific. The tricky part is to develop specific measures for each position in the organization that reflect the value-added factor of each position to the success of the NPO's mission outcomes.

For example, your company might decide that revenue growth, external customer satisfaction, operational effectiveness, financial impact, and span of control are its most important business success drivers. In the simplest form of strategic work valuation, jobs are then strategically valued in relation to each of these drivers.[13]

When using SWV, jobs need to be classified on several levels of impact on mission outcomes. Circuit City measures jobs as drivers, moderate contributors, or sustainability adders to organization results, or jobs that are limited in their value added to the organization.[14] This valuation, combined with market factors, results in a very organization-specific valuation of jobs. Obviously, from a strategic perspective, this approach can assist in hiring and layoff situations.

After the employee factors and pay structure requirements are determined, an NPO should monitor and continuously update the factors and requirements in order to remain successful in recruitment and retention policies.

Recruitment

It is a fact of life in organizations that position vacancies occur because of resignations, firings, and creation of new positions. This can cause the often unpleasant task of hiring new employees. Often, NPOs fall lowest in the pecking order for quality hires. Competition often means having to offer the highest compensation package, but compensation is not always the most important factor.

The nonprofit sector employs close to 11 million people, or seven percent of the workforce. It is increasingly eclectic, with people from the for-profit and public sector in addition to people who have only worked in the nonprofit sector. Nonprofit professionals looking for new positions likely seek advancement opportunities, higher salaries, or a different organizational culture. People with for-profit backgrounds looking for nonprofit positions are often looking for more meaningful work or deeper relationships with colleagues.[15]

Understanding employment trends, including the fact that many people desire a higher purpose in life than compensation, is an opportunity for NPOs to find excellent recruits and determine ways to relate them to organizational success.

Retention

Employee retention is difficult in any industry, and the nonprofit sector generally pays less than private and public organizations. This is somewhat counterbalanced due to the fact that many nonprofit workers choose to work for NPOs because of a commitment to social change and to helping people. In fact, employees are motivated by factors like organizational energy, effective communication, and loyalty in addition to compensation. Nevertheless, these non-monetary motivations are not reasons to forget the responsibility that NPO boards and executives have to maximize compensation.

Raises

Pay raises have a number of purposes. At a minimum, pay raises preserve employee purchasing power. They are also used to motivate employee performance. Finally, raises may be used as a reward. Raises can come in many forms. Across-the-board percentage increases are the commonest, easiest, and perhaps most equitable approach to increasing the salaries and wages of current employees. At the direct opposite of across-the-board raises is the concept of merit increases based on quality performance evaluations. Such performance increases can be based on individual effort or teamwork. Often, in plentiful years, a combination of the across-the-board and merit raises can be a strategic method of keeping morale up while rewarding good performance. It gives employees the ability to preserve their purchasing power and encourages performance at the same time. Regardless of the approach, a pay raise policy should be part of the compensation plan and should be based in the budget and the strategic plan.

Tough-Time Strategies: Layoffs, Salary Freezes, and Salary Reductions

The tough-time side of this discussion is the effect of bad budget times on employee recruitment and retention. The ultimate consequence is, of course, layoffs, the policy of last resort for most managers. Before that decision has to be made by an NPO, other steps should be taken. A tough-time strategy should freeze salaries first before using layoffs to try to make it through the tough times. Freezes do not make employees happy, but if they can stave off the layoff monster, freezes can be endured. An even more complex challenge is the step of reducing salaries as a way of keeping everyone employed. Sometimes, of course, an NPO's recruitment and retention policy comes into direct conflict with a tough-time strategy. If highly valued employees need to be retained, freezing or lowering salaries will complicate matters. Thus, an NPO will have to make a decision to reduce or freeze the salaries of nonessential employees while maintaining or even increasing essential employees' salaries.

Types of Pay

Five common types of pay include salary, hourly wage, overtime, bonuses, and commission.

Salary

A salary generally means a regular periodic payment by an organization to an employee who has a real or implied contract to receive a portion of an annual cash compensation for performing specified activities. The proverbial *white-collar* worker is associated with the receipt of a salary.

Hourly wage

Wages generally are conceived of as *piecework* and are usually determined in hourly units. The words *blue-collar* are associated with hourly personnel.

Overtime

Hourly employees are commonly eligible for overtime pay for working more than 40 hours in a week or on holidays. According to the U.S. Department of Labor, employees covered by the Fair Labor Standards Act (FLSA) must be paid overtime pay for hours worked in excess of 40 in a work-week at a rate not less than time and one-half their regular rates of pay.[16] The Act does not affect the number of hours of overtime employees work during any period of time. While it is true that FLSA does not require overtime pay for work on Saturdays, Sundays, holidays, or regular days of rest, as such, it is often the practice of employers to pay at rates above an employee's normal rate for overtime worked during those periods.[17]

Bonuses

Bonuses comprise incentive payments over and above base salary. In most organizations that use variable pay, bonuses are awarded to employees working either alone or in teams based on the level of their contribution to organizational productivity, mission outcomes, safety records, output quality, or other measures deemed important to the success of the organization. This type of incentive pay and pay for performance are quite common in the business sector but not so much in the government and nonprofit sectors. Essentially, it says to an employee, "The more and the harder you work, the better you will be paid." That, of course, depends, or should depend, on accomplishments. Theoretically, such a system works best in a competitive job market when unemployment is low. A system of bonuses or other type of pay incentive may help in recruiting and retaining quality employees. Such a system also allows an NPO to minimize the annual base pay and give generous increases as the annual budget permits without committing the budget in the long term to higher base salaries. Of course, the base salary has to be evaluated each year to make sure that the combination of base pay and potential bonuses remains competitive.

Commissions

In some NPOs, certain employees prefer getting paid a commission based on a percentage of money raised for the organization. While the Association of Fundraising Professionals is opposed to commissions in lieu of salary, fundraising positions are occasionally outside the usual pay structure. An NPO may find that paying a commission to certain employees is an effective pay plan. The types of employees who fit this type of pay plan include those with fundraising responsibilities. Fundraising activities may include seeking donations, planning special events, grant applications, and other related activities. Commissions can motivate some employees to work at their peak level. It is not uncommon for grant writers and fundraisers to get a percentage of the money they raise for the NPO. In some NPOs, all or a portion of salary for fundraising employees may be paid through commissions. Some common types of commissions include the following:

- **Straight commission:** The fundraiser receives a percentage of the money raised with no fixed salary portion.

- **Base plus commission:** The fundraiser may be guaranteed a minimal amount of salary as a base and paid a prescribed amount of money for each dollar raised above the minimum salary.

- **Draw against commission:** The fundraiser is paid a draw or an expected amount of commission. If the amount of commission money falls below the amount prescribed, the fundraiser will pay back the difference between the commission earned and the amount expected from the draw.

Executive Compensation

In a book about NPO budgets and financial strategies, it is important to talk about those who receive the highest salaries—executives. In recent years, the compensation of executives in all the sectors of the economy has been criticized and investigated. The nonprofit sector is no exception. Generally, the publicity has come in critiques of seemingly excess salaries of national organizations. James E. Rocco and A. Bowman point out that these critiques got their start in the 1990s "in response to controversies regarding excessive compensation, such as the widely publicized United Way of America national director scandal and the 1993 series of articles in the *Philadelphia Enquirer* entitled 'Warehouses of Wealth.'"[18] Regional, state, and local agencies do get their fair amount of publicity on compensation. The IRS has taken notice. Nonprofits are subject to scrutiny by the IRS for disqualified persons, excess benefit transactions, and the questionable presumption of reasonableness.[19]

Federal legislation in 2006 redefined disqualified persons as those in a position to exercise substantial influence over an exempt organization and increased penalties for those who participate in what GuideStar® describes as an "excess benefit transaction" (a financial transaction in an amount that exceeds the market rate) in violation of the rules. Charities may pay reasonable compensation for services provided by officers, executives, and staff. Under this scrutiny, investigations of executive salaries have occurred in most major subsectors of the nonprofit sector. Congressional leaders have demonstrated an interest in hospital executive compensation.[20]

It is not illegal and perhaps not even unethical for executives to be paid handsomely for their leadership roles. Given the scrutiny and bad publicity that executive compensation can evoke, however, a different tack might work best. Based on these facts and so as not to put undue pressure on an NPO budget, it is probably good policy to pay executives within the range of executive pay that is found within the subsector and the community in which an NPO is situated.

SUMMARY

This final chapter has dealt with the delicate issue of employee compensation. Compensation includes salary, benefits, and retirement packages. NPOs need to be strategic about their compensation packages. Wages need to be studied and markets should be monitored in order to create a wage and salary structure that can be understood and appreciated by employees. A pay structure provides a way for an NPO to organize, monitor, and analyze labor markets. Likewise, benefits help recruiting and keeping employees. Benefits like health care, life insurance, and disability payments tend to be expensive and strain NPO budgets. Many smaller NPOs have to minimize benefits. Yet benefits add to the attractiveness of a compensation plan. Retirement is another issue discussed in this chapter. Retirement plans range from full retirement packages with generous wages and benefits to enabling employees to buy into mutual funds through a sponsored 403(b) or 401(k). Finally, a compensation plan, because of the importance of employee morale, needs to be administered professionally. These responsibilities include recruiting and retention, maintenance of the pay structure, and executive salaries.

DISCUSSION QUESTIONS

1. Consider the salary structure of the organization in which you are employed or volunteer, or consider another organization that you have researched and with which you have become familiar. Does the organization do anything to maintain its salary structure to remain competitive in the market for quality employees? If so, what does it do? How does it do it? When was the last time, if ever, that the organization conducted a survey of salaries in its market? What factors did the organization study? Did the findings indicate the need to increase salaries? How else was that survey used? Did the findings of the survey influence changes in the organization's salary structure? If the organization has not conducted a market salary survey, what factors should be studied?

2. Barbara Reinhold, a career coach, states that "an increasing number of people are leaving the cohort that *Utne Reader* has identified as stressed wage slaves who are seeking deeper meaning and usefulness to their work and lifestyle. They are looking for balance." Reinhold observes that business functions in the profit and nonprofit sectors overlap and that individuals will be able to find careers helping others while doing what they like to do.[21] This should ring a bell for any NPO manager, or person aspiring to become one. These individuals may be a source of quality employees for nonprofits. There is a sticky point to this niche group. Assuming that the salaries offered for comparable business-sector positions are usually going to be greater than in the NPO sector, discuss how NPOs can compete for this source of quality employees. What is an appropriate strategy?

EXERCISE

For this exercise, use Table 12.1 and consider the following. The fictitious Knotfer Prophet Agency is having recruitment and retention problems that have led to a request by the executive director to the governing board for a local salary study. She has seemingly unfillable vacancies at the program manager level and high turnover at the development assistant level. The board limits the study in the following way: Do it in confidence and on the cheap. Using the study guide she developed three years ago, the executive director finds the following:

- A wide range in salaries below and above the average salaries of her program managers, program aides/receptionists, and her executive director position

- A relatively tight range of salaries around the rest of her employees

- Average salaries of program managers are equal to her program managers and development director

- Average salaries of development assistants is $2,000 below the average salaries of her development assistants, but $1,000 above her program assistants

- The average salaries of executive directors is $4,000 above her own salary

The executive director calls you, her friend and executive director of a competitor agency, for consultation and advice. It just so happens that you are paid a higher salary than she. What would you advise her as to what the data mean and what she should recommend to her board? What additional information should she have in order to make reasonable recommendations to the board?

INNOVATION

While there may be influences on compensation-setting from national boards in NPOs that have local branches, local governing boards generally are responsible for compensation policies in their organizations. Rocco and Bowman note that "Innovative compensation practices include cash compensation and recognition plans."[20] The following are examples of innovative cash compensation or recognition plan options:[21]

- Individual incentives
- Team or group incentives
- Bonuses
- Spot awards
- Special cash recognition
- Special non-cash recognition

The discussion here provides examples of paying bonuses and providing benefits without busting the budget.

Bonuses

One-time bonuses can bust the budget. NPOs that are in a situation where a board is anticipating a fairly generous amount of revenue in the following fiscal year, but expects budget troubles in the one after that, might take a strategic approach to rewarding employees, especially if the outlook for the third year out is positive and permanent raises can be offered. That approach is to pay performance bonuses in lieu of permanent raises. It would be wise for the NPO in that situation to maximize the amount of each bonus. It would probably be helpful to codify a policy for giving bonuses.

Benefits

Many small NPOs have a challenge paying reasonable salaries and a further challenge offering high-cost medical and other benefits. An innovative strategy is to help employees individually purchase the benefits they value the most in their particular circumstances. The particular suggestion is to offer cash in lieu of benefits. The NPO board can even use its knowledge of the community to help employees find a low-cost and effective alternative to a company-offered benefit. For example, board members may know well-placed individuals in the local insurance industry who could put together health insurance options for the individuals. Similarly, the board could use its knowledge of local resources to find a financial broker to put together options for organizing 401(k) or 403(b) retirement options. The board would be serving the NPO's employees and perhaps retaining valuable personnel with low-cost assistance options as described.

NOTES

1   Lloyd Harger, *Workers' Compensation, A Brief History* (Tallahassee, FL: Florida Division of Workers' Compensation, 2007).

2   Herrington J. Bryce, *Financial and Strategic Management for Nonprofit Organizations* (San Francisco: Jossey-Bass, 2000).

3   Carter M. McNamara, *Field Guide to Leadership and Supervision* (Minneapolis: Authenticity Consulting, LLC, 2007).

4   Paychex®, "Exempt vs. non-Exempt: Identifying Employee Classification,'" 2007. Online at http://services.paychex.com/exempt.pdf (accessed April 28, 2008).

5   Insure.com "The Basics of Short-Term Disability Insurance," 2007. Online at http://insure.com/ (accessed April 28, 2008).

6   Historical Text Archive, "The History of Life Insurance," 2005. Online at http://www.historical textarchive.com (accessed April 28, 2008).

7   National Coalition on Healthcare, "Health Insurance Cost," 2008. Online at http://www.nchc.org (accessed April 28, 2008).

8   U.S. Department of Labor, "Health Plans & Benefits—Employee Retirement Income Security Act – ERISA," 2007. Online at http://www.dol.gov (accessed May 20, 2008).

9   Susan M. Heathfield, *Why Organizations Have Pay Structures,* Microsoft Office Access. Online at http://office.microsoft.com/en-us/help (accessed May 20, 2008).

10 Ibid.

11 Ibid.

12 Ibid.

13 Ibid.

14 Ibid.

15 Nonprofit Recruitment Services, "Frequently Asked Questions," 2007. Online at http://www.nonprofitrecruitment.com (accessed April 28, 2008).

16 U.S. Department of Labor, "Employment Standards Administration Wage and Hour Division." Online at http://www.dol.gov/esa/whd (accessed May 20, 2008).

17 Ibid.

18 James E. Rocco and A. Bowman, *Innovative Compensation Practices in Nonprofit Organizations* (Avondale, MI: Applied Research and Development Institute International, 2007).

19 GuideStar®, "IRS Increases Enforcement Focus on Nonprofit Executive Compensation," 2007. Online at http://www.guidestar.org/ (accessed April 28, 2008).

20 Ibid.

21 Barbara Reinhold, *Toxic Work: How to Overcome Stress, Overload and Burnout and Revitalize Your Career* (New York: Plume, 1997).

22 James E. Rocco and A. Bowman, *Innovative Compensation Practices in Nonprofit Organizations* (Avondale, MI: Applied Research and Development Institute International, 2007).

INDEX

A

A-133 Single Audit Act, 139
accounting
    balance sheet, 119–121
    basis, 109–111
    chart of accounts, 111–112
    combining and combined
    financial statements, 107
    debits and credits, 117
    documentation, 122
    double-entry, 115–117
    financial and fiscal
    administration network, 15–17,
      98
    financial reporting, 100–101
    financial reporting hierarchy,
      101–106
    function, 99–100
    functional expense allocation,
      121–122
    funds, 112–114
    funds *versus* accounts, 114–115
    journals and ledgers, 118–119
    management analysis of
      financial statements, 107–109
    reasons for, 99
    reporting requirements, 121
acid test ratio, 158
American Institute of Certified
Public Accountants (AICPA), 31,
  138
American Society of Agency
  Executives (ASAE), 157
American Stock Exchange (AMEX),
  247
arts and culture subsector, 6
ASAE. *See* American Society of
  Agency Executives
auditing profession, 148–150
audits
    A-133 Single Audit Act, 139
    assessing financial condition,
      150–156
    economic value, 137
    engagement letter, 140
    entrance conference, 140–141
    exit conference and final report,
      143–144
    field work, 142
    final report, 143
    financial and fiscal
      administration, 132–133
    financial ratios, 157–158
    function, 135–137
    implementing changes, 145
    independent, 139
    independent process, 139–140
    internal, 138

preliminary review, 142
preparing for, 145–146
program, 142
purpose, 133–135
results, 142–143
successful, 147–148
types, 137–138

B

balance sheet, 119–121
bank statements, 146
basis, accounting, 109–111
benefits, 305–306
billings, revenue management, 180
BLS. *See* Bureau of Labor Statistics
board
    members, 85–86, 264–265
    minutes, 146
    procedures affecting yields, 152
    responsibilities, 172–173
bond indebtedness, 292–293
bonuses, 317
borrowing, 292–293
bounded rationality, 77–78
budget
    audits, 146
    big picture, 72
    board members, 85–86
    calendar, 74–75
    classic rational decision
      making, 77
    decision-making models,
      75–76
    definition, 68–70
    evolution, 78

    financial and fiscal
      administration network, 68
    fiscal year, 70
    importance of, 15–16
    monthly cash flow, 72
    organizational differences,
      89–90
    performance budgeting, 78–79
    pie chart, 69
    process, 72–74
    program staff, 86
    purpose, 70–72
    realistic decision making,
      77–78
    revenues and expenditures,
      87–88
    risk, 258
    shortfalls and rebudgeting,
      86–87
    trends and projections, 88
    types, 75, 78
    United Way example, 74
    variance analysis, 88–89
    zero base budgeting, 79–85
budgetary controls, 152
buildings, 153, 260–261
Bureau of Labor Statistics (BLS),
  205
business budget factors, 75–76
business ventures, 270–271

C

cafeteria plans, 308
CAFR. *See* comprehensive annual
  financial report

calendar, 74–75

capital budgeting
    budgetary factor, 75–76
    overview, 280–281
    strategic plan, 281–282

capital campaigns, 291–292

capital debt policy, 294–295

capital decision making
    cost and benefit streams,
      283–284
    discounting, 284–286
    importance of, 282–283
    internal rate of return, 289–290
    net present value, 288
    payback period, 286–288
    summary, 290

case management procedures, 152

cash
    Check Clearing for the 21st
      Century Act, 233
    control theory, 244
    delaying payments, 232
    effective use of, 243–244
    electronic wire transfers,
      232–233
    importance of, 230
    inventory cash management
      model, 241–243
    managing needs, 233–234,
      240–241
    payment strategies, 230–232
    planning cash flow, 238–239
    shortages, 239–240
    surplus, 240
    transaction cost, 243–244

cash flow budgets, 234–237

cause-related marketing, 177–179

CB. *See* cost-benefit analysis

centralizing accounts, 230

chart of accounts, 111–112

Check Clearing for the 21st Century
    Act (Check 21), 233

classic rational decision making, 77

combining and combined financial
    statements, 107

commissions, 317–318

community norms, 71

compensation
    accidental death or
      dismemberment, 307
    administration, 311
    benefits, 305–306
    bonuses, 317
    cafeteria plans, 308
    commissions, 317–318
    components, 303
    defined benefit, 310
    defined contribution, 310
    disability insurance, 306
    Employee Retirement Income
      Security Act of 1974
      (ERISA), 308–309
    executive, 318–319
    exempt and nonexempt
      employees, 304–305
    Health Insurance Portability
      and Accountability Act,
      308–309
    hourly wage, 316
    job descriptions, 311

lay-offs, 315–316

life insurance, 307

long-term disability paid leave, 306–307

medical and hospitalization insurance, 307–308

overtime, 316

overview, 302

pay structure, 312–314

raises, 315

recruitment, 314–315

retention, 315

retirement plans, 309

salaries, 311, 315–316

short-term disability leave, 306

types of pay, 316–318

uses, 302

wage and salary structure, 303–305

competitive bidding, 221–222

compliance with code, 153

comprehensive annual financial report (CAFR), 101

Consumer Price Index (CPI), 205–206

contracts, 146

control theory, 244

controlling expenditures, 217

corporate partnerships, 268–270

cost, 60–61

cost and benefit streams, 283–284

cost-benefit analysis (CB), 211–214

cost-effectiveness analysis, 214–217

cost for service, 152

costing, 217–218

CPI. *See* Consumer Price Index

criteria-based spending decision making, 211

current debt ratio, 158

D

debits and credits, 117

debt, 60, 145, 152–153

decision-making models, 75–76

default risk, 247–248

defined benefit, 310

defined contribution, 310

delaying payments, 230–232

Delphi technique, 186–187

determining prices, 181–184

deterministic forecasting, 190

direct deposit, 232

direction, 71

director's liability insurance, 264–265

disability insurance, 306

disclaimers, 265

discounts, 207–210, 284–286

documentation, accounting, 122

donations, 59, 145–146

donors, dependency upon, 256

double-entry accounting, 115–117

E

education and research subsector, 4–5

electronic wire transfers (EWT), 232–233

Employee Retirement Income Security Act of 1974 (ERISA), 308–309 employment practices, 261

employment rate, 3

endowments, 293

engagement letter, audits, 140

entrance conference, audits, 140–141

equipment, 145, 153

ERISA. *See* Employee Retirement Income Security Act of 1974

EWT. *See* electronic wire transfers

executive compensation, 318–319

exempt employees, 304–305

exit conference and final report, audits, 143–144

expenditures, 60–61, 152

expert forecasting, 186

external sources, dependence upon, 152

F

Fair Labor Standards Act (FLSA), 305

FASB. *See* Financial Accounting Standards Board

federal budget factors, 75–76

fee for service, 152, 171

fees, 146

fidelity bonds, 265

field work, 142

final report, audits, 143

Financial Accounting Standards Board (FASB), 31, 101

financial and fiscal administration. *See also* audits; budget

    accountability, 21

    activities, 11

    board member responsibilities, 21–22

    closed environment, 11

    communication, 26

    definition, 10

    ethics, 24–26

    financial manager, 11

    Form 990, 29–30

    grants, 30–31

    Internal Revenue Service 501(c)(3) designation, 28–29

    leadership, 24

    money, importance of, 13–14

    network, 14–17, 68, 98

    organizational role, 17–19

    Pareto optimality, 11

    rational theories, 11–12

    real-world theories, 11–13

    Sarbanes-Oxley Act, 31

    sector comparison, 31–33

    shareholders, 11

    staff member responsibilities, 23

    state agency oversight, 30

    technology, 27–28

    value, risk and rewards, 19–20

    volunteer responsibilities, 23–24

financial evaluation

    A-133 Single Audit Act, 139

    assessing financial condition, 150–156

    audit program, 142

    audit results, 142–143

    audit types, 137–138

    auditing profession, 148–150

economic value, 137
engagement letter, 140
entrance conference, 140–141
exit conference and final
    report, 143–144
field work, 142
final audit report, 143
financial and fiscal
    administration, 132–133
financial ratios, 157–158
function, 135–137
implementing changes, 145
independent audit process,
    139–140
independent audits, 139
internal audits, 138
preliminary review, 142
preparing for independent
    audits, 145–146
purpose, 133–135
successful audits, 147–148
financial markets, 246–247
financial ratios, 157–158
financial reporting, 100–101
financial reporting hierarchy,
    101–106
financing capital projects
    bond indebtedness, 292–293
    borrowing, 292–293
    capital campaigns, 291–292
    endowments, 293
    grants, 292
    pay-as-you-go, 291
    pay-as-you-use, 291
fiscal year, 70

fixed costs, increase in, 152
FLSA. *See* Fair Labor Standards Act
forecasting
    example, 190–192
    failure, 193–194
    revenue, 184
    types, 185
Form 990, 29–30
fraud, 261
functional expense allocation,
121–122
funding sources, 167
fundraising
    consultants, 174
    events, 146, 170
    responsibilities, 172–174
    risk, 259–260
funds, 112–113
funds *versus* accounts, 114–115

G

general liability policies, 264
generally accepted accounting
    principles (GAAP), 99–101,
    137–138, 147
generally accepted auditing
    standards (GAAS), 99–101,
    137–138, 147
Government Financial Officer
    Association, 70
grant contracts, 146
grants, 59, 145, 169, 292
grounds, 153, 260–261
group purchasing, 223

H

health care costs, 153

health care system, 12

Health Insurance Portability and
    Accountability Act (HIPAA),
    308–309

health services subsector, 4

hold harmless agreements, 265

hourly wage, 316

I

identifying funds and accounts,
    113–114

in-kind contributions, 145

indemnification, 265

independence in appearance, 148

independence in fact, 148–149

independent audits, 139

initial public offering (IPO), 246

insurable risk, 264–266

internal audits, 138

internal rate of return (IRR),
    289–290

Internal Revenue Service 501(c)(3)
    designation, 28–29

Internet banking, 233

inventory, 146

inventory cash management model,
    241–244

investment management
        financial markets, 246–247
        importance of, 244–246
        risk, 247–249
        strategy, 249–251

investment planning, 60–61

investment risk, 247–249, 259

IPO. *See* initial public offering

IRR. *See* internal rate of return

J

job descriptions, 311

journals and ledgers, 118–119, 146

K

kiting, 233

L

lay-offs, 315–316

leases, 146

ledgers, 146

legal limitations, 174–175

legal requirements, 263

liability, 261

life insurance, 307

liquidity risk, 248

local budget factors, 75–76

local change, impact of, 207

long-term debt, 152

long-term disability paid leave,
    306–307

long-term forecasting, 185

M

management analysis of financial
    statements, 107–109

managerial accounting, 100

maturity risk, 248–249

medical and hospitalization
    insurance, 307–308

medium-term forecasting, 185

memberships, 60, 170–171

Mental Health Parity Act, 309

money, time value of, 204–206

monthly cash flow, 72

monthly payment plans, 232

N

National Association of Educational Buyers, 220–221

national change, impact of, 207

net present value (NPV), 288

New York Stock Exchange (NYSE), 246

Newborns' and Mothers' Health Protection Act, 309

noncompetitive procurement, 222

nonexempt employees, 304–305

nonprofit budget factors, 75–76

nonprofit organization (NPO), definition, 2–3

nonprofit sector finances, 3–4

NPV. *See* net present value

NYSE. *See* New York Stock Exchange

O

OMB. *See* U.S. Office of Management and Budget

opportunity costs, 75, 207–210

organizational differences, 89–90

overtime, 316–317

P

Pareto optimality, 11

partial payments, 230

pay, types of, 316–318

pay-as-you-go (PAYGO), 291

pay-as-you-use (PAYUSE), 291

pay structure, 312–314

payables, 145

payback period, 286–288

payment strategies, 230–232

payroll, 146

pension liability, 153

performance budgeting, 78–79

performance management subsystem, 204

personnel productivity, 152

philanthropy, 166

pie charts, budgetary, 69

planning cash flow, 238–239

pledges and membership dues, 180

policies consistent with affordability, 153

political issues, revenue management, 184

population size, 153

portfolio allocation strategies, 249–251

PPBS. *See* program and performance budgeting system

preliminary review, audits, 142

price, 207–210

procurement

    competitive bidding, 221–222

    definition, 219–220

    group purchasing, 223

    model, 220–221

    noncompetitive, 222

    overview, 218–219

professional liability insurance, 264–265

program growth per expenditure, 152

program and performance budgeting system (PPBS), 79

program staff, 86

property, 145

property insurance, 265

public support, 179

R

raises, 315

realistic decision making, 77–78

receipts and invoices, 146

recruitment, 314–315

regional change, impact of, 207

religious organizations, 5–6

reporting requirements, accounting, 121

request for bids, 219

request for proposal (RFP), 219–220

request for quotation (RFQ), 219–220

retention, 315

retirement plans, 309

revenue collection procedures, 152

revenue estimating procedure, 152

revenue management

    administration, 179–180

    administrative and political issues, 184

    billings, 180

    board responsibilities, 172–173

    cause-related marketing, 177–179

    collection, 180

    Delphi technique, 186–187

    determining prices, 181–184

    deterministic forecasting, 190

    expert forecasting, 186

    fees for service, 171

    financial and fiscal administration, 166

    forecasting example, 190–192

    forecasting failure, 193–194

    forecasting revenue, 184

    forecasting types, 185

    funding sources, 167

    fundraising consultants, 174

    fundraising events, 170

    fundraising responsibilities, 172–174

    grants from foundations, 169

    grants from government, 169

    legal limitations, 174–175

    long-term forecasting, 185

    medium-term forecasting, 185

    membership dues or fees, 170–171

    philanthropy, 166

    pledges and membership dues, 180

    public support, 179

    selling assets, 171–172

    short-term forecasting, 185

    social entrepreneurship, 170

    staff responsibilities, 173–174

    tax credit case analysis, 196

    tax credit policy, 194

    traditional donations, 167–169

    trending, 187–190

trends and new ideas, 176
unrelated business income,
    176–177
Youth Opportunity Program,
    195–196
revenue to benefit growth ratio, 153
revenues and expenditures, 87–88
revenues per clients, 152
rewards, 75
RFP. *See* request for proposal
RFQ. *See* request for quotation
risk
        budgets, 258
        buildings, grounds, and
            equipment, 260–261
        business ventures, 270–271
        corporate partnerships, 268–270
        dependency upon donors, 256
        downside, 268
        employment practices, 261
        fraud, 261
        fundraising, 259–260
        insurable, 264–265
        investment, 247–249, 259
        legal requirements, 263
        liability, 261
        logic, 267
        management, 262–263
        overview, 256–258
        reducing, 263–264
        related businesses, 266
        responsibility distribution, 263
        tax-exempt legal status, 271–272
        turning down revenue
            sources, 260

unrelated businesses, 266–267
upside, 267–268

S

salaries, 311, 315–316
Sarbanes-Oxley Act (SOX), 31,
    149–150, 207
satisficing, 77–78
SDR. *See* social discount rate
Securities and Exchange
    Commission (SEC), 246
short-term disability leave, 306
short-term forecasting, 185
shortages, cash, 239–240
shortfalls and rebudgeting, 86–87
sick leave records, 146
social and legal services subsector, 5
social discount rate (SDR), 210
social entrepreneurship, 170
SOX. *See* Sarbanes-Oxley Act
staff responsibilities, 173–174
stakeholder values, 71
state budget factors, 75–76
Statement of Cash Flows, 238
stocks, 246
strategic plan
        defined, 42
        external factors, 52–53
        financial and fiscal
            administration, 58
        importance of, 16, 40
        internal factors, 53–54
        money, goals, and objectives,
            54–57
        operational versus capital

budgeting, 57–58

process, 44–45

purpose, 43–44

revenue planning, 59–60

role of, 40–42

steps for creating, 47–51

strengths, weaknesses,
    opportunities, and
    threats, 45–46

surplus cash, 240

T

tax credit case analysis, 196

tax credit policy, 194

tax-exempt legal status, 271–272

tax-related documents, 146

time value of money, 204–206

traditional donations, 167–169

transaction cost (TC), 243–244

trending, 187–190

trends, 88, 176

tuition, 146

U

United Way of America (UWA), 74,
    132

unrelated business income, 176–177

U.S. Office of Management and
    Budget (OMB), 20, 31, 210

utility costs, 153

UWA. *See* United Way of America

V

vacation records, 146

variance analysis, 88–89

W

wage and salary structure, 303–304

waivers, 265

Whatcom Council of Nonprofits,
    14–15

Women's Health and Cancer Rights
    Act, 309

workers' compensation, 265

world change, impact of, 207

Y

Youth Opportunity Program (YOP),
    195–196

Z

zero balance account (ZBA),
    230–232

zero base budgeting (ZBB)

advantages, 84

case example, 80–84

decision unit, 80

definition, 79

disadvantages, 84–85

evaluation, 80

line-item budgeting,
    compared to, 84

packages, 80

purpose, 79–80

rank, 80

steps, 80–83

zero base, 80

Activity-Based Cost Management in Government, Second Edition

Gary Cokins, CPIM

Activity-Based Cost Management in Government, Second Edition, can help you finally determine the true costs of your outputs. This invaluable resource helps public sector managers understand why current costs are at certain levels and mixes and predict future resource demands. A must-have for government managers who want to create optimal performance. The second edition includes all-new content on risk management and performance management using strategy maps and the balanced scorecard, as well as new, up-to-date examples showing the utility of ABC/M.

ISBN 1-56726-181-7 ■ Product Code B817 ■ 384 pages

Quick Reference to Federal Appropriations Law, Second Edition

John E. Jensen

This second edition provides a quick reference to the fundamentals of appropriations law, including examples of how those principles have been applied in practice. Adapted from the extensively researched *Principles of Federal Appropriations Law* (developed by the U.S. Government Accountability Office), the book focuses on core appropriations law subjects, explains the law in a condensed and accessible format, and provides updates pertinent to the law.

ISBN 1-56726-176-0 ■ Product Code B760 ■ 269 pages

Federal Financial Management Library

This hand-picked compilation of financial management regulations keeps you abreast of the ever-changing rules for managing federal funds. Available in your choice of format—CD-ROM, online, or both—and fully searchable and indexed, *Federal Financial Management Library* (FML) ensures that you are up-to-date with the latest regulations and guidance.

Order *Federal Financial Management Library* together with *Principles of Federal Appropriations Law* (FAL) for a special price! You'll receive both resources in your choice of format, giving you *Federal Financial Management Library's* wide range of financial management regulations and *Principles of Federal Appropriations Law's* focused appropriations law content.

Online with Quarterly Updates: Product Code OQ105
CD-ROM with Quarterly Updates: Product Code CQ105
CD-ROM and Online Combination: Product Code OQ105C
FAL/FML Single User Online: Product Code OQ106
FAL/FML CD-ROM: Product Code CQ106
Combination FAL/FML Single User CD-ROM and Online: Product Code OQ106C